W9-AWM-932

The **COMPLETE** IDIOT'S Guide to

Making Money on the Canadian Stock Market 🍁

♦ Learn the steps to building wealth

♦ Practical strategies for investing in your future

♦ Make your money work for you!

Stephen Nelson & Christy Heady

An Alpha Books/Prentice Hall Canada Copublication

Prentice Hall Canada Inc., Scarborough, Ontario

Canadian Cataloguing in Publication Data

Nelson, Stephen, 1968-
    The complete idiot's guide to making money on the Canadian stock market

ISBN 0-13-779134-8

1. Investments.   I. Heady, Christy.   II. Title.

HG5152.N44 1997   332.6   C97-931868-8

© 1997 Prentice-Hall Canada Inc.
Scarborough, Ontario
A Division of Simon & Schuster/A Viacom Company

Prentice-Hall, Inc., Upper Saddle River, New Jersey
Prentice-Hall International (UK) Limited, London
Prentice-Hall of Australia, Pty. Limited, Sydney
Prentice-Hall Hispanoamericana, S.A., Mexico City
Prentice-Hall of India Private Limited, New Delhi
Prentice-Hall of Japan, Inc., Tokyo
Simon & Schuster Southeast Asia Private Limited, Singapore
Editora Prentice-Hall do Brasil, Ltda., Rio de Janeiro

ISBN 0-13-779134-8

Managing Editor: Robert Harris
Acquisitions Editor: Jill Lambert
Copy Editor: Rob Glen
Editorial Assistant: Joan Whitman
Production Coordinator: Julie Preston
Art Direction: Mary Opper
Cover Design: Kyle Gell Art and Design
Interior Illustration: Judd Winick
Cover Photograph: Richard Laird/Masterfile
Page Layout: Gail Ferreira Ng-A-Kien

1 2 3 4 5   RRD   01 00 99 98 97

Printed and bound in the United States of America

This publication contains the opinions and ideas of its authors and is designed to provide useful advice in regard to the subject matter covered. The author and publisher are not engaged in rendering legal, accounting, or other professional services in this publication. This publication is not intended to provide a basis for action in particular circumstances without consideration by a competent professional. The authors and publisher expressly disclaim any responsibility for any liability, loss, or risk, personal or otherwise, which is incurred as a consequence, directly or indirectly, of the use and application of any of the contents of this book.

Visit the Prentice Hall Canada Web site! Send us your comments, browse our catalogues, and more.
www.phcanada.com

*I would like to dedicate this book to
Kathy Nelson, Kathryn Grant and Debbie Nelson.*

Contents

Foreword

Only 10 or 15 years ago, "investing" was something rich people did. Although most Canadians did set aside some savings for a rainy day—usually in the form of safe investments such as GICs, Canada Savings Bonds, etc.—they didn't really think of themselves as "investors." And they didn't feel an urgent need to understand what was going on in financial markets—it had little to do with them.

The world has changed a lot in recent years. Canadians have come to understand that they have to take greater personal responsibility for their retirement income. They have had to become investors. They have had to become more hands-on, more aggressive —and therefore more knowledgeable—about how to invest their savings for the future.

There is no lack of information out there about investing and investments. As a matter of fact, the problem is that there is probably too much information out there! Our newspapers, magazines, radio and television bombard us constantly with economic and financial information—not to mention ads for an endless number and variety of "investment vehicles." How can the ordinary person make sense of it all?

As an economist, I spend a lot of my time speaking to various groups about what's going on in the Canadian economy and what's happening in financial markets. I am always impressed by two things. First, there is a huge hunger out there for knowledge and information. People really do want to understand all about interest rates, inflation, government policies, and ultimately how these things affect their investments. Second, people want to be talked to in plain English (or French). They don't want to hear a lot of jargon and complex theories. They want and need straightforward, concrete, down-to-earth explanations of what's going on. They want to be talked to in a way that they can relate to and easily understand.

This book tries to do just that. It is easy to read, sometimes even fun, and it explains in simple and basic terms most of what an average investor should know about investing. For beginners it's a great way to get started!

Ruth Getter
Senior Vice President and Chief Economist
TD Bank

Introduction

I once knew a gentleman who wanted to invest a little money he had. He wasn't wealthy by any means, but he wasn't stupid either. He knew that his little bit of money, wisely invested, could be working a lot harder for him than it was parked in his savings account. He also knew that he needed to learn about investing if he was to do it wisely. So he bought books—he had more books on investing than anyone I knew—and as far as I know, his money is still parked in the bank. Why?

He never got past Chapter 3 in any of the books he bought. They were dry; they were tedious; they made history books on 17th century France look fascinating by comparison. And they made this gentleman, who wasn't stupid, feel like an idiot. I wrote this book for him and for the thousands of others like him who know their money could be making more money, but don't know where to start.

I know you're not an idiot (after all, you bought this book). That's the first assumption I've made about you, and I'm presumptuous enough to make a few other assumptions, too. For example:

➤ You're not an economist and you're probably not a stock broker or even a certified public accountant.

➤ You work hard for your money and you can't afford to lose much of it.

➤ You are smart enough to realize that unless you provide for the future, the future may be very bleak indeed.

➤ The very though of buying stocks—let alone futures or options—sends a prickle of fear down your spine.

Although the stock market looks like a shark tank and you feel like bait, you CAN make it work for you, and that's what this book is all about. It contains the fundamental information you need to make sensible decisions about your money. It offers tips—not hot tips on a real deal ("trust me"), but tried-and-true tips on investing from pros who've been there. It gives you useful worksheets and formulas that help you plot your course through sometimes choppy waters. And it isn't boring. Yes, you can get past Chapter 3 without falling asleep. Here's how it works.

Part I, The Stock Market Tycoon, grounds you in some basics. It helps you establish your financial goals, determine an acceptable level of risk, learn how to research different investment opportunities, and get disciplined about spending and saving (so you have money to invest).

Part II, The New Kid on the Block—Megabuck Bank, helps you get the most out of your bank accounts (chequing and savings), and understand how both fit into an overall investment plan.

Part III, Stocks—The Granddaddy of All Markets, introduces you to your first really scary (and potentially really profitable) investment tool. This section helps you understand what stocks are and how their performance can build or evaporate profits from your investment dollars.

Part IV, IOU—Learning the Basics of Bonds, walks you through another popular investment tool—government and corporate bonds—complete with tax considerations.

Part V, Mutual Funds Mania, shows you how to make even small amounts of money grow through managed portfolios, how to pick reputable mutual funds, and how to select the best time for mutual fund investments.

Part VI, Futures and Options, explains the risks and opportunities in this volatile area of investing and helps new investors understand the culture of this particular investment avenue.

Part VIII, Make That Money Grow, provides specific strategies for investing dollar amounts from $100 to $10,000, plus tax tips for handling profits from your investments.

Plus, you get an appendix of "freebies" that may be available to you just for becoming a corporate shareholder, and a glossary of investment terms that will help you understand how "money talks."

While you may not need to read this book cover to cover, I strongly recommend that you read Part I before you dive into a specific investment area that interests you. From there you can pick and choose, based on your goals and how much risk you can handle without losing sleep.

Extras

In addition to clear and interesting explanations and advice, this book offers other types of information that point you in the right direction, help you avoid dangerous and costly traps, define confusing jargon, or provide sidenotes that may simply be of interest. Look for these easy-to-recognize signposts in boxes:

Definition

Yes, it's true. The stock market is full of mysterious and unnecessary jargon, but you should get familiar with some of it. These boxes will put you in the know, so you can talk to your broker without embarrassment, and impress your friends at cocktail parties.

Tips show better ways to get things done—ways to save money or time. Think of them as a friendly word in your ear.

Cautions help you avoid costly mistakes so you don't end up like this pitiful character.

Bet You Didn't Know

These little boxes contain interesting or useful background information about investment opportunities or the fascinating world of the stock market. It's information you can ignore ... but you probably won't want to.

The Complete Idiot's Guide to Making Money on the Canadian Stock Market

Part I
You—The Stock Market Tycoon

Imagine you're rich. I mean really loaded. You're forty-five years old, retiring with $1 million to your name, and plan on playing golf—every day, of course—for the rest of your life. Or you bought your dream vacation house and plan on spending the rest of your life on vacation.

Sound impossible? It's not. You can do this if you learn how to invest wisely. This part of the book will show you that it doesn't take a lot of money to start out—just a little know-how.

Before you start, you need to know yourself very well. What are your financial goals? How much risk can you handle? What bad spending habits do you have to break before you can invest a dime? What you do today will affect you for the rest of your life. Making mistakes will cost you, especially in investing. But doing nothing is the biggest mistake of all. So, are you ready? Let's find out more about you.

Chapter 1

You Can Get There from Here

In this chapter

➤ How to motivate yourself to wealth—even on a limited budget!

➤ How long it takes to double your money

➤ Top Ten Tips for Successful Investing

It's Saturday night, and you're at your local convenience store with your ice-cold Slushee, bag of potato chips, and lottery ticket in hand. As you fill in the numbers on your ticket, you pray that "today is the day." You start fantasizing about what you're going to do with all that money. Buy a yacht and sail the Caribbean. Go on a shopping spree at your favourite mall. Or send all six of your kids to Harvard med school with their tuition paid in full!

Really, folks, let's be serious! You have a 1 in 7 397 685 chance (or something like that) of winning a zillion-dollar lottery. You can't bet the farm that you are going to win all that dough. Sure you can dream, but if you want to make your dreams a reality, you're going to have to do more than fill in the little boxes on a lottery ticket.

Winning the lottery may be the quickest path to wealth, but *playing* it is not. If you spend $7 a week on lottery tickets and never win, you are throwing away $28 a month. That's $336 a year, which can be almost a week's worth of after-tax pay for some Canadians. That's like working a week for free—you might just as well set your paycheque on fire and watch it burn.

What if you take that same twenty bucks and invest it? You can invest as little as $25 a month in a stock or mutual fund and watch it grow into hundreds and possibly thousands of dollars.

What's a C-Note?

A $100 bill—a "century note." There are one hundred years in a century, and one hundred dollars in a C-Note.

All You Need Is a C-Note

Let's take a $100 bill and see what it can do. Suppose that on the 15th of each month you invest $100 into the fictitious Sky's The Limit mutual fund—faithfully, no matter what the change in price of the mutual fund.

One hundred dollars a month invested over a twelve-month period is $1,200. Easy enough. Assume that you live in a perfect world and the price of Sky's The Limit mutual fund keeps increasing. Now check out Table 1.1.

Table 1.1 Watching the C-Note Grow

When Do I Invest?	How Much Do I Invest?	What's the Price?	How Many Shares Do I Own?
January 15	$100.00	$15.00	6.67
February 15	$100.00	$16.00	6.25
March 15	$100.00	$15.00	6.67
April 15	$100.00	$17.00	5.88
May 15	$100.00	$18.00	5.56
June 15	$100.00	$18.00	5.56
July 15	$100.00	$19.00	5.26

When Do I Invest?	How Much Do I Invest?	What's the Price?	How Many Shares Do I Own?
August 15	$100.00	$20.00	5.00
September 15	$100.00	$20.00	5.00
October 15	$100.00	$22.00	4.55
November 15	$100.00	$21.00	4.76
December 15	$100.00	$23.00	4.35
Totals:	$1,200.00	$18.67 average price/share	65.51
Total amount I invested:	$1,200.00		
Value of my portfolio now:	$1,506.73		
Net profit:	$306.73		

From Table 1.1, you can conclude that if you were to invest $100 a month into a mutual fund whose price kept rising, at the end of a year you would have a profit. Keep in mind that prices of mutual funds can rise and fall.

Mutual funds aren't the only investments to consider. There are stocks, bonds, and options. Each of these specific investments may work for you, based on your financial goals, your initial investment, your risk-comfort level, and your age. In this book, you'll get the best answers to your financial questions and learn which investment products are best for you. You'll also discover how to generate some decent returns on your money with a little time and effort.

A **mutual fund** represents a pool of different stocks and/or bonds.

WHAT?

It may look like Greek to you now, but the language of investments is easy. You can learn to make money in the stock and bond markets and understand and practice this new language. It's the same as learning how to play the tuba, taking up underwater basket-weaving, or making a cheese soufflé in ten minutes or less; the jargon of investing is easy once you know how to do it.

Investing and Saving—Not the Same Thing

If a twenty-five-year-old were to invest a little over $100 a month until age sixty-five, and his investment earned 12% annually, he would have a million bucks by the time he retired. Even if you are in your forties, $600 a month for the next twenty-five years would get you a million bucks, too.

Can you save your money over the same time frame and have a million bucks? Good question.

You can always save money. Whatever is left over after you've paid all your expenses can be savings. That's good; most people try to have money left over. But if it's tucked away in a noninterest-bearing chequing account, what good is it? It's just sitting there, earning no interest.

Investing the money is a different story. As an investor, you do your homework to see what investments suit your style, your level of risk, and your financial goals. You can earn more if you invest it. You can even double or triple your money. But you can also lose it all. You'll learn later in this book that there is more risk to investing than just losing money.

Typically, when you think of saving money, you think of a savings account. Deposit your money and earn around 0.25% to 2% interest. You can sleep at night knowing all of your cash is there. Some of you might even stash your cash in an old shoe box or a special hiding place under your mattress—no interest earned there, though!

If you were to invest your money, where would you put it? Many people choose stocks, bonds, and mutual funds when they invest their money. Good thinking, folks!

To see the differences between saving and investing, take a look at Table 1.2. This shows what would happen if you allocated $100 a month to a savings account versus what happens when you invest the same amount over certain periods of time, assuming the following:

➤ Money under your mattress earns no interest (0%).

➤ Savings accounts earn less than 2% interest.

➤ All dividends and capital gains from an investment are reinvested.

Table 1.2   Save or Invest?

Return	5 years	10 years	15 years	20 years	30 years
0%	$6,000	$12,000	$18,000	$24,000	$36,000
2%	$6,315	$13,294	$21,005	$29,526	$49,348
5%	$6,829	$15,592	$26,840	$41,275	$83,573
8%	$7,397	$18,418	$34,835	$59,294	$150,030
10%	$7,808	$20,655	$41,799	$76,570	$227,936
12%	$8,247	$23,334	$50,457	$99,915	$352,992

Table 1.2 charts the results of saving your money in the two following ways:

➤ **Under your mattress (0%).** You would have $36,000 at the end of thirty years. $36,000 is a lot of money, until you compare it to ...

➤ **A savings account (2%).** Earning 2% or less on a savings account in the 1990s has become a reality. Saving this way, you can turn a deposit of $100 a month over the next twenty years into almost $30,000. So it's better than leaving your money under the mattress and earning 0%. But there's a better avenue to take.

Table 1.2 also shows what could happen if you invested your money in one of the following:

➤ **Stocks, bonds, or mutual funds.** Any of these investments can boast higher returns than saving your money in a savings account. Just look at the table. If you invested your $100 a month every month—even at a 10% annual return—after fifteen years, you'd more than double the amount earned over leaving it under your mattress. After thirty years of investing, you'd have six times the amount sewn up in your bed for the same period of time.

The Process for Successful Investing

So you want to be investment-savvy? Most of us want to be smart investors, and all of us want to be rich investors. Why not? As a smart investor, you control your investments and don't let fear or greed get the better of you. You work too hard for your money to throw it away. If you're a rich investor, then it shows that your smarts have paid off.

But you can't be a rich investor without first being a smart one. Smart investors know that knowledge is power. They're not looking for an immediate payoff but have a stick-to-it attitude that guarantees wealth and success. The two most important words in managing your money and creating your wealth are *getting control*. The more you learn about what some of the investment products are and how they work in different economic and financial climates, the more control you'll have in creating your own wealth. You might even be able to dazzle a few new acquaintances at cocktail parties, too.

This isn't a cakewalk, though. You have to commit to the following steps first:

1. **You have to want to learn.** Motivation is the starting point of all achievement. You have this book, that's motivation right there. Believe you can do it, because you can.

2. **Get rid of the negative emotions—fear and greed.** Many people are afraid of investing, usually because of a lack of knowledge or confidence. Others are greedy, only caring about improving the bottom line. These same people let their investments control them rather than controlling their investments. Get rid of these emotions, and you can control your financial destiny.

3. **Set some goals.** What do you want? Where do you want your money to take you? You must set specific financial goals at the outset—such as paying for your children's university tuition, paying down the mortgage, retiring at an early age and living comfortably, or buying your dream home. You cannot invest just for the sake of watching your money grow. You'll see how to set a goal and how to reach it in Chapter 3.

4. **How much money is it going to take to reach these goals?** How much will your new home cost? Do you have any money for your child's post-secondary education? Take your goals from the previous step and figure out how much money each will require

8

5. **Figure out where you are financially.** Are you deeply in debt? Can you barely make ends meet? Are you scared of really knowing what your financial situation is? It's not uncommon—believe me! By using the recommendations in Chapter 3, you will be able to find out where you are financially and how much you can afford to invest.

6. **Determine how much you can afford to lose.** This step in the process of successful investing concerns risk. By establishing your tolerance for risk, you will be able to pinpoint which investments you should be in.

7. **Plan for the long-term.** Success in investing doesn't happen overnight. You are going to have to work at creating your wealth.

8. **Do your homework.** You've got the motivation, you know where you are financially, and you know how much risk you can take. Now what? Time to do your homework. You need to learn as much as you can about as many different types of investment products that are out there. This may entail:

   Definitely reading this book.

   Reading the financial sections of daily newspapers.

   Subscribing to a few investment newsletters on the investments of your choice.

   Taking a course or two in basic investing.

   Watching television programs that talk about investing.

   Buying computer software programs specifically for budgeting and investing.

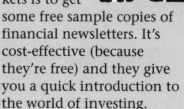

The best way to start learning about the financial markets is to get some free sample copies of financial newsletters. It's cost-effective (because they're free) and they give you a quick introduction to the world of investing.

9. **Start small and start early.** You don't need a million to make a million. It only takes a little bit. Recall that as little as $100 a month can do. Even if you only have $50 or even $25 a month, you can still continue the process of successful investing. The earlier you start, the better. Why? You will have more time on your side to make your money grow—and you will benefit more from potentially rising financial markets. Don't think it's too late: it's better late than never.

10. **Constantly monitor your investments.** You can't just sink a week's pay into stocks or bonds and ignore it. You have to set aside time to monitor your investments and keep up with the latest financial information. Once you learn where to find your stock symbol or bond quote in the newspaper, you'll be hooked.

Your Financial Toolbox

Think of what a toolbox looks like. Not very big, but it can hold a lot. Now, open the lid, and inside there's a top shelf. You can store a few things in there: pencils, fishing line, bolts, and a few lugnuts or whatever. Pull up the lid and underneath you find several shelves that open like an accordion. These shelves are at different levels. Many times a handyman puts the heaviest items on the bottom, such as a hammer or phillips-head screwdriver. The lighter items are left on top.

The concept of investing works in the same manner. Each investment product sits on a different shelf in a financial toolbox. What goes into each shelf depends on how risky it is, how much of it you own, and how long you own it.

Within this toolbox are the investment products. You may have heard how you can make money investing in these products: buy low and sell high! It's an old trick, but one that works. But what are you buying and selling? You are trading investment products, such as stocks, bonds, mutual funds, options and futures. I have dedicated a section later in the book to each of these products.

The Big Payoff

Let me ask you a question. If I could give you a million dollars today—right now—or a penny that you could double in value today, tomorrow, and every day thereafter for the next thirty days, which would you pick? Most folks want the upfront cash. The smart ones, however, would take the penny. Why? Because if you took the penny today and doubled its value each day thereafter for the next thirty days you will have almost $5.4 million dollars. Really.

It's easy to figure out. On a piece of paper, write down the next thirty days, starting with Day One and ending with Day Thirty. At the beginning of Day One put down .01, for one penny. Day Two should have .02 next to it because doubling one penny gives you two pennies.

How much does two pennies give you? Four. Put that down for Day Three. Complete your worksheet, making sure you double each day's amount.

Why does this work? Because of the magic of compounding. It is one of the most powerful ways to double, triple, and even quadruple your wealth.

There's a tale of a young boy who used to buy used Matchbox cars for $1.00 at garage sales. He would clean them up and make them look brand new. Then the boy would turn around and sell each of them for $2.00 apiece to the next ru-grat that came to his house. That kid made 100% profit on his initial investment. What a grand idea. (Eventually his mother found out what he was doing and was miffed, but boy, was his stockbroker father proud.)

Compounding is the money you earn on the interest you earned in the previous period. To maximize the benefits of compounding, let an investment compound over a longer time period. The more time you give it to work, the better.

WHAT?

The kid doubled his money because he knew the basic essence of compounding without even picking up an investment book. Not everyone can do that, especially when you're trying to make money in the markets. Oh, sure you can make 200% profit on some of the market's riskiest investments, but you could also lose all of your money—and more!

Compounding works if you understand its theory. The more you invest, the more compounding goes to work for you. Now, to practice its theory, you must:

➤ Have already established the time horizon for your financial goals.

➤ Exercise the self-discipline—like $100 a month, every month, for example.

➤ Learn the Rule of 72.

One of the biggest secrets to learning how the method of compounding works is understanding the Rule of 72. You don't need to break out the calculators or even sign up for a statistics course to see how this works.

The Rule of 72 tells you how long it will take you to double your money. This rule has been used by many, many financial advisers. The formula is pretty easy. Take any fixed annual rate of return and divide that number into 72. The end result should be the number of years it will take to double your money. Keep in mind the rule is based on a fixed annual rate of return.

Use some math. A $1,000 investment with a 10% annual rate of return would take 7.2 years to double and grow to $2,000. Figure it out: 10.0 divided into 72 = 7.2.

Buying and Selling Your Way to Success

It's funny, but many investors don't follow the process for successful investing. Instead, they look for a "get-rich-quick" investment, but that investment usually tends to leave them without a big payoff.

The big payoff in investing comes from knowing an old trick—one that's easy to grasp: Buy low and sell high!

Generations of experts have calculated financial formulas and tested hypothetical theories, but no one has designed one specific set of rules except for this one!

Unfortunately, statistics indicate that a high percentage of all investors lose money in the stock market. Many investors lose money in the other financial markets as well, especially if they don't do their homework and follow up on their investments. Why do so many people lose money? For example, in the case of investing in stocks, they buy stocks at too high a price and let greed overcome their sense of reality. Or maybe they get really greedy and want more profit. So they don't sell the investment and the price of it drops. Then the investor has a loss.

When you buy low and sell high, the big payoff is a profit. This is also known as a capital gain.

The Slow and Steady Method

Where else is there a payoff? In *dividends*, for one. These are typically quarterly payments sent to stockholders that represent a company's profit. For example, when you buy stock, you become part owner in the company, and your proportion of ownership depends on how many shares you buy.

As a part owner, you may share in the company profits when the company sends you a dividend cheque. Technically, it is the proportion of net earnings (kind of like a profit) from a company paid to you. So, as a stockholder, not only do you benefit from the price of a stock rising (the buy low and sell high concept), you also get a perk—a dividend.

It's in Your Best Interest

You can also make money from *interest* payments you receive from some investments. Typically, these interest payments come from fixed-income investments, which include Guaranteed Investment Certificates (GICs) and all types of bonds— e.g., Canada Savings Bonds (CSBs), Government of Canada Bonds (GOCs).

In order to encourage Canadians to invest in dividend-paying shares of Canadian companies, a dividend gross-up and tax credit system exists. Dividends received are grossed up by 25%. The taxpayer obtains a credit against his or her federal tax based on this grossed-up amount. Provincial taxes are then deducted.

Interest payments are usually paid to you every six months. The amount of interest you receive depends upon the interest rate that is given on the bond. Many investors choose fixed-income securities as a way to earn steady income.

Investing for a Rainy Day

The old saying was "saving for a rainy day." Not in the 1990s.

Today, "saving for a rainy day" means "investing for retirement." Why should you place so much emphasis on retirement, especially if it's ten, twenty, thirty, or even forty years away?

Because it will be here sooner than you know it. Many folks can attest that retirement comes too quickly. Today's senior citizens who live on a fixed income are faced with very, very limited budgets. Their incomes have fallen so dramatically because they either didn't plan for retirement properly, saved their money instead of investing it, or counted on the Canada Pension Plan (CPP) to be their cure-all.

According to Statistics Canada, the average income for a senior citizen, after transfer payments, and after tax, is less than $18,000 a year. Can you live on that?

If you are getting ready to retire or are already retired, it's not too late. In fact, it's never too late! Start working your plan as if it were day one. Check out the top ten steps in the process of successful investing and plan accordingly.

If you're a baby boomer, graduate from the mentality of spending everything you're earning to investing for retirement. You are in your peak earning years but have a shorter amount of time to invest for retirement than you had ten years ago. You can still reach your million by retirement; it's just going to take a few more dollars for you to invest per month to get there.

Those who have the longest time—and therefore the power—to plan for retirement are you twenty- and thirty-year-olds. Remember, only $100 a month invested every month over the next forty years can practically get you a million bucks.

Don't believe that CPP will take care of all of your financial necessities when you retire. Receiving CPP benefits should be looked upon as a "bonus" during your retirement years. It is quite possible that there will be no money left in the CPP twenty, thirty, forty years from now when you retire. If you work your investment plan to its fullest potential, you won't have to count on CPP. (You should still apply for benefits, though, when the time comes.)

The Least You Need To Know

➤ You don't need a gazillion dollars to begin your investing program. Even $100 a month will do it. As you keep reading this book, you'll find out you can work with even less!

➤ The top ten steps in the process of successful investing include (among others): motivation, setting some financial goals, determining how much money you're going to need for these goals, learning how to do your homework, and then doing it!

➤ Fear and greed can overwhelm your investment decisions. Control them both and you control your financial destiny.

➤ Understand that unless you were fortunate to have Uncle Louie leave you a fortune in his will, you're going to have to work at creating your wealth.

Chapter 2

Everyday Economics

In this chapter
➤ How economics affects everything you do—especially investing
➤ Economic buzzwords
➤ The language of money

Remember the time Grandpa George pulled you aside, took the cigar out of his mouth, and bellowed, "Kid, when I was your age, the deficit was only three dollars and twenty-nine cents! And a litre of gas was a nickel. Plus, we had to walk to school uphill—both ways—in our bare feet, through ten-foot snow drifts." You also might've been lucky enough to hear that unending, grandparental hymn, "A penny saved is a penny earned."

These people speak of how bad things used to be for a reason: they lived through one of the most depressing financial times of the century—the stock market crash and the Great Depression. Terrible unemployment. War rationing. They can attest to poverty and explain how the basic essentials of life that used to cost a few pennies now cost a bundle. That generation can also discuss how our economy and financial markets have changed over the years. They probably can even tell stories of a few financial windfalls that they've enjoyed. Listen to them!

Bet You Didn't Know

The most outstanding economics book, *The Wealth of Nations* by Adam Smith, was written the same year the first United Empire Loyalists—1124 people from New England—arrived in Halifax. What year was that? 1776.

Today, you hear about our economy every day in the news, and read in the papers that the deficit is a zillion dollars. Or that the Bank of Canada raised interest rates. What does all this mean? How does it affect you and your investment decisions? Plenty.

You should care about economics. Why? If you understand

➤ Where we are in the business cycle

➤ The general direction of interest rates

➤ The economic indicators

...then you will be able to make better decisions for your investments. Many investments are affected by these three factors.

First, if you know where you are in the business cycle, you will have a better understanding of how well or how poorly companies are doing. This may help you choose stocks, corporate bonds, and mutual funds to invest in, since stocks and corporate bonds are issued by companies and mutual funds invest in both stocks and bonds.

The cardinal rule of economics? Learning that there is no such thing as a free lunch! There is always a cost involved. Know this and you understand the first lesson in economics.

Second, if you follow the general direction of interest rates, you will be able to determine at what point in time you should be investing in bonds. For example, if interest rates are really low, would you want to put your money in an investment product that doesn't pay a high rate of interest—such as a bond—for a really long time? Probably not. But on the other hand, if interest rates are high, you may choose to invest in a bond so you can get higher interest payments.

Third, following the major economic indicators will help you, because economic reports affect financial markets. You need to combine your understanding of where the economy is in the business cycle with the economic news of the day, in order to anticipate how financial markets will react and then make your investment decisions accordingly. Very often, what we think of as "good news" is perceived as "bad news" by the markets. An economic report saying that the economy is growing at a good clip sounds like good news, doesn't it? Not necessarily. If the economy is growing too quickly, markets can react negatively, because they are worried about inflation. So it's important to follow economic indicators for two reasons: to understand how the economy is doing and where it is in the business cycle. Then you can make intelligent decisions about your investments.

What Do Inflation and Recession Have To Do with Me?

Prosperity is when the prices of the things that you sell are rising; inflation is when the prices of things that you buy are rising. Recession is when other people are unemployed; depression is when you are unemployed.

> —Anonymous, taken from *Economics: Private and Public Choice* by
> James D. Gwartney and Richard L. Stroup.

A perfect economic world would be a pretty stable environment: steadily increasing business production, steady prices, and full employment (i.e., when the rate of unemployment is low at about 7 or 8 percent—-it never gets to zero). But you don't live in a perfect world—you live in a business cycle.

You can make better investment decisions by finding out where the economy is in the business cycle. In the following figure, the business cycle looks like nothing more than a squiggly line drawn by your two-year-old on your dining room wall. This line reveals a lot, however.

When you hear reports that the economy grew at a rate of 3% during the first quarter of this year, what does that

"Normal" employment When about 92 to 93 percent of the entire labour force is working, employment is "normal."

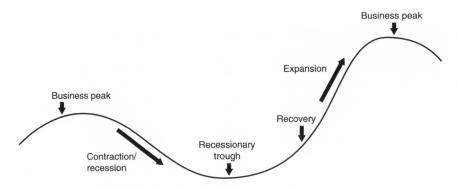

Riding the roller-coaster of the business cycle.

The **business cycle** reflects changes in the general level of economic activity as measured by certain economic indicators, such as the gross domestic product (GDP), the final measure of goods and services produced in the country within a year.

mean? When unemployment is at its highest level in six years, what does that indicate? The answers are in the business cycle.

A business cycle is a roller-coaster motion that shows whether the economy is on its way up or down. This changing motion has to be measured by economic indicators that not only tell you whether the economy is moving up or down but also give more detailed information on how different parts of the economy are doing.

When businesses are operating at a good capacity level—meaning their production of goods and services is up, running, and steadily humming along—the economy is expanding, and possibly heading toward a business peak. On the other hand, if business starts to slow down a bit and sales of goods and services drop, the economy may be entering the contraction part of the business cycle and possibly heading toward a recession.

Economics + You = Understanding Financial Markets

So what does all this have to do with financial markets? Several things.

First, when you invest in a stock, a corporate bond, a stock or bond

18

mutual fund, or even futures and options, what are you investing in? Businesses. Determining the position of the economy in the business cycle helps you determine how these businesses are doing.

For example, suppose general business production is on the upswing. Sales are rising everywhere. I own a company that makes Nighty-Night sleepwear for kids. My business production has been steadily increasing as mothers buy their children the sleepwear that I make. The profits of my company are rising, too. That's good news for the company's stock, and the stock price rises also. You buy stock in my company, and you're a happy camper as the stock price rises.

A period of rising prices is **inflation**, meaning it costs you more to purchase a typical bundle of goods. You'll see later in the book how inflation affects your buying and investment decisions.

Then the people who I buy my material from tell me that they have to raise their prices by five percent. Why? Because it now costs them more to buy cotton from their supplier to make the material that they sell to me. I still need this material in order to continue my business. If it's costing me five percent more to produce the same number of pajamas, and I don't raise my price, then I make less money in profits. This hurts my company's stock price, which means the price of the shares of stock that you own in my company drops. I probably could raise my prices on the sleepwear to try and increase profits, but that can backfire because mothers may not want to buy their kids expensive pajamas.

This is a pretty cut-and-dried example of how the economy's position in the business cycle can affect financial markets—in this case, the stock market.

Let's take this example one step further. Suppose that I do raise my prices on the sleepwear that I distribute to stores and consumer demand does drop a little—not a lot, but enough to make a small dent in my production. As prices of

Technically, the **unemployment rate** is the percentage of persons in the labour force who are not working but are either actively seeking a job or waiting to begin or return to a job.

19

WHAT?

A **recession** is a decline in economic activity. Economic activity is made up of all the goods and services that are produced.

my products and possibly other company products rise, talk of inflation starts. Because of the higher prices on these products, everyone's dollars purchase less than they did. Inflation essentially causes a decline in your purchasing power.

What happens if sales fall for most companies and they're not getting as much money coming in? The production of goods and services decreases. If my company, Nighty-Night sleepwear, reduces the number of pajamas it manufactures, then it might need less workers—I might have to lay some of them off. Those workers then become unemployed, which causes the unemployment rate to rise.

At this point, the economy approaches the recession part of the business cycle. Economists usually say it takes about two successive quarters (six months) of declining performance or no growth for a downturn to be labelled a "recession." That means that production in many businesses is contracting. As an investor, you probably don't want to invest in a company that is experiencing a decline in production.

Second, think of one of the most important factors affecting the economy—interest rates. If you follow the general direction of interest rates, whether they are rising or falling, they can help you determine what types of investments to look for.

For example, there are investments that are interest-rate sensitive, meaning for every blip up or down an interest rate takes, the value of those investments will be affected. An example? Bonds. Bonds are IOUs. You know when you have an IOU to pay, you have to pay the amount you borrowed plus interest. The interest rate on these bonds fluctuates (rises and falls).

Here's the point. If the general direction of interest rates in the economy is rising or falling, it will affect investments that carry an interest rate, such as bonds, and their value (or price) will be affected.

The Power Players

Businesses play a big part in the economy. But there are other power players who affect your investment decisions, whether you're trying to earn a gazillion percent on your bond investments or figuring out when is the best time to invest.

Who are these players? The federal government, for one. The Bank of Canada, for another, which monitors our nation's financial system and sets interest rates. Our foreign friends who lend our governments money and make investments in Canada have an impact, too. Finally, there's another player—you. You'll see why in a minute.

Big Brother

The federal and provincial governments have a major impact on our economy in several ways. First, they receive money, or revenues, by taxing you. Then they take this money and spend it on a number of things: bridges, transportation, education, social services, health care, and so on.

> **Revenues** are money received before expenses are taken out. WHAT?

Governments keep a budget similar to a family one. You work at a job and get a paycheque. That's your income. Governments rely on revenues from the taxes that they collect from you. That's their income. If they don't collect enough money from taxes, they can borrow it from you by selling you government securities (more on this in Part IV).

You have expenses—food, clothing, rent or a mortgage, weekend jaunts to Tahiti—and hope that you can meet these expenses and, of course, have a little left over. That's balancing your budget. Governments do the same thing—well, sort of. They try to balance the books every year, but the federal and provincial governments have had a hard time balancing their budgets in recent years. They have been running *budget deficits*.

> When the government spends more than it takes in, it's operating with a **budget deficit**. WHAT?

But the governments' deficit situation is changing rapidly—for the better. Only a few years ago —in 1992— the federal government and every single provincial government ran budget deficits, with the total deficit amounting to $66 billion. Since then, all of these governments have been working to reduce and eventually eliminate their deficits. In the governments' fiscal year ending March 31, 1997, the combined deficit of the federal and provincial governments had been reduced to $23 billion—less than half of what it was 5 years earlier—and five of the ten provincial governments had balanced budgets or surpluses.

 The total amount of the federal government's debt is often referred to as our **national debt** (the total of all the annual budget deficits over time). But provincial debt is also a large number.

So there is good news on the deficit front. But let's take the next step. If you add up all the past deficits, you come up with the total government debt. As of March 31, 1997, total federal and provincial debt amounted to $842 billion. To put this amount in perspective, it is 5% more than the value of all the goods and services produced by the Canadian economy! Even though the amount of total government debt is so large that it is hard to relate it to the day-to-day financial transactions that most of us do, it still must be repaid. And until it's repaid, the Canadian governments will have to keep paying interest on it.

You learned that every time governments have to borrow money, they sell government securities, such as Treasury bills, Canada Savings Bonds, etc., to people. Bingo! Here's where investing and the financial markets enter the picture. When a government sells these securities, it is actually borrowing the money. Therefore, the government must pay interest. The federal government spent $46 billion in interest on its debt in the fiscal year ended March 31, 1997 while the provincial governments handed over $20 billion in interest payments to investors.

So what does this have to do with making money? Plenty. When you buy a government bond or other security, you've invested in the government. That's the investing part. Because this money is out of your pocket, you're not spending it on groceries, or homes, or anything else. It isn't circulating out there in Canada. Money becomes scarce—the money supply is shrinking. That's the economics part. (Hang in there. This makes sense in a minute.) If the money supply shrinks, interest rates go up. Couple that with the government borrowing more money—well, that just pushes interest rates higher. Nine times out of ten, a change in interest rates has a major impact on the financial markets and ultimately, your investment decisions.

The Bank of Canada

Speaking of interest rates, let's check out what the central bank—the Bank of Canada—does. If you asked an economist how the central bank spends its time, the answer would be "it runs monetary policy." The primary job of the Bank of Canada is to keep the rate of inflation low and steady. The Bank and the federal government have set a target range for inflation in Canada: the annual increase in the Consumer Price Index (after changes in food and energy prices are taken out) is to be no less than 1 per cent and no more than 3 per cent each year.

Economists call the total stock of money that is circulating in the economy the **money supply**. Your personal money supply is money that you can access quickly and easily—the dollar bills in your pockets—plus what you have in your piggy bank, chequing account, savings account, and so on.

The main tool used by the Bank of Canada to control inflation is to change the rate of interest it charges for overnight loans to a group of "primary" investment dealers to finance their inventories of securities. This interest rate is actually a range of 50 basis points, or half a percentage point (for example 4.0–4.5 percent). Whenever the Bank of Canada observes that inflation may be rearing its ugly head, it raises this "operational target band for overnight funds." On the other hand, if inflation is low or falling and if the economy needs a boost to growth, the Bank will lower the operational target range.

When the Bank of Canada raises the overnight rate, two things are accomplished. First, it provides a signal to financial markets, as well as individuals and businesses, that the Bank is acting to slow the economy down by raising rates. (If the Bank lowers the rate, it sends a signal that it is trying to stimulate the economy.)

Second, when the overnight rate is raised—making short-term credit more expensive—it leads to increases in other, longer-term interest rates, such as 3-month or 6-month interest rates. The point of getting these interest rates to rise, of course, is that as credit becomes more expensive, people—and companies—put off buying goods and services, which helps slow the economy down. And that helps to keep inflation down. The Bank will continue to raise rates until it accomplishes its objective of stopping inflation from rising. Some people and some companies will pull back their spending in anticipation of the changed conditions ahead, even before the higher cost of borrowing affects them directly.

You may have heard about the Bank of Canada moving toward a "tighter" or "easier" monetary policy. All it means is that when the Bank raises interest rates it is "tightening" (like pushing on the brake pedal); and when it lowers interest rates, it is "easing" (like pushing on the gas pedal).

Sometimes you will hear about the "Bank Rate" in the financial press. This is the rate of interest charged by the Bank of Canada to a chartered bank if it needs to borrow money for a brief period in order to pay other banks at the end of the day when all of the transactions among the banks are settled. The Bank Rate is automatically set at the upper end of the range of the overnight interest rate.

Another interest rate that is often mentioned in the press is the "prime rate." Although this interest rate isn't directly related to the Bank of Canada, it generally does move in the same direction as the Bank Rate. The prime rate is the rate of interest charged by the chartered banks on loans to their best and most credit-worthy customers. Although the prime rate applies to corporate loans most of the time, occasionally financial institutions will relate an interest rate on a personal loan to the prime rate.

The Bank of Canada does a number of other things besides set interest rates. It monitors and adjusts growth in the money supply, smoothes out changes in the value of the Canadian dollar in foreign exchange markets, manages debt for the federal government, and has some supervisory responsibilities for financial institutions in Canada.

Our Foreign Friends

Canada is a trading nation. In fact, international trade plays a more important role in the Canadian economy than it does in Japan, Germany, the United States, and many other industrialized countries. Therefore, what happens in the economies of our major trading partners is very important both to the Canadian economy and to the many individual companies which sell goods and services to other countries. The United States is by far Canada's largest trading partner, accounting for about 80 percent of Canada's merchandise exports.

Canadian exports have always included many tangible items such as automobiles or refrigerators or copper or wheat, as well as some newer items such as computer software. These items are labelled "merchandise" exports. But Canada is increasingly involved in international trade in services—or "non-merchandise" exports—such as consulting services or financial services.

There is another aspect to the international side of Canada's economy, and that is *foreign investment*. Traditionally, Canada looked to foreign investors to supply a large part of the investments needed to make the Canadian economy develop and grow. These investments are of two types. *Direct investment* consists of the purchase or construction of a factory by a foreign investor (e.g., Toyota building an auto plant in Ontario). *Portfolio investment* is the purchase of Canadian stocks or bonds by foreign investors.

Foreign investors have also lent a lot of money to Canadian governments, who have had to borrow money abroad to finance their budget deficits. As a result of these various types of foreign investments, there have been large outflows of interest payments and dividends from Canada each year to other countries in order to provide the foreign investors a return on their Canadian investments. It has also meant that foreign investors have had quite a lot of influence over the Canadian economy.

Times are changing. Foreigners still invest in Canada, but Canadian investors increasingly invest in foreign countries. And Canadian governments are borrowing less from abroad because they are reducing or eliminating their budget deficits. The result is that when you add up the capital inflows and outflows, they are much closer to being in balance than they used to be.

This doesn't mean that our international economic and financial relationships are any less important than they have been in the past, but they are different. International trade is growing rapidly throughout the world. In fact, trade is growing faster than any one country's economy. Firms from other countries are working hard to sell goods and services in Canada and Canadian firms are working equally hard to sell Canadian goods and services to foreign markets. By participating in international trade, Canadians raise their own economic prosperity.

You

Now for that last factor that controls the economy. You stare at it in the bathroom mirror every day. It's you—the consumer. The decisions you

WHAT?

Look at your paycheque stub. See that little box labelled Gross Pay? That's your gross income. Now check out all the little boxes where taxes are taken out, as well as unemployment insurance premiums and Canada Pension Plan premiums, etc. What you're left with is **disposable income**.

make on a day-to-day basis influence the economy. In fact, consumer spending accounts for about two-thirds of total economic activity.

How consumers behave has a huge impact on how the economy—and financial markets—perform. Suppose that for some reason (perhaps because their credit cards are tapped out) consumers decide to spend less. Then businesses will produce less goods and services and their profits will decline. The prices of their stocks fall. Companies may lay off some workers, and the unemployment rate rises. That makes consumers spend even less. At this point, the government can step in to stimulate the economy by lowering interest rates. Lower interest rates tend to get the economy going again—consumers spend more and businesses increase production. Profits rise and stock prices along with them.

Check In with Dr. Econ

Because changes in the economy affect financial markets (although some say that it's the other way around), there are critical economic reports that need to be monitored in the same way that a doctor monitors your vital signs. Each can send the price of an investment sky high, or knock the bleep out of it! Here's a thumbnail sketch of a few economic buzzwords and phrases that you should know.

If you really want to follow the direction of the economy and determine where we are in a business cycle, follow the economic indicators listed here. Then watch the financial markets to see how they react. It's a great way to familiarize yourself with the relationship between economics and financial markets.

The Gross Domestic Product (GDP) is a measure of the total output of goods and services produced in the Canadian economy in a given period. It provides the most comprehensive measure of the health and growth of our economy.

The Consumer Price Index (CPI) tracks the changes in the prices of food, housing, clothing, transportation, electricity, and other items that most consumers purchase. If the price of your favourite breakfast cereal rises, it will be reflected in the CPI. Economists and market watchers use the CPI as an indicator of inflation.

The labour market —or employment —report provides information on how many new jobs are being created as well as on how many people remain unemployed (the unemployment rate).

Set 'Em Up, Knock 'Em Down

Economics is about people and the choices they make. Think of the economy and the financial markets as dominoes: when the first one gets hit, all the others are affected. Remember the Nighty-Night sleep-wear example? The first domino that was struck was my material supplier. As he increased his prices, I had to make changes to compensate for the price increase. That was the next domino. As more changes were made, more dominoes were affected.

Understanding where the country is in the business cycle affects your investment decisions. Once you understand economics and how these important economic reports affect your investments, you'll make better educated decisions as an investor.

The Least You Need To Know

> ➤ Economics isn't boring. In fact, if you know how our economy operates, you can make educated investment decisions.

> ➤ The economic reports that the government releases give a good indication of the strength and weakness of our economy.

> ➤ The biggest players in our economy are consumers, businesses, government, and foreign investors.

> ➤ In the world of investing, there are many different investment products, which are also known as securities or instruments. These include bank products, stocks, bonds, mutual funds, futures, and options.

"A bull market tends to bail you out of all your mistakes. Conversely, a bear market makes you pay for all your mistakes."

—Richard Russell

Chapter 3

Your Personal Financial Battle Plan

> ## In this chapter
> ➤ How to determine your financial goals and the plan to reach them
> ➤ A financial rule you can't afford to live without
> ➤ Where to find money to invest

When a general designs a strategy for his army during a war, he has a plan. He doesn't lead his troops into combat without doing his homework. He has to evaluate the strengths and weaknesses of his armies before, during, and after the conflict.

What about your plan? You want your money to work as hard for you as you do for it. Making an investment plan is half the battle. Not only does it tell you where you stand financially right now, it will help determine where you want to be in the future. This chapter helps you put together your personal financial battle plan.

Setting a Goal—And Figuring Out How To Reach It

So where do you want to go? What do you want? It's time to set some goals.

Setting goals isn't difficult. Think back to grade school when you were the top contender in the 6th grade spelling bee. You had a goal of getting through the word "zoophagous" (yes, it's a real word!) and winning the championship. Or in high school when you were on the football team, you set a goal to score the most touchdowns in a single quarter. All you are doing now is applying the same discipline to your investment plan.

Don't put off making a financial plan until tomorrow. Tomorrow never comes, you know.

Take out a piece of paper. Divide up the time frames and what your goals are into four categories: Five years, Ten years, Twenty Years, and Thirty Years. Write these down. It may look something like this:

➤ **Five years** Pay off school loans, auto loans, any bad debt.

➤ **Ten years** New home.

➤ **Twenty years** University education for the kids.

➤ **Thirty years** Your retirement—and enjoying it!

Now, next to these goals write down how much money each goal is going to require. Don't be surprised by your results. Unless you already have the money socked away somewhere, most people will have to put up additional funds to reach these goals. The amount of the additional funds will determine what types of investment products you will buy and sell.

To continue with the example, it may look like this:

➤ **Five years** Pay off school loans, auto loans, any bad debt: $3,000.

➤ **Ten years** New home (twenty-five percent down payment, $200,000 home): $50,000.

➤ **Twenty years** University education for one child: $40,000 (really!).

➤ **Thirty years** Retirement: $1,000,000.

Good. Add these all up. Here, the total is $1,093,000. Okay, more than a million bucks. Do you have this total amount stashed away in a bank account or a brokerage account? If you're like most hard-working people, the answer is no.

DON'T WORRY! You can have that amount. You are in the midst of planning your work and working your plan. Now, can you see why investing is so important? You need to use the magic of compounding and the essence of time to work for you to attain these goals.

Don't change your goals. Do not look at the bottom line and say "Oh, these numbers are too high. I'll never get there." With that attitude, you won't. But this book will help you get there. How? Discipline.

Buying a Home

Let's take the goal of buying a house. Ah, the Canadian dream. This is the most expensive purchase you can make. But it is probably the biggest investment you can make, too. There's a lot of pride in home ownership—not to mention the potential for appreciation through the years.

It will take more money to save for a house than any other major purchase. If the median price of a three-bedroom, two-bath home in your area is $200,000, you may need up to twenty-five percent of that for a down payment—that's $50,000. For many hard-working people, that's more than an average annual salary. If you save $250 a month over the next ten years and earn an annual rate of 8%, you'll almost make it, having saved $46,146 at the end of those ten years.

Even though you can get a mortgage with as little as five percent down (for first-time homebuyers), try to put down as much as possible. In fact, if you can meet the standard twenty-five percent down payment, it might be a good idea. Why? This way you avoid paying private mortgage insurance, which insures the insurer for lending you the money to buy a house without a lot of money as a down payment.

But what if you want the house sooner? Well, then you're going to have to allocate more than just $250 a month and/or invest in an investment product that pays a better return than 8%. You may wish to refer back to Table 1.2 in Chapter 1 as a guide or you can check out the "Investment Pyramid" in Chapter 5, which lists investment products, their level of risk, and the type of annual return you can expect.

Let's Get Organized!

If you are becoming concerned about having enough income for retirement, you are not alone. But, don't despair; time is on your side. You are figuring out your goals now—years before you plan to reach them. This part of the process lets you know the following:

➤ What your goals are.

➤ When you want them.

➤ How much they'll cost.

➤ How much you'll need to invest to get there.

A Few Tools To Help

Before you start digging into your desk drawers that are filled with your financial records, please be aware that there are a few tools to help you become organized—and none of them is a shovel!

The key to organizing your finances in the 90s is the computer software package. They range from simple to downright computer nerdy. Each computer software package is designed specifically for you with one goal in mind: To help you GET CONTROL (there's that phrase again) of your finances.

Most financial software packages enable you to:

➤ Pay your bills electronically.

➤ Create a budget and track your expenses.

➤ Create and monitor your own personal investment portfolio.

➤ Update investment security prices (via modem, typically).

➤ Figure out how much you'll need for your children's university education.

➤ Assist you in planning for retirement.

The only thing these programs can't do is make you breakfast.

You can take full advantage of a financial software program—by projecting your budget on an annual basis and consistently managing your investment portfolio; or you may only wish to get your financial records in order. In any event, transferring the mess from your desk to your computer will pay off!

Here are two financial software packages out on the market that can assist you in organizing your financial life.

➤ **Microsoft Money 97 and Money Guide** Available for DOS and Windows. This simple, convenient program helps you put your financial house in order through personal financial education and planning. You can pay bills, check bank account balances, chart your investments, or plan your retirement. Money 97 has enhanced its online banking features, providing access to more banks and financial institutions. In fact, the banking features are the most solid aspect of this package. The program's Financial Wizards hold your hand through specific tasks, such as mortgage financing and setting savings goals. When tax time rolls around, Microsoft Money can generate a tax report to help you fill out your tax returns. Microsoft Money sells for approximately $90 and is available across Canada.

You don't have to be a computer whiz to work with these software packages. In fact, if you aren't sure about purchasing one, see if you can get a "demo" disk that will explain the features.

➤ **Quicken** Available for Windows, DOS, and Macintosh, Quicken is an extremely popular and easy software package to use for those of you who have a hard time balancing a chequebook. The package provides you with features to pay your bills electronically. Also, this financial software makes it easy for you to track your investments and create financial records, such as an asset and liability worksheet. This program updates security prices for you on all of your investments listed in your portfolio. It's available through computer stores, warehouse clubs, and discount stores Canada-wide and retails for approximately $70.

The two financial software packages mentioned above are among the most widely known and used. They are compatible with many of the banks' online services. For a list of some other helpful sources to get your financial house in order, check out the Appendix.

A Look at Your Budget

Imagine you're in a brand-spankin' new mall and you just found out that your favourite store is having its grand opening. Unfortunately, the mall is more than three kilometres long and you don't know where the store is located. So you search for a mall directory. Once you arrive, what's the first thing you do? You find that little red dot that says "YOU ARE HERE" before you go any further. Why? Because in order to get to your favourite store, you need to know where you are standing right now.

Before you can improve your financial condition and start investing, you need to complete the following three steps:

1. Clean up the mess and get organized—it's not difficult, trust me.

2. Add up the pluses and minuses—good debt versus bad debt.

3. Create your own budget.

Clean Up the Mess

Getting organized is the key. At one point or another, many people have had the motivation to sort out their financial affairs. Some even go as far as making a New Year's resolution to develop a sound financial system for themselves and their families. This usually lasts about as long as a New Year's diet; although I'm sure people stick to their diets better than they maintain their financial records.

Don't worry. This won't be nearly as painful as dieting. If you've kept pretty good records over the years, pat yourself on the back. Nearly six in ten Canadians do not organize their financial records. The numbers increase for those people who do not even balance their chequebooks. If you have set up a filing system, great! But if your underwear drawer is stuffed with unopened envelopes that hold your monthly bank statements, we may have a problem!

First, let's make this easy. You don't need years and years' worth of information. Just use information and receipts from the past six months or even three months. The important thing is to get started. You'll be able to project for the remaining months of the year what you'll spend.

Some of you may want to be super-organized and get together all the information that you'd need if you were preparing your tax returns. The idea is not to be overwhelmed but just to be organized. You can't make educated investment decisions if you don't do the following:

➤ Start with organized records.

➤ Create a budget that you can work within.

➤ Learn how much money you can afford to invest.

The first step to organization is a file cabinet. Using a shoebox is okay, but after time you'll need more organized storage space. Because it is suggested that you keep this material for six years, in case of re-assessment by Revenue Canada, you need to set up an annual filing system. These materials should include (but are not limited to) the following:

➤ Copies of your old tax returns.

➤ Copies of cancelled cheques paid to Revenue Canada for income tax payments.

➤ Paycheque stubs.

➤ Copies of the T-4s that you receive from your employer(s).

➤ Copies of the T-5s that you receive from dividends and interest that you have earned.

➤ Bank statements and brokerage statements (if you have any yet).

➤ Chequebook registers (make sure you start a new one each year).

➤ Records of any deductible expenses (e.g. tuition, charitable donations, interest on investment loans).

Make sure all of these records are stored safely in a file cabinet in a folder labelled "Tax Returns for 19__." Do this from now on. Second, gather your tools. Purchase a three-ring binder, twelve paper-dividers with tabs, a hole punch, a stapler, a box of legal-size envelopes, and a box of extra-large 8 1/2" x 11" envelopes.

Label one drawer of the filing cabinet for tax returns, the other "January to December." Put the twelve dividers with tabs in the three-ring binder. Label the tabs with the months of the year. Every time you receive a bill—telephone bill, electric bill, charge card bills—put the tear-off stub of the bill in this three-ring binder.

For example, suppose it's November 9th and you just received your telephone bill. Tear off the bill payment portion and put it with its envelope and your payment. Next, using your stapler and paper punch, staple together the parts of the bill that you save and punch three holes in it. Write your cheque number on it and the date you sent the payment. Finally, put it in the three-ring binder, and you're on your way to organization!

Do this with all your bills. You can even paper punch bank statements, paycheque stubs, and any loan statements and place them in the corresponding months.

Those of you who like to save all your receipts can do so with envelopes. For example, I like to save all my bank machine receipts. At the end of every month, I put them in date order, cross-reference them with my cheque register, staple them together, and put them in an envelope marked Bank Machine Receipts. I do the same thing with taxi receipts, gas receipts, grocery receipts, and clothing receipts.

Why? Is it because I'm an organizational freak? No way! Because if all of my receipts are in order, at the end of the year I can add them up and figure out how much I spend on each annually. Believe me, it really puts your financial affairs in perspective when you find out that you spent more money on clothes than you did on groceries in a single year!

Adding Up the Pluses and Minuses

Now that you have this information organized, you can start determining where you are financially. That means figuring out your pluses and minuses. By doing the exercises in this chapter, you can see how your assets (the pluses) match or mismatch with your liabilities (the minuses). Here are some terms you should know before you embark on adding it all up:

Assets. What you own, such as the equity in your house, your car, your furniture, your property, your bank accounts and your kids! (Just kidding on the last one.) Basically, assets are your possessions.

Liabilities. What you still owe on your house, your car, credit cards, unpaid taxes, student loans. If you owe it, it's a liability. There are good liabilities (good debt) and bad liabilities (bad debt).

The more debt you are burdened with, the longer it will take to dig yourself out of a hole. Your first priority should be to ELIMINATE nonproductive debt.

Good Debt. What you still owe on your house. Why is it a good debt? Because the value of the asset (the house) can appreciate. The more you pay off on this good debt, the more equity you will have in your home.

Bad Debt. What you still owe on your car, your credit cards, and student loans. These debt monsters don't work for you; they work against you. Plus, it's bad debt because the interest rates are extremely high. Pay off the highest interest rate items first (usually your credit cards).

The name of the game is to have as few

bad liabilities as possible and increase your assets substantially. You can do this by building wealth through your investment planning; however, that does not mean also increasing your credit card debt or buying another car. That only defeats your entire plan.

> Your **investment portfolio** represents the sum of all of your stocks, bonds, mutual funds, options, futures, etc., that you have invested in.

Let me give you an example of how bad debt works against you. Assume you made a $1,000 purchase last month on your 19.8% VISA, and you don't pay it off in full when the bill comes next month. You're the meet-the-minimum-payment type of consumer. At that rate, it will take you about fifteen years to pay off that thousand bucks. (This is how credit card companies make their money.) Also (get this!) there are additional thousands in nondeductible finance charges.

Let's take it one step further. You have started building an investment portfolio of a few stocks, a couple of bonds, and a mutual fund or two. The average annual return you make on your entire investment portfolio is 12%. Not bad!

Here's where the bad debt attacks you, even if you are investing your money. If you're making 12% interest but are paying off a credit card balance of 19.8% on your $1,000 purchase, the money you make on your investments turns into minus 7.8% (12% – 19.8%)! You end up working even harder for that $1,000 purchase.

Of course you want to invest your money. However, it is equally important to get rid of the bad debt first. You can't get ahead in this investment race if you still have one foot stuck in the ground. Once you reduce bad debt, your net worth will increase. You will also feel a sense of security with your growing net worth and will be able to change jobs and meet personal emergencies as they arise. Use the worksheets in the following figures to determine where you stand.

Once you figure out your financial property and your personal property, you can calculate your total assets. Then add up how much you owe on your liability worksheet. That sum is your liability statement. Now subtract your liabilities from your assets and you should have a positive number. That's your net worth. If it's negative, you're not alone. Thousands of Canadians have a negative net worth. This process shows that there is more to good finances than merely increasing your net worth through wise investing. That's just one small part of the entire picture.

Financial Property	Date Purchased	How Much Did You Pay?	Today's Date	What's It Worth Today?
Bonds (type)				
Bond mutual funds (type)				
GICs				
Chequing accounts				
Coin collections				
Money market mutual funds				
Pensions & profit sharing plans				
Savings accounts				
Savings bonds				
Stocks				
Stock mutual funds				
Government bonds				
Other				
Total Financial Property				

A financial property assets worksheet

Personal Property	Date Purchased	How Much Did You Pay?	What's It Worth Today?
Appliances (washer & dryer, etc.)			
Automobiles			
Boats, campers			
Computers			
Furniture			
Fur coats			
Home			
Home furnishings			
—curtains			
—rugs			
—tableware (glasses, dishes)			
—blankets			
—lamps			
—silverware			
Jewelry			
Paintings			
Stereos			
Televisions			
Miscellaneous			
Total Personal Property			

A personal property assets worksheet

What You Owe	To Whom	Interest Rate %	When Is It Due?	How Much Do You Owe?
Bills, bills, bills				
—electric				
—gas				
—retail stores				
—telephone				
—other				
Loans to family				
Loans to friends				
Automobile loans				
Bank loans				
Credit cards				
—credit card #1				
—credit card #2				
—credit card #3				
Furniture loans				
Student loans				
Mortgage				
Home equity loans				
Miscellaneous				
Total Liabilities				

A liabilities worksheet

Creating Your Budget

Tracking where all your money goes is important. Figuring out your assets and liabilities to calculate your net worth assists you in determining how you spend your money. To keep these expenses in line, create a budget. Keeping a budget gives you insight into any nasty spending habits you might have. You can't afford a champagne lifestyle when you have a beer budget!

Your net worth is where you stand financially. Add up the total value of what you own, subtract what you owe, and the bottom line is this number. Good luck!

A common misconception is that following a budget means you can't start investing. After calculating your net worth and creating a healthy budget, you'll realize that in order to invest the money, it has to come from somewhere. You're either going to have to reduce some of your expenses or get another job. Unfortunately, millions of Canadians already live in a two-paycheque family, and there are only so many hours in a day.

So where do you begin? You need to calculate your income on a monthly basis. Consider this Budget Number #1. Then, because you have organized all your receipts and financial papers from the past few months and have (I hope!) put them in their respective categories, it'll be easy to figure out how much the following regular expenses are:

Auto expenses	Car payment, auto insurance, maintenance, gas (save your receipts and payment stubs!).
Clothing expenses	Clothing, shoes, coats.
Dental expenses	Teeth cleaning, etc. (anything not covered by insurance if you have it).
Dining expenses	Restaurants, even if it's fast food (it adds up!).
Entertainment	Movies, golf, zoo.
Education	Kids' tuition, your tuition, books, and school supplies.
Gifts	Birthdays, holidays.
Groceries	Food, drugstore items (toiletries, cosmetics, etc.).

Home business	Subcategories including equipment, supplies, taxes, etc.
Household items	New things you buy for the house—furniture, plants, curtains, etc.
Household expenses	This is different from the items above. These are things you buy for the upkeep of the house, such as paint, aluminum siding, lawn maintenance equipment and services, etc.
Insurance	Life insurance, disability insurance, homeowner's insurance.
Mortgage	If you own a home, fill in your mortgage payment.
Parking	If you have to pay to park (at work, when shopping, etc.).
Rent	If you are renting, fill in your monthly rent.
Taxes	Income taxes paid, real estate taxes.
Utilities	Including telephone bill, gas bill, electric bill.
Vacations	Including airplane tickets, hotel/motel accommodations, meals, sightseeing, etc.

(These are just a few categories to get you started. Depending on your own situation, you may wish to add or delete a few.)

Calculate how much you spend on each category in a month. When you have determined each total, add them all up. That should be Budget Number #2.

Now complete this calculation to find out what you can invest each month:

Budget Number #1 – Budget Number #2 = What You Can Afford To Invest

If you break even or are "in the hole," you may have to cut some expenses. It's up to

If you want to forecast your annual budget, remember to take into account the changes in utility bills, (higher in winter, lower in summer) or non-monthly expenses, like car insurance and real estate taxes.

you to decide which expenses are necessities and which are just plain frivolous. If you are ahead of the game, congratulations!

An integral part of creating and working within a budget is monitoring—and possibly cutting—some spending habits. I can't tell you where, because I surely would hate for someone to tell me that I couldn't hit the golf course every other weekend. While I may not be willing to cut this expense, I have drastically cut expenses in other departments.

How Much Can You Afford To Invest?

Whatever money you have left over from subtracting your expenses from your income should work just as hard for you as you do for it. That's why you should choose to invest it—and you don't have to invest all of it if you don't want to. That decision is up to you. However, the more money you invest, and the longer you invest it for, the more potential it has to grow.

One of the biggest expenses you can cut right now is debt. How? Cutting up the plastic credit cards and making do with the ol' jalopy that sits in your driveway are good ways to begin.

One rule of thumb is the ten percent rule. Why ten percent? Because it's easy to figure out in the math calculations. For example, if your monthly income is $2,500, ten percent would be $250. Easy enough.

If you cannot afford the ten percent rule, try and have at least $50 a month to begin your investment portfolio. If that is too much, start with $25—but no less. (You'll learn where you can invest with these amounts in Chapter 27.) Even if it means making holiday gifts instead of buying them or staying at home on vacation, the potential reward over the long-term is greater than any gift you could buy or any sightseeing tour you could take. Use the $50 or $25 as your own guideline. Once you start trimming your expenses (or perhaps receiving more income), add to the monthly amount as much as you can.

Pay Yourself First

Treat yourself as if you were a monthly bill. On your budget worksheet, create another category. Call it the "Pay Yourself First" category. This requires you to further develop the habit of investing on a consistent basis. Before all of the other utility bills, before the kids' shoes, even be-fore Monday night Bingo, pay yourself first every time you receive your paycheque. Take this money and invest it—don't go and buy a new put-ter or take your girlfriend or boyfriend out to dinner. By earmarking it in your monthly budget, you are creating your fortune without even re-alizing it. Remember what as little as $100 can do over time?

A number of financial strategies use this principle. In fact, you can pay yourself first by using automatic deductions that are taken directly out of your paycheque before you even see the money.

Before you begin paying yourself first, have your paycheque di-rectly deposited into your bank chequing account or savings account. Why? Well, first you earn interest as soon as it hits the account and don't have to wait in long teller lines during your lunch hour to deposit your cheque. Plus, you don't see it; it's automatically deposited. No temptation!

Once you establish a direct deposit feature, sign up for an auto-matic monthly purchase plan for mutual funds. For example, take 10% from each paycheque and put it into an investment account. Again, this eliminates the temptation to withdraw a few bucks for things that you don't really need. Plus, you'll earn better rates of interest than you do in a noninterest-bearing chequing account (ha ha—you don't earn *any* interest on a noninterest-bearing account) and learn how to be dis-ciplined. Even better, this method takes advantage of dollar cost averag-ing (more on that later).

Reducing your expenses is a smart move. So is paying yourself first!

Cash You Didn't Know You Had

You have hidden cash resources that can grow into a substantial invest-ment nest egg.

If you were one of the lucky people to have refinanced your mort-gage when interest rates hit rock bottom in November 1996, you could have saved money every month. Even $50 from an $875-a-month mort-gage bill allows you to save and invest an extra $600 a year. If you invest $600 every year into a growth stock mutual fund that earns an average annual rate of 13% a year, it can grow to roughly $4,139 in five years— and that's not even counting dividends being reinvested in the fund.

You can find extra money by asking for discounts on your automobile insurance coverage. They include breaks for having air bags or antitheft equipment (such as a car alarms), for keeping annual mileage under prescribed levels, and for having no claims against your policy. Check with your insurance agent. These discounts can save you up to twenty percent of your average annual car insurance premiums. That could mean an extra $240 a year if your annual premiums are $1,200.

Another gold mine of extra money to invest is in your home-owner's insurance policies. By increasing your deductible to $500 or $1,000, you can lower your premiums and save as much as ten to twenty percent a year.

Above all, ask yourself:

➤ **How much is my net worth?** If you're competing with a negative net worth and high credit card debt, you have to get rid of both of these. Once your net worth increases, you'll be able to allocate more dollars to your investment plan.

➤ **What is ten percent of my weekly take-home pay?** Calculating this figure is easy. Once you establish self-discipline and put that amount in investments, you'll see how much your money can grow.

➤ **At what rates of return over how long a period of time do I need?** This depends on what you're investing for (the house, university education, your retirement). By determining how long you have until you reach these milestones, you'll know how conservative or aggressive you must be in your investing.

These are just a few questions you should ask yourself. As you learn more from each chapter of this book, you'll be able to judge how well your investment plan is going.

The Least You Need To Know

➤ Everyone needs a plan before he or she can make his or her dream a reality. Work your plan and plan your work!

➤ Organizing your financial records is the key to successful investing. Once you know where you stand financially, you'll be able to determine which investments are right for you.

➤ Automatically save at least ten percent of your paycheque. This strong discipline will pay off handsomely as the monies accumulate. If you can't, you should begin with $50 or $25 a month. As you trim your expenses, you will be able to add to it.

➤ Only you can determine what you are going to do with your money. Determine what you want, how much money you're going to need, and how long you're going to have to invest your money to reach those goals.

Chapter 4

Tax-Sheltered Plans for the Entire Family: RRSPs, RRIFs, and RESPs

YOU'LL BE FINE. YOU'RE COVERED.

In this chapter

➤ Registered Retirement Savings Plans

➤ Registered Retirement Income Funds

➤ Registered Education Savings Plans

All right folks, I hope you're paying attention, because this is the single most important chapter in the entire book. If you were to read only ONE chapter in this whole book (or at least remember only one chapter), this would be the one! Here, we focus on tax-sheltered plans and how to use them to your maximum advantage.

Start early and invest often. Say this to yourself ten times. The best way to build savings is to put time to work and harness the power of compounding. For instance, if at age twenty you put $100 a month into a tax-sheltered plan until

Start early and invest often. Ah, the golden rule to successful retirement planning. The best way to build savings is to put time to work and harness the power of compounding.

you reached age sixty-five, assuming a 10% annual compound rate of return, you'd be a millionaire by the time you retired!

Taxes. Taxes. Taxes. Canadians are burdened with taxes almost everywhere we turn. There's income tax, property tax, provincial sales tax, goods and services tax, tax on interest income, capital gains tax...the list goes on and on. The fact is we are taxed to death. Unfortunately, there are very few tax breaks available today. So, you should make full use of the tax-sheltered plans that the government offers...while you can.

The RRSP is definitely long-term and the crux of all retirement planning. With time on your side, you can see your investment grow substantially. Remember, doing something (something smart, that is) is better than doing nothing!

An **RRSP** is a Registered Retirement Savings Plan. It's not an investment like a stock or bond, but rather an account where you can buy and sell different investments—tax-free.

WHAT?

The RRSP: King of Tax-Sheltered Plans

One of the best tax-sheltered plans available to Canadians today is the Registered Retirement Savings Plan, or what's more commonly called the RRSP. An RRSP is not an investment like a stock or a bond, but an account that you put your money in. Inside the RRSP account, you can buy and sell different investments—tax free.

The RRSP was designed in 1957 for people who were not covered by a company-sponsored retirement plan to help them save for retirement. In fact, the government of Canada encourages Canadians to save for their retirement; with this in mind, the government has developed tax incentives for those who do invest into an RRSP.

The beauty of an RRSP is that it is a tax-sheltered investment vehicle. The amount you contribute annually to your RRSP, within your maximum allowable contribution limits, is completely tax deductible. In many cases, you can expect a significant tax reduction. For example, if you are in a 50% tax bracket, a $10,000 contribution to your RRSP would mean a $5,000 reduction in taxes paid. Even better, the investment in-

Bet You Didn't Know

If you invest $50 a month, every month for thirty years (assuming an 8% annual return) in an RRSP instead of a taxable account, you will have accumulated more than $75,000!

come earned inside an RRSP (interest, dividends, capital gains) is sheltered from current taxes. Your money grows more quickly in an RRSP because, unlike a conventional savings account, your money compounds tax-free.

Once you have set up your RRSP account at your bank, brokerage firm or mutual fund company, you are allowed to make an annual contribution of up to $13,500 or 18% of your earned income for that year, whichever is less. These contribution limits may change in the future—make sure you know what the limits are. If you are covered by another retirement plan, such as your company pension plan, you can contribute to an RRSP, provided your pension has not exceeded your RRSP contribution limit. Any excess RRSP contribution room may then be used.

You may contribute to an RRSP until you reach age sixty-nine. At that point, you can take the cash and run or you must convert your RRSP to an

RRSP Contribution Limits

(Note: These limits may change for future years.)

The previous year's unused contribution room plus:

➤ 18% of last year's earned income to a maximum of $13,500; OR

➤ If you hold a pension plan, 18% of last year's earned income to a maximum of $13,500 minus last year's pension adjustment.

Keep in mind that your RRSP contributions must come from "earned income," such as from your salary. You should receive a notice of assessment from the government stating the maximum amount you are allowed to contribute.

RRIF (Registered Retirement Income Fund) or an annuity. Both require you to withdraw a minimum amount each year. But more on that later.

To allow for any unintentional over-contributions (i.e. beyond the legislated limit) to your RRSP, each individual can have up to $2,000 in over-contributions without paying a penalty tax. Any over-contributions in excess of this $2,000 are subject to a 1% per month penalty. If you do not make your maximum RRSP contribution in a given year, according to current legislation, you may "carry forward" indefinitely the unused portion accumulated since 1991.

When you do withdraw money from your RRSP, you pay taxes at your current rate. For most people, money will be withdrawn at retirement when income tends to be lower, and therefore, personal tax rates may be lower. If, however, you withdraw money from your RRSP earlier than age sixty-nine, you will be penalized a withholding tax (at 10% or more, depending on the amount withdrawn), and you will pay income tax on that amount at your current rate.

Bet You Didn't Know

Let's say your earned income for last year was $30,000 and you are thirty years old. Your maximum RRSP contribution for this year would then be 18% x $30,000, which is $5,400. You put that $5,400 maximum into your RRSP account for this year, and at least this much for the next thirty-five years (provided your earned income is at least $30,000 over this time period and the limits remain the same). Assuming an 8% annual compound rate of return, you'd have well over a million dollars! Remember: invest early, invest often!

Foreign Content in your RRSP

One more critical thing to note regarding RRSPs. The maximum amount of foreign content you can hold in your RRSP is 20%. Foreign content means any investing you do outside of Canada—for example, U.S. stocks, European bonds, or an Asian Pacific mutual fund. It is a good idea to maximize your foreign content because it helps you to diversify your investments outside of Canada. Remember, don't put all your eggs in one basket! If you have approximately 80% of your portfolio exposed to Canada, you can maximize your foreign content and expose your portfolio to the opportunities that exist in the rest of the world. Be careful not to exceed the 20% foreign content as there is a penalty of 1% per month on any amount that exceeds the 20% limit.

When Are My RRSP Contributions Due?

Each year there is an RRSP contribution deadline which usually falls on March 1. Any contributions made before that deadline can be used for the previous year's tax return (assuming there is available room to make the contribution). Many people wait to the last minute to make their contribution and many times will not have enough money to maximize their contribution. They end up taking out a loan (you should be able to get an RRSP loan at prime as long as you pay it back over one year) and paying interest on the loan. The point is, they are maximizing their contributions.

But, there's a better way. Each month you should be allocating a set portion of your paycheque money to your RRSP. You can set up an automatic monthly mutual fund purchase plan where the money will automatically come out of your bank account and go right into your RRSP into the mutual fund that you have pre-selected. This way you are investing earlier (before the March 1 deadline!) and the money is going to work for you sooner.

Your annual RRSP contribution deadline is March 1. Don't wait until the last minute—such as March 1 or your sixty-eighth birthday—to make your RRSP contribution. The earlier in the year you make it, the longer your money will grow tax-deferred. Make your contribution as early as you can. Not only do you get a tax deduction, you still receive the benefit of tax-deferred compounding when you invest in an RRSP. This is also known as sheltering your investments from income taxes. Check it out.

On top of that, with the monthly contributions you will be taking advantage of something you may have already heard about—dollar cost averaging. But more on that later. The earlier you get the money in the RRSP the better. The bottom line: maximize your yearly RRSP contributions. If you take nothing else away from this book, take that.

Maximize your RRSP contributions! Instead of taking out an RRSP loan to maximize your RRSP contributions, have a fixed amount of your paycheque set aside each month toward a mutual fund monthly purchase plan.

Types of Retirement Savings Plans and Other Assorted Perks

Basically, there are two types of RRSPs: the Single Vendor RRSP (or what I call the conventional RRSP) and the Self-Directed RRSP. Single Vendor, or conventional RRSPs, invest in one or more of a variety of pooled funds or mutual funds which are held in trust under the plan by a particular issuer, bank, or trust company. There is usually a trustee fee charged for this type of plan.

A Self-Directed Retirement Savings Plan (SDRSP) is slightly different from the conventional RRSP. As the name implies, it is fully self-directed. This type of plan offers you maximum flexibility in meeting your financial planning objectives and taking advantage of investment opportunities. Along with savings options, you can also invest in stocks, bonds, T-Bills, GICs, RRSP-eligible mutual funds, foreign investments, and even your own mortgage.

An SDRSP can be set up at any brokerage firm and carries an annual administration fee of approximately $100. The key feature of the SDRSP is that it allows you to consolidate all your RRSP holdings into one account. So, instead of receiving five statements in the mail each month (e.g. bank RRSP statement, mutual fund RRSP statements, brokerage firm RRSP statement), you'll receive just one. Having an SDRSP will not only cut down on administration fees, but enable you to manage your money more effectively. Even better, because SDRSPs are offered mainly by brokerage firms, you will have the professional services of a broker overseeing your account.

If you are just starting out, you can set up a Single Vendor or conventional RRSP at your local bank or mutual fund company. These RRSPs are qualified RRSPs, meaning they are limited to certain investments and don't cover the broad range of products that the SDRSPs do. If you open an RRSP account at the bank, the bank usually charges no administration fees, but you will have access to a limited range of investment products. Mutual fund companies will charge you administra-

The key advantages of a SDRSP:

➤ You control every aspect of your retirement savings program (that's where the self-directed part comes in).

➤ You have access to the widest range of investment products (stocks, bonds, RRSP-eligible mutual funds, T-Bills, GICs, and foreign investments).

➤ Convenience and ease: all your RRSP investments are consolidated in one place, with one statement, for easy record-keeping.

➤ You can rely on service and sound advice from the broker overseeing the SDRSP.

tion fees, but you only have access to that particular company's mutual funds. So, as your account grows, and you contribute more into your RRSP as you approach your peak earning years, you may find the need to switch over to a SDRSP. It is never too early to set up an SDRSP, but if the value of your RRSP is approaching $10,000 to $15,000, you should consider one.

Spousal RRSPs

You can make tax-deductible contributions to your spouse's RRSP, as well as your own, in what is called a spousal RRSP. The total of both contributions (both your own and your contribution to your spouse's RRSP) cannot exceed your RRSP contribution limit.

You can use spousal RRSPs as an income-splitting vehicle that allows you to pay less tax on the withdrawals from your RRSP. The advantage at retirement will be that you and your spouse will each have taxable income. The marginal tax rate on the two smaller incomes will be lower than the rate on large income. So—if you are making the contribution—you get the tax deduction on your return, but the money can be invested in your spouse's name.

For example, Joe Smith's contribution limit is $10,000 and he contributes the ten grand to his wife's SDRSP as it is set up as a spousal account (to set up an account as spousal simply contact your broker). Joe

Spousal RRSPs allow couples to split their retirement in come, so that they collectively will pay less income tax.

will get the tax savings and his wife will have the $10,000 invested in her name in her SDRSP. When the RRSP matures, the money withdrawn will be taxed at the wife's lower rate, assuming the wife has less taxable income than the husband. Keep in mind that if that $10,000 is withdrawn from Joe's wife's account within two years of the contribution, it will be taxed at Joe's marginal tax rate. Using this strategy husbands and wives can mature their plans separately, pay tax on the funds separately, and ultimately reduce their income taxes.

Group RRSPs

If your company has a group RRSP, you can automatically contribute a substantial percent of your pre-tax dollars. The rule of thumb is to contribute the maximum amount allowable. Companies sometimes match your contribution, which allows you to save even more. The contributed monies are invested in various types of stock or bond mutual funds, depending on what the company offers.

Your company may offer a group RRSP, which allows you to save for retirement with pre-tax dollars by sheltering your money and the profits you make from taxes until you retire. If your company has one, check into it!

Remember: the advantage of any RRSP is that you can shelter all the money that is invested in the plan from taxes until you retire. At that point, you'll probably be in a lower tax bracket, not to mention the tax-free returns you have earned along the way. This is known as compounding and is an extremely powerful part of investing, especially in a tax-sheltered account.

Attention First Time Home Buyers

An RRSP offers you investment products you would otherwise not have access to. One unique opportunity is The First Time Home Buyers Plan. This Plan allows you to take up to $20,000 cash from your RRSP to use as a down payment toward your first home, if you qualify for the program. You can use either your RRSP or SDRSP to join.

Some of the requirements include: the house that is being purchased is your first and the funds have been in your RRSP for at least ninety days. The money being used from your RRSP must be paid back to your RRSP over fifteen years (or, you can pay it back sooner than that if you wish). Each year you are required to pay back one-fifteenth of the amount. Failure to do so will result in one-fifteenth of the amount borrowed being taxed at your marginal tax rate. Consult your broker or local bank representative for complete details on the program.

> Buying your first home? Check out The First Time Home Buyers Plan. This Plan allows you to take up to $20,000 cash out of your RRSP to use as a down-payment toward your first home.

I Can Hold a What in my RRSP?

Now that you have your first home, what about the mortgage? Guess what? You can even hold a mortgage in your SDRSP. If you are in a position to take a mortgage out from a financial institution, then you are a candidate to hold that mortgage in your SDRSP. First of all, you must have the capital in your SDRSP, and the RRSP must be a self-directed RSP.

The property that the mortgage covers has to meet a few requirements. For example, it has to be a Canadian residential property or a rental property that is six units or less, and the mortgage in question must be a first or second mortgage. (Consult your bank representative or broker for details.)

Basically, the process is the same as when you apply for a mortgage from a financial institution, but the main difference is that instead of the money coming from the financial institution, the money is coming from your SDRSP. Keep in mind that the terms of the mortgage in your SDRSP must be consistent with those of a normal mortgage, i.e., the interest charged has to be within the context of the market. Once the mortgage is set up in your account, your SDRSP will earn a rate equivalent to the interest on the mortgage. In other words, the money used for the mortgage will grow inside your SDRSP at the rate that the mortgage is set at.

Consult your broker to see if it makes sense for you to set a mortgage up in your SDRSP, as there are some annual fees that may apply. Keep in mind that if you set up a mortgage in your SDRSP it would be

You've Reached Your Retirement—Now What?

It is never to early to start your RRSP, but it can be too late. RRSPs have a limited life. You can maintain your RRSP until the end of the year in which you turn 69. At that time, you must convert your accumulated RRSP savings using one of the following avenues:

➤ Withdraw all funds and pay tax on the full amount in the year of the withdrawal.

➤ Purchase an annuity.

➤ Establish a Registered Retirement Income Fund (RRIF).

When you convert your RRSP to an annuity or an RRIF, you will be required to withdraw a certain amount each year (see Table 4.1).

the same as purchasing a bond in your RRSP. Think of the mortgage as a type of fixed-income product.

Table 4.1 Selected Ages and Minimum Prescribed RRIF Withdrawals

Age at end of year	% that must be withdrawn from RRIF
69	4.76
75	7.85
80	8.75
85	10.33
90	13.62
94+	20.00

Note: The above withdrawal percentages apply to RRIFs opened in or after 1993. These figures may change in future years.

So, to calculate the required withdrawal amount, you multiply the value of your RRIF plan at the beginning of the year by the appropriate percentage, according to your age.

Your Registered Retirement Income Fund

When you collapse your RRSP at age 69, while taking the money and running is more than appealing, this will result in a huge tax bill as the entire amount of the withdrawal is taxable. Purchasing an annuity is like purchasing a bond. It has a certain term to maturity and a certain interest rate. The annuity will simply pay out the prescribed amount each year. Your best option would probably be to establish a Registered Retirement Income Fund (RRIF).

> A Self-Directed RRIF gives you the same flexibility as a SDRSP, but the main difference is that you cannot make any contributions to the plan.

If you convert to an RRIF, you can convert to a Self-Directed RIF (or SDRIF) and maintain the flexibility that you had over your investments with your SDRSP. The major difference will be that you are not able to *contribute* into the plan any more, and also you are required to take a certain amount *out* each year (as described above).

With an SDRIF you will have the ability to take out more than the minimum, or control your assets in the account. If you do select the SDRIF route remember that it is your responsibility to make sure there is enough cash in the account (you may have to sell a stock or maybe purchase a bond with large enough interest payments) to meet the amount that will be withdrawn to meet the requirements.

And for the Kids

Investing for your child's university education can start as early as the day the little critter was born. If you're thinking along these lines, consider implementing a Registered Education Savings Plan (RESP).

An RESP is a unique opportunity to set aside money for the post-secondary education of a child or beneficiary. The money invested is

---

Bet You Didn't Know

Believe it or not, the average cost of tuition, room and board for a four-year university degree has skyrocketed...and the increases aren't going to cease. Experts now project that, assuming a modest 3% inflation rate over the next fifteen years, a four-year program could run you from $31,000 to $44,000 per child!

---

allowed to grow and compound, sheltered from tax. With an RESP, you contribute up to $4,000 a year to a trust which is set up in the name of a specific child or a number of beneficiaries. Although your contribution is not tax-deductible, investment income and capital gains that are earned and accumulate therein are not taxed while they remain within the plan. When the money in the plan is used to pay the costs of a qualifying post-secondary education, the student pays tax only on the earnings portion of the withdrawal. The principal portion is not taxed. Since a student's income tends to be low, it is likely that the tax on withdrawals will be minimal or may not even apply.

To put this in perspective, let's say you decide to open an RESP at a brokerage firm. You invest $50 a month for the next twenty years with an 8% annual return and you will have almost $30,000.

How an RESP Works

As the planholder (known as the subscriber), you can make annual contributions of up to $4,000 into each plan. Your lifetime limit for each RESP is $42,000. After 21 years, no further contributions are permitted to each respective plan. (By the way, if you did make the maximum $4,000 contribution per year for the next ten and a half years to the $42,000 limit at an annual return of 8%, you'd have more than $67,000.) The plan must be collapsed by the end of the 25th year following the year in which the plan was set up.

You are allowed to set up as many RESPs as you wish. However, no subscriber can make a person a beneficiary of more than one RESP. You can choose either a single beneficiary or multiple beneficiaries for your plan. However, in a multiple beneficiary plan, the beneficiaries must be related to you, either by blood or adoption. You may also designate an academic institution as a beneficiary.

You can make annual contributions up to $4,000 into an RESP, up to a lifetime limit of $42,000.

In order to receive funds from the RESP, your beneficiary must be a student at a qualifying post-secondary educational institution and enrolled in a qualifying education program. For tax purposes, the beneficiary must include a portion of educational assistance payments into income. While the subscriber of a plan cannot change, the beneficiaries of the plan can be changed by the subscriber. As the subscriber, you can have your original contributions to the plan refunded at any time, tax-free. The interest, dividends and capital gains can continue to grow sheltered from taxes until the plan is collapsed.

In the past, income earned in the plan was lost if the beneficiary did not attend a qualifying post-secondary institution within the prescribed time limits. Recent changes allow this income to be withdrawn by the contributor on a taxable basis provided that the plan is at least ten years old. These funds are subject to an additional 20% tax. In order to avoid this additional tax, the contributor may choose to transfer the contents of the RESP to his or her RRSP up to the available contribution room provided certain criteria are met.

The Least You Should Know

➤ Remember the golden rule of retirement planning: invest early, invest often! You want time on your side and the power of compounding working for you.

➤ Take full advantage of the tax-sheltered plans the government offers. These include RRSPs, RRIFs, and RESPs.

➤ The legislated RRSP contribution limit equals the previous year's unused contribution room plus 18% of last year's earned income to a maximum of $13,500

➤ Remember to maximize your yearly RRSP contributions!

➤ Don't overlook some of the unique opportunities RRSPs offer, including the Self-Directed RRSP, Spousal RRSPs, and The First Time Home Buyers Plan. Remember—you can only hold a mortgage in a Self-Directed RSP.

The White-Knuckle Experience

In this chapter

➤ How much you can afford—and can't afford—to lose
➤ What is your investment style?
➤ The trade-off between risk and reward

Let's face it, there are risks involved in everything you do these days. If you decide to eat a greasy hamburger instead of a sprout-laden tofuburger, boom! Clogged arteries. How about whitewater rafting instead of the annual family vacation to our nation's capital? Somehow being tossed around in a six-by-four-foot inner tube, trying to avoid submerged boulders, seems quite risky.

This chapter will help you assess how much risk you can, and should, build into your investment plan.

How Much Risk Can You Take?

Investing in stocks, bonds, mutual funds, options and futures is risky, too. How risky your investing becomes depends on you. How quickly do you need the money? How much can you afford to lose? What do you want from the investment? To get a very general and basic idea of what your risk-comfort level is, ask yourself the following questions:

➤ If I invest money and lose it all, will I have to get another job to support my family? Will my entire fortune be destroyed?

➤ Can I invest my money and still sleep soundly at night?

➤ In case of an emergency, will I need that wad of dough immediately? How liquid an investment is it?

➤ How long will it be until I reach my short-term and long-term goals—saving for the children's university education, buying a house, putting money away for retirement?

 Your investment's liquidity depends on how easily and quickly it can be converted into cash. Every investment product has a time factor determining this. For example, a savings account is very liquid; you can easily get at your cash. The harder it is to convert your money from an investment to cash, the less liquid the investment is.

Answers to these questions vary with each individual. Many people don't have a lot of extra money to invest. Others haven't put together a personal financial battle plan to determine how much they can afford to invest.

Take a look at the figure opposite. The least risky investments are at the base. As you climb the pyramid, the more risky it becomes. Like Mt. Everest, the higher you climb, the scarier it is. This pyramid gives you an idea of how the different risk levels are involved in investing, but there is a trade-off. The higher you travel on the pyramid, the greater the possibility for a higher investment return on your money. That's trading "risk" for "reward."

Now let's review your answers to the questions. Your answers should determine how comfortable you are with investing. Investing in stocks, bonds, mutual funds, and even options and futures can reap great rewards, but you can lose money, too.

If I invest money and lose it all, do I have to get another job to support my family? Would my entire fortune be destroyed? Assess how much money you can afford to invest without wiping out the family fortune. You want to balance out the potential risk and reward and invest when that balance is most promising. Don't risk your life savings with high expectations of unattainable returns.

Can I invest my money and still sleep soundly at night? If an invest-

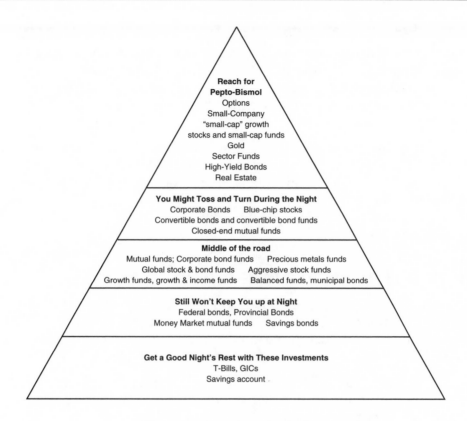

Reach for
Pepto-Bismol
Options
Small-Company
"small-cap" growth
stocks and small-cap funds
Gold
Sector Funds
High-Yield Bonds
Real Estate

You Might Toss and Turn During the Night
Corporate Bonds   Blue-chip stocks
Convertible bonds and convertible bond funds
Closed-end mutual funds

Middle of the road
Mutual funds; Corporate bond funds   Precious metals funds
Global stock & bond funds   Aggressive stock funds
Growth funds, growth & income funds   Balanced funds, municipal bonds

Still Won't Keep You up at Night
Federal bonds, Provincial Bonds
Money Market mutual funds   Savings bonds

Get a Good Night's Rest with These Investments
T-Bills, GICs
Savings account

How your investments stack up

ment is keeping you awake at night, it's not worth it. No investment is worth losing sleep over. Sell it.

In case of an emergency, would I need that wad of dough immediately? Many investors need the capability of getting at their cash immediately in case of emergency. If you need to take that wild trip to Borneo or the brake pads on ol' Betsy are wearing thin, you need cash—fast. You want a type of investment that doesn't swing wildly in price or doesn't tie up your money for a long period of time. All investors should have some portion of their portfolio allocated to cash. That means a money market mutual fund or even just a savings account earning a comparable rate of interest. In case of an emergency, you can access that money quickly.

How long will it be until I reach my short-term and long-term goals? What are you going to do with this money? What are you saving for? It's probably not just for the sheer joy of watching your investments go up and down in price. Determining your financial goals helps set your risk-comfort level. For example, if you need the money next fall when Junior starts first-year university, you won't be comfortable tying up your money in a security that doesn't mature for another ten years or more, such as a thirty-year government bond. You'd be better off putting your money into something that's shorter term, such as a one-year government bond.

If all the questions left you feeling uneasy, you can't afford to take on a lot of risk. You're a conservative investor. You need safety and peace of mind. That's okay. In fact, many conservative investors are happy with earning only 5%–6% on their money each year, knowing that any chance of losing that investment would wipe them out—financially and emotionally!

You're a Die-Hard Conservative

If you're a die-hard conservative, don't put a lot of money into any risky investments that sound promising. Stick to the lower half of the pyramid. But that doesn't mean putting all of your eggs into one super-safe investment basket...or under the mattress, either.

Why? Because that's a risk, too. If you don't diversify your portfolio, you could wind up like many poor chumps who invest in one stock and lose all of their money.

Every investor's portfolio should have different "baskets" of investments. If one of your assets takes a nosedive, you'll have alternate assets to fall back on. Your risk tolerance, financial goals, and age help determine what you'll put into those baskets.

Moderately Speaking

If you don't mind risking a little safety in exchange for a better return on your money, your investment style can be a little more moderate. You can hold on with a few market bumps. The products listed in the middle of the pyramid in the figure shown earlier typically have an average return of 8%–10%.

You Fly by the Seat of Your Pants

Finally, if you're the type of person who lives moment to moment, well, you will probably withstand a few market fallouts and still hang on for the ride just for the sake of watching your money grow. Your investment style is aggressive and sometimes speculative. The investments listed toward the top of the pyramid are the most risky. However, in exchange for this risk, the returns you may receive are quite high. Face it, you're a gambler.

Keep in mind that no matter how old you are or what your risk-comfort level is, a segment of your investment pie should always be allocated to safer financial instruments.

One theory suggests using your age as a factor in determining your investment portfolio. The older you are, the more conservative your investments should be. For example, let's say you are thirty-five years old. Subtract your age from one hundred, giving you sixty-five. This result, according to the theory, means you should have sixty-five percent of your portfolio in growth/aggressive investments (such as stocks) and thirty-five percent in more conservative investments (fixed-income instruments, such as bonds). That's just one theory and there are a zillion others that follow. You may wish to refer to Chapter 31 which discusses how you can allocate your investment portfolio.

Diversify

By putting your money into several different investments—*diversifying your portfolio*—you reduce your risk. How? If you put all of your eggs in one basket and drop the basket, they all break. Spread your eggs among different baskets, and when one of them breaks, you only have one cracked shell...and the others are still intact.

No Pain, No Gain

Unfortunately, no one eliminates risk. Remember, the greater the potential payoff, the greater the risk.

However, it's impossible to be a successful investor if you are living in fear all the time. You don't need to jump in head first. Establishing what level of risk your investment portfolio can take is based on the following:

➤ **Your age** How old are you?

➤ **Your financial goals** What is it that you are investing for?

➤ **Your time horizon** When are you planning on reaching these goals?

➤ **Your wad of dough** How much money are you allocating to investing and how much are you going to need in the future?

Here's a basic guideline to further your knowledge of how much risk you can tolerate from your investments:

How old are you? Generally, the older you are, the less risk you should take in your investments. Why? Because as you get closer to retirement, your focus shifts from investing in products that can appreciate and grow (such as stocks and stock mutual funds) to income-producing investment products, such as those that pay interest (for example, bonds). The younger you are, the more aggressive you can be in your investment approach.

What are you investing for? Post-secondary education, or a home, or whatever. If you absolutely cannot withstand losing any of the money you are investing because you need to reach that goal, then you may have to be more conservative in your approach. However, you may not have to be too conservative depending upon your timeframe for reaching the goal.

When are you planning on reaching these goals? Available time is a major determinant in factoring risk in your portfolio. If you have a lot of time to reach the goal, you may be able to take on more risk. That doesn't mean sinking Junior's university fund into pork belly future contracts, but you can be a little more aggressive in your approach as long as you follow your investments' progress on an ongoing basis.

How much money are you allocating to investing, and how much do you need for your goals? A few investments require initial minimum amounts, and you may have to slowly work your way to meet those minimums. Figuring out how much money you're going to need for those goals will help you determine if you need an investment that appreciates greatly in value, but carries more risk.

Above all, when you buy and sell an investment product, you always have the risk of losing your money. Investing is a risk, but the degrees of risk vary with each investment product.

➤ The more risk you take, the greater your potential is for a substantial reward, but you also have a greater chance of losing money.

➤ The less risk you take, the less your potential is for a substantial reward, but you also have less chance of losing money.

Now that you've established what level of risk you can handle, let's take a look at some other risks involved with making money in the stock and bond markets.

There's That Inflation Word Again

Think of inflation this way. You go to the grocery store and find that your favourite cereal, Choco-Brano, is now $6.39 a box instead of $4.59. The price went up by 39%, but that's not the only price increase you see. Oodie Fruit Doodie Fruit Juice is up to $3 a carton. Nachodoodles? Almost $4 a bag.

Or maybe you're car shopping. The last time you bought a car, the 1964 Dodge Charger was in its stellar year. Today, you'll probably have sticker shock because the average price of a new domestic automobile is well over $20,000. Ten years ago it was $13,393—a substantial increase of more than 50%!

Does this mean the country is in a financial crisis? Not necessarily. What it means is that as time passes on, most things become more expensive. How does this affect you? Your purchasing power is reduced. The same thing happens in investing. If prices are rising about 5% a year, the value of your dollar is steadily eroding over time.

Purchasing power is how much bang you can get for your buck. What you buy today for a dollar will not buy you the same product ten years from now.

Here's an example. Suppose the cost of living rises about 4% every year, and you want to invest $1,000 each year. Today's dollar can't buy the same thing five years down the road. Therefore, the loss in purchasing power of every $1,000 you invest today is cut to $822 in five years and then to $703 in ten years. That $1,000 in 1994 will be worth $822 in 1999. No fair, but it's reality.

Let's take it one step further. Suppose you invest that $1,000 every year for five years in an interest-bearing savings account that earns 3%. Think you're happy earning 3% a year on your money? Think again. If inflation is at 4% a year, you still won't come out ahead five years from now. In the long run, you're earning a minus 1% on your savings. This can also be called playing it too safe.

How Quickly Can I Get At My Money?

The most liquid investments are usually those with moderate-to-low risk—with the exception of options and futures. Options and futures are liquid investments because you can get at your cash rather quickly, however they are extremely risky. Part VI show just how risky these investments can be.

Which investments in the pyramid figure aren't too risky and are pretty liquid? Savings accounts (because they're already cash), government bonds (because they're insured by the full faith and credit of the Canadian government, and it takes one to three days to convert the securities into cash), savings bonds (you can just turn them in for cash at the bank), and money market mutual funds (they usually take one business day to convert to cash). Stocks, some bonds, and mutual funds are pretty liquid, taking about three business days to sell them and receive your money.

 No matter how much money you have to invest, make sure you allocate a portion of it to a liquid investment. This way, in case of an emergency, you can get at your cash rather quickly.

However, the more aggressive the investment, usually the harder it is to sell (except for futures and options). That means it's illiquid. A good example of an illiquid investment? Real estate. It takes time to find a buyer for your home or property. Many times if you are forced to sell an investment because you need cash quickly, you have to accept a lower price. Yes, it's unfair, but it happens.

And What About Those Interest Rates?

Interest rates on bonds, mortgages, savings accounts, and GICs have risen and fallen...and risen and fallen...and—okay, you get the picture. These investments are known as being interest-rate sensitive. Because these investments have an interest rate as a feature, the general direction of interest rates (which you learned about in Chapter 2) affects the interest rate that is on the investment product. In some cases, the general direction of interest rates directly influences the price at which you buy the investment.

Here's an example. Bond investments have a fixed interest rate and a price at which you can buy them. These fixed interest rates and the bond prices move in the opposite direction of each other. When the in-

Reinvestment risk When, because of changing market conditions, the money that you get when your investment matures or you sell it cannot be invested in another instrument that produces the same investment return, you've experienced reinvestment risk.

terest rate goes up, the bond price goes down, and vice versa. Therefore, if the general direction of interest rates, which influences the interest rates on bonds, goes up or down, the price at which you can buy or sell the bond goes down or up. And what does this mean for you? Well, if you need to sell a bond, for example, you will receive the going market price. If interest rates have risen since you purchased the bond, you will get a lower price, and vice versa.

In the early '80s, the prime rate was as high as 21.75%. GIC investors were enjoying double-digit yields of 15%–18%. Yields on bonds, mortgage rates, and other financial instruments soared. By the end of 1996 (when interest rates bottomed out), the prime rate fell to 4.75%, and all other interest rates followed. Yield-hungry investors who grew accustomed to double-digits were astonished when their investments started earning anemic rates. This type of rate environment affects you in two ways: reinvestment potential and lifestyle.

First, if you are earning double digits on your investments and they either mature or you have to sell, the yield on your investment declines when you have to reinvest, which is also known as reinvestment risk.

Here's an example. Back in the 1980s, you invested $5,000 in a five-year GIC that earned 17% annually. Because when you invest in a GIC you lock in your money for a specified period of time, you also lock in the interest rate, regardless of the rates going up or down.

Five years later when the GIC matured, the same $5,000, five-year GICs were not earning 17%, but instead were earning 10%. You couldn't reinvest your money in the same GIC and earn the same return, because interest rates had dropped. So, if you invested the money now at 10%, you would be receiving $500 a year in interest ($5,000 x 10%), instead of the $850 a year ($5,000 x 17%) you got five years ago. That's a loss of $350 a year.

Second, those investors who rely on income from their investments had to make lifestyle adjustments. Why? Because in a declining rate environment, the interest payments that you receive decline also. Therefore, there's less money received…and less you can spend.

Risk Is Not a Four-Letter Word

Unfortunately, the word "risk" gets a bad rap. It shouldn't. Risk tells you a lot about yourself. If you know how much risk you can tolerate from an investment—how comfortable you are in the investment decisions you make—and if you educate yourself about other inherent risks associated with investing, you're on your way to making your money work for you.

The Least You Need To Know

➤ Don't let your investments keep you up at night. If you can't sleep, sell!

➤ Figure out what your risk-comfort level is. Are you a conservative investor? Middle of the road? Aggressive? This helps you determine what types of investments make you uncomfortable.

➤ Diversify. You can lose all your money if you invest in just one type of financial security. Spread the risk around by investing in various types of products.

➤ Don't play it too safe. Eventually, inflation will get the best of your "safe" investments and you won't make any money at all.

And Now for the Legwork

Making money is easy once you become an educated investor. If a broker, a friend, or your Great Aunt Lorraine gives you a hot stock tip, do you invest immediately? No questions asked? Better not. You kick a few tires when you buy a new car, and you need to do a little investigating before you invest. That means homework, and this chapter explains how to research potential investments.

Learn About the Company and Market

If you had $100,000 to invest, anywhere, and you know you want to create an investment portfolio of stocks, bonds, and a few mutual funds, which stocks would you invest in?

One of the initial steps in creating an investment portfolio is deciding what you should invest in. You make this decision by determining what each investment product is, how it works, and how risky it is.

Once you figure that out, the next step is to decide which stocks or bonds you should consider. That decision is based upon investment research. Yup, folks, it's homework time. What if you don't know how to do any research? Well, you've come to the right place.

Anytime you are researching an investment, you are typically investigating a company. Why? Because that's who issues stocks, bonds, etc. Before you get out the paper and pencils, know that you already have one of the greatest resources around—your eyes. Look around you and what do you see? Many times a good investment choice will come from paying attention to your surroundings.

If, for example, you notice everyone is drinking Slurp-N-Burp soda and not Coca-Cola, you may wish to start digging up some information on the company that manufactures Slurp-N-Burp soda pop. Or if you work for a hospital, a manufacturing plant, or an automobile dealer, pay attention to any changes that take place. These changes can include new services, improved equipment, or a new line of products. Here, you are performing your own *fundamental analysis*.

You can learn about a company by contacting its headquarters and finding out where they're located. If they are nearby, you may wish to see if you can tour the facilities or at least pick up some information about what type of business the company is in.

Speak with a representative in shareholder services or investor relations to see if the company is a private or a public company. Most often, whenever you have a question regarding the company's business or past history, you contact either of these departments. They are there to serve investors. Request documentation from them such as financial reports and brochures on general company information. Find out the following:

➤ **Who is running the company?** If there has been poor management in the past, it will be indicated in the company's track record. However, if the company is managed well, chances are that good results can be repeated. If there is a change in management, you may wish to look into the background of the new managers.

➤ **How long has the company been in business?** Is it a brand-new company? If so, realize these companies are relatively risky. Companies who have a stable background and have been around for years probably won't go belly up overnight.

➤ **How profitable is it?** See if you can get at least a five-year history on its profitability. Make sure that the company isn't constantly running itself into the ground without any profits at all. The more profitable a company, the greater the possibility for increases in dividends for shareholders.

➤ **How much bad debt vs. good debt does it have?** Companies are just like you! They carry both good and bad debt. The idea is to eliminate the bad debt. Watch out for companies that carry a lot of bad debt.

➤ **Who is the competition?** Think of McDonalds vs. Burger King or Pepsi vs. Coca-Cola. How strong are the company's competitors? How much of a market share does the company have? If the company is new and entering an already saturated market, what type of competition does it face? Does its product have an edge over the others?

➤ **What are the barriers to entry?** Does it cost a lot of money to enter this market? Is there any government regulation or legislation controlling the industry?

➤ **Are there any new products or services coming out on the market from this company?** In an already-established company, new products or services can be either good or bad. Find out if the company has ever ventured into that territory before and if it faces any stiff competition.

Once you have done all your research and have answers to your questions, check out the entire market. You've done some of this already by checking out the competition. However, you should dig a little deeper to see how the industry as a whole is doing. Ask yourself the following:

➤ Is the industry a stable one or is it based on fads?

➤ How well does it perform overall in each phase of the business cycle? (Now you can see why the discussion of economics in Chapter 2 is so important to understand.)

Realize that your research will be an ongoing process. Learning about the company and the industry is just the first part. You need to consistently monitor the company after you have invested by following its performance information.

Sources of Performance Information

One day you're standing at your mailbox and open it up to find it crammed full of envelopes. There's a few bills, some junk mail, and an envelope that looks unfamiliar.

You open up the unfamiliar envelope and find what looks like a research report, but you can't make heads or tails of it—you'd have an easier time spelling out your name in a bowl of alphabet soup. Then you remember that you had contacted the shareholder services department at a company you were researching. This slick, glossy brochure and the unintelligible research reports included with it must be the information you need to wade through.

Performance information is usually given in the form of a report. It indicates the results of what the investment "did," typically expressed as a percentage.

Is this the only avenue to pursue? No. There are so many sources of *performance information* available to you that you could wallpaper your whole house with them.

Most of the resources available track the performance of individual stocks and mutual funds. Individual bonds aren't necessarily "tracked" for performance, but they are assigned special ratings based on the risks involved in each individual bond. Options and futures are both such volatile investments that most of your information will come from financial newsletters covering those markets or the day-to-day coverage found on financial television programs such as CBC's *Business World* or on CNN.

Some organizations were created solely to provide performance and statistical information to the public about companies and businesses. For advice on some of the more popular research companies that analyze stocks, turn to Chapter 20.

Ticker Talk

The most readily available source of performance information is in the financial section of your local newspaper where you'll find the biggest performance indicator, the closing price of an investment. *The Globe and Mail* and *The Financial Post*, for example, list the closing prices for thousands of stocks, bonds, mutual funds, futures, and options that traded the previous trading day. These investments are listed either by their *ticker symbol* or an abbreviation. (Or if there's room, it's completely spelled out.)

These closing prices represent the last price at which the investment security listed was traded. That price is usually what people look for—and you will, too, once you begin investing. It is one way to monitor your investments.

In addition to the closing prices, other performance information is given. These include (but are not limited to) the following:

> You use a **ticker symbol** (an abbreviation of the investment name) to get current quotes (prices) from a broker. For example, The Toronto-Dominion Bank's ticker symbol is "TD." Alcan Aluminum is "AL".

➤ **High and Low.** Typically the numbers in these columns represent the highest and lowest price of an investment during the previous trading day (yesterday).

➤ **52 Week High and a 52 Week Low.** This represents the highest and lowest price of an investment during a fifty-two-week period.

➤ **Close.** The price at which the investment closed yesterday.

➤ **Volume.** Sometimes shown as "VOL" in the table, the volume indicates how many shares, issues, or contracts of an investment traded for the entire previous trading day.

➤ **Net Change.** The difference in price from the previous day's close to that particular day's close. For example, if it was Wednesday morning and you were reading the financial table, the net change listed would represent the difference in price from Monday's close (or last price) to Tuesday's close.

➤ **Div.** This stands for dividend, which is the sum paid to shareholders out of a company's earnings.

This is just the first part of the process in learning about the sources of performance information. Make sure you don't base your investment decisions on yesterday's closing price. There are other steps you need to complete.

Information You Can Trust

If your local newspaper does not carry all of the pricing information you need, you may also look into purchasing *The Financial Post* or *The Globe and Mail*.

Established in 1907, *The Financial Post* is an excellent Canadian source for learning about the "Who's Who" and "What's What" in the stock markets. It covers all financial markets, both national and world-wide and provides comprehensive news coverage and in-depth analysis of Canadian business, finance, investment, and government. Published Tuesday to Saturday, the *Post* reports on up-to-the-minute business, finance and investment news and reports. Special features include the annual Financial Post 500, which ranks the performance of the top 500 Canadian companies. You can reach them at 1-800-387-9011 (ask for Operator 7) for more information and subscription rates.

The Globe and Mail, Canada's national newspaper, also gives you thorough coverage of the financial markets in its Report on Business section. *The Report on Business Magazine*, which is published monthly, includes the top 1000 Canadian businesses, ranked by profits. For subscription information, you can contact them at 1-800-387-5400.

If you want to keep track of performance information online, there are several database services available to you. These include the following:

➤ **Corona (Realtime Quotes) www.rtquotes.com** If you want real-time quotes on stocks, bonds, options and indices, all you need is a PC with a modem and an ordinary telephone line. This powerful tracking tool gives you historical and daily performance graphs, news, price/volume alerts, top ten gainers and losers by exchange, and much more. You can download the software from their website and sign-up for your free trial run.

➤ **Telenium (800) 665-0302.** Telenium offers free Canadian quotes and even tracks portfolios. There is an investor relations file for listed companies, along with software tools to assist private investors. It even provides an extensive list of GIC, Mortgage and RRSP rates for leading financial institutions across Canada.

➤ **ChartSmart Software www.chartsmart.com** ChartSmart offers quotes, charts, and filters over 4000 VSE, ASE, TSE, and ME securities. It includes daily and weekly performance bar charts. You can download the complete software free off the net and take a one week free trial.

➤ **Contact your broker.** Most brokerage firms are now offering online quotes and stock performance information. Even better, you can get access to your brokerage accounts and track your stocks.

Interpreting Performance Information

Consumers' lives are filled with numbers. We rate performance on everything these days. Thumbs up or down for the latest movie release. Two or three stars for a restaurant review. Even automobiles and appliances are rated by consumer magazines.

It doesn't stop there. Investment products are given a thumbs up or down, too. In the world of stocks, you hear about "buy," "hold," or "sell" recommendations from investment analysts. When it comes to bond investing, companies like the Canadian Bond Rating Service (CBRS) and the Dominion Bond Rating Service (DBRS) rate all types of bonds by giving them a credit rating in the form of a letter. As for mutual funds, futures, and options, their performances are rated, too.

All of the performance information is given, but how do you figure out which end is up? Here is a basic primer to understanding what performance information tells you.

➤ **Total Return.** The stock reports you review are plagued with numbers. But there is only ONE—just one—number that tells you about the performance of the investment: total return.

Total return gives the sum of the price appreciation and income derived from an investment. For example, if you invested in a stock that indicates a total return of 12%, the twelve percent is what you earn from the appreciation in price of the stock (the stock price moving up) and the income that is derived from the stock (in the form of dividends that you receive).

Now, when you have stocks that don't pay any dividends, the majority of performance (total return) comes from the price appreciation. Those stocks that are high-paying dividend stocks focus on income, not price appreciation. Therefore, the majority of the total return comes from the income derived from the dividends that are paid to shareholders.

➤ **Annual Return.** Annual return is the total return measured over a twelve-month period. When you see an annual return of 10%, that means the investment earned ten percent—either in price appreciation, income or a combination of both—over a period of twelve months.

➤ **Cumulative Return.** The cumulative return is expressed in a period of three years, five years, ten years, etc. The BIGGEST mistake is for investors to look at the performance of a mutual fund, let's say, that states there was a 165% return over a period of five years. That does NOT mean that every year for five years you earned one hundred and sixty-five percent a year on the investment. Rather, the cumulative return amount is the total of all the annual returns for the number of years specified.

➤ **Average Annual Return.** This return number represents the cumulative return number expressed as what you would earn for each year given. For example, if the cumulative return of a mutual fund was 30.85% for three years, the average annual return would be 10.28%, or the cumulative return divided by the number of years.

Getting A Prospectus and Attempting To Understand It

Getting your hands on a mutual fund prospectus is easy, and it's something that's required if you want to buy an investment. All you have to do is contact the fund company (the shareholder services or investor relations department) for information. It is required by law for you to receive a prospectus before you invest one cent in a mutual fund.

If you wanted a prospectus from a company regarding its stocks or bonds, the only way you can get it is if the company is having an initial offering. When a company is coming out with its very first stock or bond issue, it'll hire a large full-service brokerage firm to sell its stocks or bonds. The announcement and sale of these securities is known as an Initial Public Offering (IPO). If the company has already had an initial offering in the past and wants to do it again, it will hold a secondary offering.

Legal Jargon and Mumbo Jumbo

What do you do with the prospectus once you receive it? Time to pick it apart. It is possible to have a full-time job reading prospectuses and translating the "legalese." Some prospectuses have pages and pages of information that look like they were written in Swahili.

Understand that each prospectus is designed to give you the name of the company or mutual fund, its purpose and policies, company history, its investment objectives, any costs involved (such as management fees), and a description of the management team.

Without going into too much legal detail, here are a few basics that you should look for when you are reading a prospectus.

➤ **Before you purchase an investment, you must legally receive a prospectus.** In the case of a new stock or bond offering, this is true; otherwise, if you just wanted to buy shares of stock that "aren't new" (they've already been traded out in the marketplace) you won't receive a prospectus. However, you should obtain the company's annual report. Or, in the case of a mutual fund, you will receive a prospectus.

➤ **If the investment pays dividends/interest payments, make sure the rate and timing are indicated.** It's important to know when your dividends and interest payments are paid out and what the rates are likely to be. These dates will help you determine when you'll be entitled to receive the dividend and/or interest payment and how much to expect.

➤ **Make sure a performance table is given.** There should be performance information given on a prospectus. For example, a mutual fund prospectus may include a ten-year performance history of the fund's change in price, the dividend income earned, and the capital gains distributions paid.

➤ **Where to buy the investment.** If there is an initial stock or bond offering and you request a prospectus, the names of all the brokerage firms that you can purchase it through will be listed on the front page.

➤ **If it is a mutual fund, make sure the investment objectives/methods are listed.** This means you should watch for any restrictions that may be given in the prospectus, such as if the mutual fund limits itself to investing

> The **annual report** is a formal financial statement issued by a company, which shows its assets, liabilities, and earnings. This report gives an indication of how the company stood at the close of the business year and if it made any profits. A **prospectus**, on the other hand, is a legal document that describes the investment objectives, costs involved (if it was a mutual fund investment), and management.

in certain types of stocks or bonds. It should also tell you what kinds of stocks or bonds it will not buy.

➤ **If it is a mutual fund, make sure the risks are spelled out.** The prospectus should tell you how volatile the change in the price of the mutual fund is. Plus, make sure it tells you if there are any strategies that involve the use of futures, options, or derivatives (a risky, volatile form of futures and options). Fund managers use these as a way to prevent losses or as a "hedging" strategy; be careful though, as derivatives can be very risky.

➤ **Read up on company business.** In the prospectus, the business should be described: does the company invest in widgets, gizmos, or thingamajigs?

➤ **What type of experience does management have?** This is key. If the management listed in the prospectus have no experience in the company or in the industry, it should be noted.

➤ **In a mutual fund prospectus, make sure you read the fine print about fund expenses and management fees.** The fund's second largest single expense is the management fee, which is the percentage of monies paid to the fund manager for, well, managing the fund. The way the fee is calculated is stated in the prospectus.

➤ **Finally, call the company if you are having trouble understanding the prospectus.** Call the shareholder services or investor-relations department of the fund or company with your questions. Many times they will provide you with the "Statement of Additional Information," which must be made available to you.

Using a Broker or Other Investment Counsellor

There are a lot of brokers who are more than willing to give you advice. Whether you need a full-service broker or a discount broker, or you're going to do it on your own, you should always monitor your own investments. Blindly giving your money to Mort, your sister-in-law's cousin, or family broker extraordinaire is not a good idea.

Full-Service Brokers

Full-service brokers are nowadays referred to as Investment Advisors (IA) or Investment Executives (IE). All of the major banks own full-service brokerage firms and exist in the market with a couple of smaller independent firms. The key advantage in involving a full service broker or an IA in your investment decisions comes from the "value-added" he or she brings to the table.

For example, a good IA will help you establish an investment strategy and, if required, hold your hand through many of the exercises mentioned in this book designed to lead you into developing an investment strategy.

Once you and your IA have developed the investment strategy and implemented it, the IA's responsibility will be the constant monitoring of the portfolio and the overall investment environment. This is where you will receive the "value-added"— not only is your IA monitoring your investments but you have access to a professional who can answer any questions or discuss the investing of any additional monies. Keep in mind that if you choose to deal with an IA, this does not mean you don't have to do your homework; you should always do your own homework and know what is happening in your portfolio.

There are good IAs and not so good IAs, just as there are good lawyers and not so good lawyers, just as there are good doctors... well you get the picture. When looking for an IA, many people rely on word-of-mouth, whether it be a referral from your banker or your lawyer or some other acquaintance. More to the point, you can phone up a brokerage firm and simply ask to speak with an IA. Keep in mind it is important to consider more than just one IA; it is probably a good idea to get a few names and talk to each one before you make any decision.

A full-service broker can offer you a "value-added" advantage by helping you develop an investment strategy and then consistently monitoring it. In addition, any questions or queries you may have will be addressed by a professional.

When selecting an IA it is important that you feel comfortable with the person you choose. Some of the questions you may want to ask include those related to his or her work experience and education. Make sure that you are comfortable with his or her investment philosophy. For instance, if the IA in question specializes in options trading and you want a portfolio of conservative mutual funds, he or she may be a very nice person but this probably is not the IA for you.

Discount Brokers

Like the full-service brokerage market, the discount market is dominated by the big banks; each bank has their own discount brokerage firm.

The "discount" in the term "discount brokers" refers to a discount in commissions, but remember, the biggest difference in dealing with a discount broker over a full-service broker is that discount brokers do not offer advice—or the same level of service. But if you are an investor that actively trades equities and you do all your own research, then it might make sense for you to use a discount broker.

With full-service brokers there is no standard commission rate. Even better—full-service rates may be negotiable.

Also, keep in mind that the full-service rates may be negotiable, depending on the individual broker, and the services involved. Furthermore, the difference in commissions charged on mutual funds and fixed-income products can be even smaller.

Some of the advantages to a discount broker, however, include the ability to access your account electronically (coming soon to a full-service brokerage firm near you) as well as the ability to trade through an automated system. Not to mention that a lot of the discount firms are open seven days a week, twenty-four hours a day.

Deciding between full-service and discount? Some factors to consider: the time you have to monitor your investments, your ability to research stocks, and your overall experience and knowledge of the markets.

The type of investor you are and the service you require will determine whether you should use a full-service brokerage firm or a discount brokerage firm. For instance, if you do your own stock analysis, have time to monitor your portfolio, and know exactly what stocks you want to buy and sell, (and when to buy and sell them!) then a discount broker may be your best bet. But, for investors with little or no time to monitor their investments, no access to or limited knowledge of stock research and performance, or who simply need a professional to oversee their portfolio, a full-service broker is the best choice.

Other Players

There are also independent mutual fund sales people and financial planners that offer you similar services. But, unlike full-service and discount brokerage firms that are regulated by what is called the SROs (Self Regulatory Organizations), these professionals are not members of any regulating body. I am not telling you to avoid mutual fund sales people or financial planners; but rather, make sure you are thorough in doing your homework when you choose to use any type of professional, whether it be for your investments or your household plumbing.

Shopping for a Broker

Here's a list of additional tips to help you choose, and wisely use, a broker:

➤ First come, first hired, first fired. Don't hire the first broker on your list without investigating others. Interview several before choosing just one. Just like hiring that new babysitter for the kids, you don't want Helga the Horrible or Bubbles (no last name, of course) with no experience to watch your children. You need to find a financial professional that you feel comfortable with, and that you can afford.

➤ Don't rely on cousin Mort. Make sure you know what type of broker (experienced or inexperienced) you are dealing with. Ask what professional degrees or credentials the broker has earned.

➤ Check on a professional's work history. If you want to find out about your broker or your brokerage firm's work history, contact the Investment Dealers Association of Canada (IDA), or your provincial securities commission. Their phone numbers and addresses are listed in the Appendix.

The Least You Need To Know

➤ Before you invest, you need to learn as much information about a company as possible, including what type of business it's in, who its competitors are, and if it's planning to introduce any new products or services.

➤ The easiest way to remember how to decipher performance information is to think of it as the investment's track record.

➤ Getting a prospectus—and understanding it—shouldn't be difficult as long as you know you should look for key points, including any expenses or fees (if it's a mutual fund prospectus) and how long the company has been in business (if it's a prospectus from an initial stock or bond offering).

➤ Whether you choose to use a full-service broker, a discount broker, a mutual fund salesperson, or a financial planner is up to you. Just remember to be thorough in doing your homework when selecting someone to overlook your finances.

Chapter 7

Kick the Spending Habit!

In this chapter

➤ How a bad habit can cost you plenty

➤ You might have more bad habits than you think

➤ How to tell good habits from bad ones

So you say you're a good shopper and a smart saver. You clip coupons. You only buy the items on sale during your trips to the grocery store. And you always wait for Scratch 'n Save Day at The Bay. Those habits are honourable. You're saving money, no doubt, but there is a hidden evil that lurks inside all of us that we don't know about—the "see it-buy it" monster.

Think about when you go on a diet. You monitor your fat intake and your calorie intake. You make sure you're getting enough exercise and eating the right kinds of food. Now apply this to spending, saving, and investing. You determined what your personal financial battle plan is in Chapter 3. You know how much your net worth is and have a good idea of how much you can save and invest. However, an integral part of that plan is to monitor—and possibly cut—your spending habits. This chapter will inspire you to take a good, honest look at how you spend your money and will help you find ways to kick any over-spending habits you have.

That Trip to the Mall Costs More Than You Think

You're at work and the clock reads high noon. It's time for lunch for most folks, but not for you. You know that it costs an average $6 per day, $30 per week, to eat your lunch out of the office. You are trying to keep your spending habits to a bare minimum. So, you take out the piece of fruit you brought from home and decide to go for a walk. Good. Not only is that nutritionally healthy, but you're also getting exercise.

On your lunch break, your walk finds you in front of your favourite Sports store, chock full of sporting goods at discount prices. Let's take a peek, you say to yourself. Fifteen minutes later, you're leaving the store with $132.11 worth of merchandise and heading toward the cashier. Ah, but you saved money on lunch, right? Wrong! It would have been cheaper for you to eat out. It's good that you've started your personal financial battle plan, but now it's time to evaluate your financial habits.

Kick the Habit

Have an extra five bucks in your pocket? Is it burning a hole there? Do you feel compelled to spend it? The worst kind of "see it-buy it" mentality is using your credit card for unnecessary purchases. Don't rationalize that just because you have credit available on your plastic, you can (or should) buy now and pay later.

Let's take a $1,000 credit card purchase, for example. At an annual percentage rate of 19.8%, it takes close to fifteen years to pay off that

Bet You Didn't Know

The average weekly amount of money spent on dining out for lunch is close to $30 a week. Brown bag it, folks!

initial purchase if you only meet the minimum payments; plus, there's thousands in nondeductible finance charges tacked on. Instead, forego the $1,000 purchase, and invest the money. If you put $1,000 a year in a moderate investment paying 8% on average for ten years, guess what you'd have at the end of the decade? About $16,000. Not bad.

It is foolish to spend lavishly now and count on Canada Pension Plan (CPP) benefits as the only source of income for later years. Many industry experts believe the CPP won't be there to help in the long run. According to Revenue Canada, the average monthly CPP benefit for the 1994 taxation year was approximately $400. That's it. Can you live on that? I doubt it. And that's in prior years' dollars. What about the future?

Never pay for groceries or any other perishable items with a credit card. If you only make the minimum payment amount, that bag of mallomars, a head of lettuce, and four rolls of toilet paper could be financed for the next four months.

There are ways to cure bad spending habits:

➤ First, use the power of your own mind and self-determination. Your imagination and goal-setting can be strong motivators. Imagine how you'd feel if you had an investment account worth $25,000, or even $50,000. Picture how rewarding it is to have money that you worked so hard for grow into a substantial nest egg. Motivate yourself to believe this substantial nest egg is more profitable and rewarding than a closet full of designer clothes or a glitzy new automobile.

➤ Second, count the number of credit cards you have in your wallet. Five, six, maybe eight? Getting rid of the plastic (with the exception of one or two major credit cards) is imperative. Make sure you only use these during an emergency. You'll be amazed to see how not using your credit cards can help cut costs.

➤ Third, reduce some of your living expenses. Watch your telephone and utility bills. Place your telephone calls at the times of day when rates are cheaper, if necessary. Unplug appliances that aren't used during the day. Don't leave lights on when you're not at home. Keep eating out to a minimum. These may seem like small sacrifices, but they add up.

If you must have a credit card, don't apply for more than two credit cards at a time. Why? Because every time you apply, the credit card company checks into your credit report, and the inquiry is recorded. If there are a lot of inquiries, then you'll be denied credit from other issuers and lenders later on.

One way to track your spending habits is to keep a pocket-sized notebook with you at all times. Every time you run to the drugstore or even the food-mart at the gas station, write down all of your purchases and tally them up at the end of the week—yes, that includes your beef jerky sticks and that carton of chocolate drink. Put the total into a "miscellaneous" category on your budget worksheet.

➤ Fourth, if you are in the market for a new automobile, consider buying a new used car—as long as you know the history behind the car—instead of a brand new car. Why? Because a brand new car depreciates 20% the moment you drive it out of the lot. Remember, a car is NOT an investment. In fact, you can save hundreds of dollars if you purchase a used car instead.

Keeping Up with the Joneses

Bud and Ethel Jones just bought a brand new, sporty, two-door BMW. The car is fully loaded. Their down payment was only $1,000, and they financed the rest for the next sixty months. They live a lifestyle of "bigger is better" and hee-haw at their friends who don't have sporty cars and flashy clothes. If a neighbour buys a new ten-speed for his child, Bud and Ethel seek out the most expensive mountain bike for theirs. Rather than taking the family on a camping trip to Algonquin, the Joneses fly to Paris.

Is it important to keep up with these Joneses? Not at all. They may be swimming in debt before long if their spending habits keep up the way they've been. Their financial future is completely destroyed. The Joneses are a status symbol family—big house, expensive car, and at least five credit cards, which I'm sure are maxed out.

Keeping up with the Joneses is the quickest way to destroy your financial future. If you try to keep up with them, how would you do it? Get another job? No, the one you have already takes sixty hours per week. You would probably have to use your credit cards, thus sinking you and your family further into debt. Don't abuse your credit cards. Using them to pay for everything—from groceries to furniture—can be bad for your financial health. All a credit card does is allow you to purchase more than you can really afford.

If I could tattoo one phrase on the inside of your eyelids it would be "Get Rid of Your Debt!" Folks, keeping up with the Joneses just digs a deeper hole for you to climb out of.

An Alternative to Spending—Investing

Creating instant wealth is not easy, unless of course, you win the lottery. We already know what the odds are with that. Creating long-term wealth is a different story, calling for patience and determination. Even if your annual salary is less than $25,000, you can afford to save money. The best solution is the ten percent solution. You should start practicing this financial habit right away. It's a good one! Putting away ten percent of your income into an investment vehicle that yields a pretty good total annual return makes it possible to retire quite comfortably.

Begin immediately. Don't tell yourself that you'll do it after you finish paying off the kids' dentist bills. Start today. Implementing this habit guarantees that you'll put you and your family ahead of all other obligations. It doesn't mean that you skip paying the electric bill. In fact, treat your ten percent solution as a bill. Whenever you are doing your bills, write a cheque out to yourself first and put it away—in an RRSP, for instance. Or set up an automatic investment account with a mutual fund for your RRSP, as you'll learn in Part V.

Put your ten percent into an account that you won't touch, such as a growth stock mutual fund. Once you learn more about the different types of investments that can grow over time, you will be better equipped to make a decision as to where to invest. Even if there's a job layoff in the family or a serious financial emergency, this money should really be left untouched. Tell yourself that there is no financial emergency great enough that would ever make you touch that money. You are planning for your future. Remember, put it in and leave it there!

What you're doing by investing is breaking the cycle of living paycheque-to-paycheque. You know the feeling. Even before your paycheque is directly deposited to your bank account, it's already spent. You can always outspend your paycheque, but that doesn't mean you should. Get out of that rut! If you pay everybody else first and try and have fun with what's left over, you'll never get anywhere. If you have the discipline to continue building your nest egg with the ten percent solution, you won't live paycheque-to-paycheque anymore.

Obviously, those who begin practicing this ten percent ritual at an earlier age will find that it takes less money to create a fortune. These individuals have years to plan their work and work their plan, which puts them in a good situation because retirement comes quickly—sometimes too quickly. Canadians are getting older, especially the majority of the population in our country, the baby boomers. You are a baby boomer if you were born between 1946 and 1964, and there's about nine million of you out there. This generation has graduated from the mentality of spending everything they've earned to trying to invest for retirement. They're in their peak earning years but caught with a shorter amount of time to save for retirement.

Start as soon as you can. In fact, start now!

The Least You Need To Know

➤ Debt reduction is key in the '90s. If you don't stop using your credit cards to pay for everything—even nights out on the town— you'll wind up under a mountain of debt.

➤ Don't try to keep up with your neighbours financially. Status symbols are out, and getting rid of debt is in! Face it, there will always be someone who has more than you. Accept and be proud of your accomplishments.

➤ Just think ten percent. Try and invest ten percent of your paycheque and watch the money grow over the long haul!

Chapter 8

How To Divide Up Your Investment Pie

In this chapter
➤ How often should you monitor your investments?
➤ Using asset allocation to diversify
➤ Does your portfolio earn an A+?

Should you buy stocks? Mutual funds? What about bonds? How about dabbling in futures and options trading? Learning which investments are right for you is instrumental in building your nest egg. Determining how much of each investment should be in your portfolio is called *asset allocation.* For you, asset allocation will mean creating the right portfolio mix based on your age and financial goals, the risk involved, and current market forces. It is more important to select the correct asset allocation for your own portfolio than selecting the individual

Be careful of the investment pro that tells you about a "sure thing" that you should invest all your money in. Sure things are about as reliable as a plane with no wings. Remember: diversify, diversify, diversify!

Remember this folks: too many people worry about which individual stocks to buy before they have worked out their asset allocation. Once you have your asset allocation, the selection of securities becomes a lot easier!

Generally, asset allocation (and not the individual securities) is said to account for 80% or more of the variation in the total returns of investment portfolios!

securities within each asset class. This chapter shows you how to wisely allocate your dollars among various investments to control risk and maximize returns.

It's a Percentage Thing

Establishing the right asset allocation mix enables you to take advantage of several different types of financial markets. For example, if you have forty percent of your portfolio invested in stocks, thirty-five percent in bonds, and the remaining twenty-five percent in cash, you've taken sufficient precautions against the possibility of stocks and bonds declining in value. (You'll learn how to set these percentages for your portfolio later in this chapter.)

Once you determine your asset allocation, it's not set in stone. You might find that last year's financial strategies don't work this year. Maybe this year's financial strategies will need some fine-tuning before they'll work next year.

Why? Tax changes, for one. Another reason for changing financial strategies is that your goals have changed. Maybe the kids left the nest, and it's time to sell the house and buy that condo on the golf course.

Whatever the circumstances, deciding what your asset allocation mix should be will help you achieve these goals. Whether you have $100, $1,000, or even $100,000 to invest, you should diversify your portfolio to protect you against market fluctuations and economic uncertainties.

Slicing Your Investment Pie

Once you've determined your investment profile, including your level of risk, it's time to slice up the investment pie. The goal is to give the investor the highest return with the least amount of risk. Your asset allocation mix is based on a number of factors, the biggest of which is risk. If the market has a problem, ask yourself how much risk you can bear? Are you going to be able to sleep at night if you see your portfolio take a 10% loss? That will really drive your decision. Even the professional portfolio managers use risk tolerance as a guideline in choosing the right asset allocation mix.

When you are creating a sound asset allocation mix for your portfolio, all you are doing is figuring out how your money should be divided up among different investments.

Answer the following questions to help you decide how much you should have invested in each category:

1. **How much of a risk-taker are you?** You already have a pretty good idea based on your answers to questions in Chapter 5. You know that the more the risk, the more the return you can expect to receive. If you are more aggressive in your investment approach, a higher percentage of your money can be allocated toward equities. However, if you are more of a conservative investor, a greater percentage can be invested in fixed-income securities. Remember, your asset allocation is not set in stone. You can adjust it at any time in the future, for whatever reason.

Base your percentage of stocks, bonds, and cash on your tolerance for risk. Look for a mix that will give you less volatility and a higher return. You want the greatest return for the least amount of risk.

2. **How old are you?** There used to be an old trick to determine what your asset allocation mix should be. "Your age should equal your percentage of fixed-income securities. The rest should be in stocks." For example, if you are thirty-five years old and you followed this rule, thirty-five percent of your money should be in fixed-income securities and sixty-five percent should be in stocks. The older you become, the more money you should allocate to fixed-income securities.

3. **What is your time horizon?** A long-term investment plan is a

Ask yourself what would be the minimum return, on average, that you would be satisfied with over the time horizon you have identified for yourself. Then, take a look at your asset allocation you have chosen. Will you be able to achieve that return with your current asset allocation? If not, you have to either lower your return expectations or increase your tolerance for risk.

key factor when you are beginning to earmark your money. If you have a long-term investment horizon, such as a five- to ten-year timeframe, you should allocate more to equities. If you have a shorter time horizon, understand that equities can give you a substantial negative return; therefore you would want to allocate a majority of your assets to fixed-income securities. Keep in mind that over the long run, equities have outperformed fixed-income securities. Because every investor is different, you need to set your own parameters and decide what the result should be—whether to invest for growth or income or both.

Diversification should be practiced by all investors because it reduces risk. The reason for the reduction in volatility is that stocks increasing in price tend to offset any negative effects of those investment securities that are decreasing in price.

Timing—A Strategy Not for the Beginner

For centuries, financial gurus have theorized about what it takes to make a handsome profit. These market wizards spent their lives timing the market, but even if they hadn't and instead just let their money ride over a long period of time, they would still have come out ahead.

For example, examine the stock market over just the past ten years using the TSE 300, which is an index that's made up of three hundred different Canadian stocks. Suppose you invested $10,000 only ten years ago and did nothing. You didn't time the market; you just let your ten grand ride. That initial $10,000 investment ten years ago would be worth almost $27,000 today. There were some pretty big bumps in the stock market along the way, but at a rate of nearly 9% compounded annually on the TSE 300, you'd have almost tripled your dough after ten years—without market timing.

Timing the market is a very involved process and should mainly be left to the graph-paper wizards, but it is interesting to read about. One ingredient to market timing includes studying the patterns of market cycles. Just notice the strange phenomenon that occurs when you get a bunch of financial Einsteins in the same room. You can count on one of them bringing up the subject of market cycles.

Why do market cycles exist? They just do. It's best to understand the basic concept of the economic and financial cycles that market watchers study. I'm not talking about how the sun moves with the moon and stars, but rather how investors make money by basing their trading decisions on the technical analysis of studying market and economic cycles.

The most interesting study is found in the *Kondratieff Wave Theory*. This is important because most economists and big time investors ask themselves a continuing pressing question: Where are we in the Kondratieff cycle? All you need to know is that a Russian economist named Kondratieff created this cycle. To be brief, his theory says that the cycle is expected to take from fifty to fifty-four years to be completed, and is mixed with large economic growth, war, high long-term borrowing, and inflation. Historians call it a "half-century business cycle."

The *Elliott Wave Theory* uses cycle analysis to make investment predictions. It records repetitions of price patterns to predict major moves in the market.

It's not important for you to follow your trading patterns according to a Russian economist or track a few repetitious patterns, but rather to understand that just as there is a business cycle in economics, there are cycles in the financial markets.

Dollar Cost Averaging Beats Averaging Down

Let's get funky. Okay, let's not and say we did.

As you are learning the rules of investing, the language of money is quite simple. Making money will be even easier as you continue on your journey through this guide. Along the way, you will find a few warnings, too. Heed them.

One danger involves the difference between dollar cost averaging and averaging down. Dollar cost averaging is a smart investment strategy. All you do is make fixed regular investments in a stock or mutual fund—regardless of whether the market is rising or falling. This strategy works in your favour no matter what the market does. Averaging down is not the same principle. The idea is to constantly purchase shares in an investment as the price of the investment continues to spiral downward, with the hope of it rising again. Often the investment keeps going down.

Let me explain it by using an example. If you purchase one hundred shares of stock at $20 a share, your total investment is worth $2,000. If the stock drops to $15 a share, your total investment is worth only $1,500. Suppose you purchase additional shares, let's say another one hundred shares at $15. Your total expense is calculated as $2,000 from your initial investment plus another $1,500 from your second purchase for a grand total expense of $3,500. By now, your average cost on the total two hundred shares is $17.50 per share. Because the stock is currently trading at $15 a share, it has to rise to $17.50 per share for you to break even on your investment.

An A+ or an E for Effort?

Managing your investment portfolio is based on a few simple concepts: How much money should you invest? What's the best strategy for you? Can you meet your long-term financial goals? And how can you put yourself in a position to properly gauge how your stocks or stock mutual funds are faring?

The best way to determine how well your portfolio is performing is to use a benchmark. As an investor, it is important to understand how your investments are judged. A benchmark measures the standard of performance reached by other investors. Sometimes this is referred to as a market average or an index.

The most commonly used index in Canada is the TSE 300 Composite Index which is a market-value weighted index of 300 Canadian stocks. The TSE 35 stock index was introduced in 1987 and consists of 35 of the most widely traded large-cap stocks on the Toronto exchange, many of which are household names (see list of company names). Because the TSE 35 is so narrowly based, it is not always the best benchmark to use. There are many indices that you can use as benchmarks.

Probably the most commonly quoted stock indicator worldwide is the Dow Jones industrial average, which is a U.S. index that represents

Companies Comprising the Toronto 35 Index

Abitibi-Price	Moore Corp
Alcan Aluminum	National Bank
Barrick Gold	Noranda Inc.
BCE Inc.	Northern Telecom
Bombardier Class B	Nova Corporation
Bank of Montreal	Placer Dome
Bank of Nova Scotia	Renaissance Energy
Canadian Imperial Bank	Rogers Communication Class B
Canadian Oxy Petroleum	Royal Bank
Canadian Pacific Ltd.	Seagram
Canadian Tire Class A	Talisman Energy
Dofasco Inc.	TransAlta Corporation
Imperial Oil	Toronto-Dominion Bank
Imasco Ltd.	Teck Corp Class B
Inco Limited	Thomson Corporation
Laidlaw Inc. Class B	TransCanada Pipelines
MacMillan Bloedel	TVX Gold
Magna International Class A	

Source: TSE Index Operations

only thirty blue-chip stocks. It often says surprisingly little about the day-to-day direction of the entire market. Because the Dow is so narrowly based, it's usually a poor benchmark against which to compare an entire portfolio's performance. The Standard and Poor 500 (S&P 500) is a U.S. index comprising 500 American stocks that gives you a far broader measure of market activity than the Dow Jones Industrial Average.

Market analysts have devised dozens of stock indices, ranging from the Standard & Poor 500 to indices that focus on just one sector, such as gold, automobiles or financial services. Because it is such a broad measure of market activity, many portfolio managers use the S&P 500 as a benchmark for the U.S. market. If you have any investments outside of North America, however, you might want to use the Morgan Stanley Capital International Europe Australia Far East (EAFE)

Index. This is the most prominent index used to track stocks outside of North America.

If you're trying to beat the market, it's not too tough as long as you're looking at a long-term time horizon. In 1996 alone, which was a banner year for the markets, the TSE 300 gained 24.1% while the S & P 500 gained 30.3%.

What about the professional money managers—those investment pros that you can take advantage of through mutual funds? The average domestic stock market mutual fund gained 21.2% last year. The average U.S. stock market mutual fund returned 17.6% last year. For the average international stock market mutual fund, the figure was 12.3%. That's the beauty of investing in a mutual fund—professional management. For those professional money managers who outperformed the averages, give them an A+.

A flurry of portfolio managers are paid well just to keep up with these indices. For example, there are a number of mutual funds, called index funds, that mirror how the TSE 300 performs. You won't get a bad return on them. In fact, you can make a lot of money with them if you invest in them over the long run. Give these investment pros an E for effort.

Mutual funds are a great way to gain access to different sectors. There are mutual funds that will expose you to conservative blue-chip stocks that will mirror the TSE 35 or the TSE 300. Whether you're looking for more aggressive, small-cap funds or for exposure to companies based outside of North America or for specialized sector funds (e.g. technology, metals, etc.) there are mutual funds to suit your objectives. Once you determine your asset allocation, mutual funds offer you a wide selection to give you exposure to each asset class.

Investing over the long run is one of the biggest secrets to making money on the stock markets. It takes a long run to average out the bull runs and bear markets. If you are investing over the long haul, hold on. You can weather it...and come out ahead.

Happy Birthday to You!

C'mon everybody, sing! (On key, please.) Happy Birthday to you! Happy Birthday to you! It's time to check your portfolio! I hope your stock and bond investments grew!

Make an appointment with your Investment Advisor at least once a year (on your birthday, perhaps) to review your investment portfolio thoroughly. The appointment date doesn't have to be on your birthday; many people find RRSP season (typically January 1 to March 1, March 1 being the deadline to make your RRSP contribution for the previous year) a good time to sit down with their advisors. This review should be in addition to the regular monitoring that you do. Treat this day as a special day for yourself. Yes, you are one year older, and that changes many things (your health, your state of mind, and your financial affairs). Why not take advantage of this day, and thoroughly check on your investments?

Take an hour or two to go through your records. Have you been living within your means? Are you contributing to your company's retirement plan? Have you adjusted your portfolio as you achieved your goals and your responsibilities changed?

Whatever the case, controlling your financial independence is sustained by keeping this appointment. It's the art of practicing self-discipline. Not only are you reviewing your portfolio on a regular basis—such as when you check your stock quotes or put your mutual fund statements in order—but this extra birthday attention that you give to your financial affairs will pay off handsomely in the future. You can also change any other pertinent financial records then. If you have made a will or bought a new piece of property, account for it during your annual review. Feel the sense of accomplishment as you check off items on your "Financial To-Do" list.

The Least You Need To Know

➤ Asset allocation is a form of diversifying your investment portfolio and protects you against market fluctuations. Remember: the correct asset allocation is more important than the individual selection of securities in each asset class.

➤ Learn how to properly gauge your investment portfolio by following some of the key indices. The TSE 300, the TSE 35, Dow Jones Industrial Average, and the Standard & Poor 500 are just a few.

➤ Do not try to time your investments. Often, the "buy-and-hold" approach fares better for investors than shimmying in and out of securities.

➤ The three main factors that'll determine your asset allocation mix include how much risk you're willing to take, your age, and your time horizon.

Part 2
The New Kid on the Block—Megabuck Bank

Many people have asked me, "Why write about banking if you're covering the stock markets?" The answer is simple. Banks have infiltrated the markets' turf. Banks are catching up to their brokerage house competitors by offering comparable investment products.

Competition is hot now. Even trust companies and credit unions have stepped up to the plate, offering investment products that would make your grandparents feel like they stepped into a time machine. This new kid on the block is here to stay. You understand the basics of what a bank can do—offering savings and chequing accounts and all types of loans. As we continue through the '90s, the banking industry will evolve into a much stiffer competitor, giving other financial institutions a run for their money. This section will help you learn how bank products can fit into your investment portfolio and how you can save a few dollars, too.

I KNOW HE TAKES IT A LITTLE SERIOUSLY, BUT HE'S THE BEST INVESTMENT BANKER AT THE COMPANY...

Banking in the '90s

Picture this. You enter your bank lobby and suddenly you're surrounded by the cutting edge of technology—fax machines, modems, PC networks, TV screens galore, and robot tellers (okay, not really robot tellers, but machines that spit out money at the touch of a few buttons). What is all this? Buck Rogers in the 21st Century?

Nope, just a modern-day bank lobby. Forget the bank brochures that you used to pick up and read for information. Bank lobbies are rigged with television monitors providing information on all bank products and services via video information channels. Everywhere you look there's a monitor. Waiting in line? Another video monitor. Want to know what's happening on the markets? Check the monitor.

Now imagine it's four in the morning. You are wide awake because you can't remember the amount of cheque number 132. (You forgot to enter it in your cheque register last week.) Easy enough—just dial your bank's twenty-four hour, seven-day-a-week hotline. Press a few buttons (don't forget your personal access code) and get your answer. Talk about technology!

This chapter takes a look at the services that today's banks provide and how those services can fit in with your investment battle plan.

You Can Take That to the Bank

Most people have already been exposed to a bank. Remember when you were little and your parents opened your first savings account for you? In fact, Canada's banks employ about 206 800 Canadians in over 8,000 branches and manage more than $900 billion in assets, according to the Canadian Bankers Association. The Canadian banking system is one of the most efficient, reliable and low-cost banking systems in the world.

Even if you don't have a chequing or savings account, you'll have to deal with a bank at some point in your life. When unexpected emergencies arise, it helps to have cash in a savings or chequing account. Whether you earn a whopping 10% or even a measly half percent on your cash instruments, your account can't fall in principal value—unlike stocks, bonds, and mutual funds. Cash is king when stock and bond prices are falling.

You learned in Chapter 5 about the role liquidity plays in your investment planning. Even if you are a big-time futures player, you still need a place to park your cash for a relatively short time between your investment trading adventures. Why not in your bank? One of the best places to keep your cash on hand is in an interest-bearing account that pays competitive rates. If you don't have an immediate need for the cash (e.g. paying the bills or this month's rent), one option would be to deposit it into a money market mutual fund. These accounts will earn you higher interest rates than most deposit accounts, and you will still have access to your cash if you need it. Contact your broker for more details.

Banks now offer mutual funds. Ask your bank representative for more information and a prospectus.

As investors of the '90s are gaining more independence regarding their finances, all financial institutions—banks, brokerage firms, financial services companies, and mutual fund companies—are competing for their cash. This has caused the banking industry to change, and you've probably witnessed a few of these changes: new bank products, different fee packages and advanced computerized services.

Many of you have already learned some aspects of smart banking in the '90s, such as implementing strategies that help you not to incur any additional fees or charges. For example, if you maintain a minimum balance in a chequing or savings account, you aren't slapped with a "below minimum balance" fee. Many of you know that when you use your bank's ABM (automatic banking machine) rather than a competitor's ABM, you avoid getting nicked with an ABM charge. Others have taken advantage of a bank's direct deposit feature and get that extra day's worth of interest from their paycheque. These are all good—but the world of banking offers so much more these days.

As banks are vying for your dollars, they're trying to stay as competitive as ever. How? By paying better interest rates on your interest-bearing accounts than the next guy. Banks also aim to provide customers with the same services (or better) as their competitors. The banking industry has been booming over the last few years, and enjoying record profits.

Let's use an example to illustrate one avenue banks use to make money. You're a bank customer at my bank and have a noninterest-bearing chequing account, a savings account, and a one-year GIC that pays 4.75%. You're in the process of buying a new car and need a loan. So you come to my bank, and I charge you 7% for a $15,000, forty-eight month loan.

Now let's do the math. Let's say you put all your money in that GIC that earns you 4.75%. And you are paying 7% to borrow money (that's what I collect from you at my bank.) The difference between the two is called the *spread*. This means the bank is making 2.25% on these transactions.

If the spread widens, my bank will make more money. In other words, if the rates that I pay my customers on their investments drop, while the rates that I

> The difference between the interest rates paid to customers on their investments and the interest rates that the bank collects on its outstanding loans from customers is called the **spread**.

charge my customers on all types of loans stay pretty steady, then I will make more money. On the other hand, if the spread narrows, my bank won't make as much money because the rates that I pay to customers' accounts and the rates that I charge on all loans will fall into a pretty small range.

The Stock Market Players Are Shakin' in Their Boots

Canadian stock market contenders never really had to worry about the banking industry stepping on their toes until a couple of years ago. Since June of 1992, federal legislation has removed many of the barriers surrounding financial institutions. Following global trends, banks, trust and loan companies, and insurance companies can compete directly with each other. Certainly, the activities of Canadian financial institutions are changing.

Most of the major banks own full-service as well as discount brokerage firms. Look for any joint services your bank may offer with their brokerage firm.

The Bank Act now permits banks to compete in new sectors of the financial services industry. This means that the banks have moved into the securities industry. In fact, most of the major banks own full-service brokerage firms as well as discount brokerage firms. Bank-owned investment dealers have become heavy hitters; in fact, as of 1995, banks held a 24% market share of Canadian mutual funds. Banks can now offer investment counselling and portfolio management services, in addition to regular banking services, all under one roof. In addition, the Bank Act allows banks to offer non-banking financial services, such as insurance and trust operations.

The Hi-Tech Bank

With the evolution of technology, your computer can be your bank. The future of banking and investing is here: PC Banking. With a connection to the Internet, you can access all of your bank accounts. For instance, The Toronto-Dominion Bank recently introduced TD Access PC, North America's first fully integrated banking and brokerage software. Pay bills, transfer funds, generate account reports or export your

Bet You Didn't Know

Canadians made 63 million information requests at ABMs during 1995, 11.1% more than in the previous year.

financials to a financial software package such as Microsoft Money or Quicken—all at the touch of a button!

For you non-computer geeks out there, don't worry; just pick up your phone and you can do all of the above, and more. Apply for a loan, order cheques, invest in GICs, purchase mutual funds, you name it. And, of course, you can visit your local automated bank machine (ABM), to access your accounts twenty-four hours a day, seven days a week.

Snazzy Cats in Blue Suits

With the stiff competition between the big banks these days, many of the banking fees are being discounted, and even waived in some cases if you can maintain a minimum account balance, e.g., $1,000. Many banks are now offering flat-fee banking which gives you flexibility by allowing you as many transactions as you wish for a fixed monthly rate. Here is a quick list of some of the fees that may be charged to your account:

➤ **Account closing fees.** Account holders had a fit when their banks charged $10 and $15 on noninterest-bearing chequing accounts when they tried to close their accounts within six months. Make sure that when you open your account, there are no fees that you'll be hit with if you decide to close it.

➤ **Bounced cheque fees.** These are still rising across the country, and they probably always will. The fee for a bounced cheque can run up to $20 at your local bank. That's dinner for four at McDonald's. Yikes!

➤ **Foreign ABM fees.** These are ABM transactions that you make at a rival cash station across town. ABM fees and charges range from $1 to $2. Who has control of these fees? You do. Don't use your ABM card at a foreign ABM station and you won't get nicked with any more charges. Twenty-five percent of bank customers don't know what it costs to use an ABM card.

➤ **Loss of interest below a particular balance.** Get this. Some banks tell you that they won't pay you any interest on your savings account if the balance falls below a certain level, such as $50. Avoid stashing your cash in these types of accounts.

➤ **Overdraft fees.** Not only can you get charged a possible $20 bounced check fee, some institutions charge you additional monies—the average is $3 for each day you're overdrawn.

I'm not telling you this for my health. You should start paying more attention to the bank fees you pay. Find out what your account really costs you. You can use the following techniques to bank wisely:

➤ Review all fine print that your financial institution gives you when you open your account.

➤ If your banking habits don't fit your institution's fee schedule, start shopping around. For example, look for lower minimum balance requirements and reduced ABM fees as you check out the competition. The savings can really add up.

➤ Establish relationship accounts. By keeping high balances in a combination of chequing and savings accounts, GICs, and so on, you can qualify for benefits, such as discounts on bounced-cheque charges and waived annual fees on bank credit cards.

Choosing the Bank Product for Your Needs

The following are the basic products that are offered by banks today, some of which have been discussed earlier in this chapter:

➤ Savings accounts.
➤ Chequing accounts.
➤ GICs (guaranteed investment certificates).
➤ Canada Savings Bonds & Provincial Savings Bonds
➤ Mutual funds.

Savings accounts are good for temporary cash havens when you are in the process of determining where you're going to invest your money. They are also a good place to stash some cash while the financial markets are volatile or when Aunt Gertie leaves you $100,000 and you haven't figured out how to spend it yet.

Chequing accounts come in all shapes and sizes these days. Unlimited cheque writing, overdraft protection, free ABM use up to ten transactions per month—you name it, it's out there. Chapter 11 explains the basics of a chequing account and how to find the best deals.

GICs and bonds pay some of the higher interest rates of any bank product, for a relatively small minimum investment. Touted as a safe investment, GICs and bonds enable you to lock into a specific interest rate for a certain period of time. Remember when you were little and instead of getting a toy for a birthday present, you got a piece of paper with your name on it that looked like a cheque? It was probably a savings bond. I know two little boys out there who have made a killing at their birthday parties because relatives buy them these bonds. Savings bonds, e.g., Canada Savings Bonds (CSBs) or provincial savings bonds, offer market rates of interest, and you pay taxes on the interest in the year you earn it. Plus, you can buy them with as little as $100. You'll learn about these in Chapter 22.

When it comes to mutual funds—do your homework. Ask for the prospectus detailing the funds. Check the fund's historical performance, asset holdings and objectives.

The Least You Need To Know

➤ Banks have captured a share of the Canadian stock market's target market. In fact, most of the major banks own full-service and discount brokerage firms.

➤ You'll have to deal with a bank at some point in your life. As part of your investment planning, make sure that you allocate a portion of your investment portfolio to cash for emergency purposes. The percentage depends upon you and your situation. We'll talk more about asset allocation later on.

➤ Know and understand the different services that your bank offers you. Savings accounts, chequing accounts, guaranteed investment certificates (GICs), and savings bonds are common products you'll see at your bank. You now see banks offering mutual funds as well.

**Every human being, even if he is an idiot,
is a millionaire in emotions.**

—Isaac Bashevis Singer

Chapter 10

So Long, Savings

In this chapter

➤ The evolution of the savings account

➤ When should you have a savings account?

➤ Savings accounts for the '90s

When I was a little boy, my idea of fun was to make as many bank deposits as I could and watch the interest accrue in my passbook savings account. Even if I only had two bucks to deposit, I'd stand in line at a teller window, anxiously waiting for the teller to stamp my new, bigger and better, balance in my little passbook. Boy, I thought I was rich as I watched the money grow.

It wasn't until I deposited a cheque from a relative that I understood how the banking industry really worked. Boing! The cheque bounced. My little passbook savings account was hit as if by a torpedo gone astray. I didn't get the money from the deposit, of course, because the cheque bounced. Reluctantly, I took my passbook to the teller and she made the adjustment. It was a horrible scene, but I think I've recovered.

Bet You Didn't Know

In 1995, Canadian bank customers made more than 730 million withdrawals and 130 million deposits.

Except for the bounced-cheque tragedy, watching my savings account grow was a great learning experience for me. I learned the concept of depositing money and earning interest on my deposits. This chapter covers the basics of how savings accounts work and how to use them (or not use them) wisely as part of an overall investment plan.

The First Savings Accounts

Actually, the world of banking began many, many years ago. In about 4 B.C., I believe, the Greeks invented the bill of exchange. This was for merchants only and was the equivalent of today's savings accounts or

Most banks offer accounts with special privileges— e.g., free withdrawals— to young people (usually age 19 or younger). Ask your local bank representative for details.

an automated banking machine (ABM). A merchant could deposit a sum of money (coins in those days) with his banker. The banker would then give him a letter in exchange for the coin deposit. When the merchant had to make a road trip—for vacation, to shop at outlet stores (just kidding), or for a business trip—he would take the letter to another banker in another city and collect money. This was how the bill of exchange worked.

Today things are much different. Savings accounts have evolved since the old letter of interest credit. For one thing, we can receive interest on our deposits, albeit not very much. In today's environment, the average rate paid on a savings account is less than one percent— much less than yesteryear's rate of 5.25%.

The interest that accrues in your savings account is based on two principles, the method of compounding and the starting date set by the bank. In the banking industry, compounding is set on a daily, monthly, quarterly, and annual basis. Table 10.1 shows how the method of compounding works.

Table 10.1 How Much Bang for Your $1,000?

Rate	Annual	Quarterly	Monthly	Daily
3.00%	$1,030.00	$1,030.34	$1,030.42	$1,030.45
4.00%	$1,040.00	$1,040.60	$1,040.74	$1,040.81
5.00%	$1,050.00	$1,050.95	$1,051.16	$1,051.27
6.00%	$1,060.00	$1,061.36	$1,061.68	$1,061.83
7.00%	$1,070.00	$1,071.86	$1,072.29	$1,072.50
8.00%	$1,080.00	$1,082.43	$1,083.00	$1,083.28

If you understand the methods of compounding, you'll come to this conclusion: the faster the reinvestment, the more money you'll earn in the end. Look at how much more money you have if you earn 4% on $1,000 compounded daily versus having it compounded annually! This principle applies to all investments that use compounding.

You don't need an accounting degree to learn the different types of compounding that many banks and trust companies use.

Depositing your money into a savings account keeps it safe from loss of principal and can stabilize your investment portfolio. Safety is an integral part of investing, and a savings account can provide that. However, safety shouldn't be the only requirement you look for in an investment.

When you sign up for a bank account, see what type of compounding method is offered. The more frequent the compounding the more you will earn.

Keeping It Liquid

During your investment planning—and actually for the rest of your life—you need to have a portion of your investment portfolio kept liquid; that

Keep in mind that if you have money that you want to keep liquid but don't need right away, you may consider putting your moola into a money market mutual fund. It usually takes one business day to access your money if you need it, and you'll receive a higher rate of interest. You can invest in these money market funds through your broker.

is, readily available. These liquid accounts should be interest-bearing accounts that provide income and preservation of capital. If an unexpected emergency arises, this account provides the safety net, but it also provides a good parking place when you're trying to decide which investment to purchase.

In the past, investors kept this portion in a savings account. Today, savings accounts offer rates that are much lower than in the past, and have difficulty in keeping up with inflation. The yields that are paid on savings accounts are typically about 0.25%–2%, well below those of quality bonds.

The bottom line? Unless you have a very small amount of money to save, it may be wiser to open an account that pays higher interest rates and returns. So skip the toasters and lollipops and search for a better source of returns on your liquid account.

One More Word of Advice

When selecting a bank or a broker, look closely at the banks that have established relationships with their brokerage firms, i.e., a brokerage firm that is owned by a bank or has a connection with a bank or financial institution. If this relationship between bank and brokerage exists, many transactions become simple and convenient, such as transferring funds from your bank account to your brokerage account and vice versa. Remember that higher yielding money market mutual fund your broker can offer you from Chapter 9? Of course, this alone is not a reason to choose a particular institution to do business with, but something that should be considered.

The Least You Need To Know

➤ Gone are the days when you could earn 5.25% on a passbook savings account. Today, savings accounts offer a less than one percent yield.

➤ Make sure you know what type of compounding method your savings account uses. The more compounding that takes place, the more you earn.

➤ Try to keep any savings you don't need in the near future in a money market mutual fund. They offer higher returns than savings accounts.

➤ Look for any relationships your bank might have with a brokerage firm.

The easiest way for your children to learn about money is for you not to have any.

—Katharine Whitehorn

AND WHEN YOU OPEN **THIS** ACCOUNT YOU GET A BEAR...

Chapter 11

Checking Out Chequing Accounts

In this chapter

➤ Types of chequing accounts

➤ Where are the best chequing account deals?

➤ How to rethink your chequing account

I'll never forget the time during my first year of university when a friend of mine and I were in the grocery store, and he wanted to buy a candy bar. He didn't have any money with him and wouldn't take a loan from me, so he wrote a cheque for fifty cents.

He got his candy bar, but it cost him more than fifty cents—the cheque bounced. His parents were furious. "What's the matter? Don't you have two quarters?" they screamed at him. I wanted to laugh, but that fifty cent candy bar cost him an extra $18 because he didn't have available funds in his chequing account to cover it. I hope he savoured every last morsel.

Bouncing a fifty cent cheque is not, obviously, a smart use of a chequing account. This chapter identifies other chequing account faux pas, and explains how you can avoid them.

You'll Always Need One

Despite how expensive chequing accounts have become, you always need some type of chequing account to pay bills. For example, when you pay the rent, are you going to send $700 in cash to your landlord? I don't think so.

A chequing account is part of your investment plan for several reasons. First, you need it to buy other investment securities. For example, let's say you open an investment account at a brokerage firm. You want to buy one hundred shares of stock in your favourite health care stock, Bugsie's Drugsies, the newest mail order prescription firm that just went public. You purchase one hundred shares at $27 a share and you owe your broker, Dave, $2,700 plus commissions. How are you going to pay for it? In cash? No. You write a cheque to the brokerage firm and it is deposited into your account. (You'll learn, later in the book, when money is due after you place a stock trade.)

The second reason for having a chequing account is convenience. The average household grocery bill is $100 or more. It isn't convenient (or safe) to carry that kind of cash around with you. Most grocery stores take cheques and/or debit cards.

Third, having a chequing account helps you keep track of your expenses. You can follow your budget closely if you itemize your transaction record in your chequebook. Keeping track of your expenses is a big part of your investment plan because it details whether you should cut certain spending habits.

Now that we've established good, solid reasons for having a chequing account, let's take a look at the different types that exist.

➤ **Chequing/Savings Accounts.** These accounts provide both interest and chequing services.

➤ **Personal Chequing Accounts.** These accounts pay little or no interest but include monthly statements and return cancelled cheques.

➤ **No-charge Chequing Accounts.** The no-charge applies as long as a minimum balance is maintained.

➤ **Tiered Chequing Accounts.** The interest rate paid on these accounts increases as the minimum balance increases.

With this range of options, you can choose the best combination for your own personal needs.

118

Managing Your Cash

Remember those stock market players who were shakin' in their boots because of bank mutual funds? They've put up their dukes and are offering alternatives to your bank's basic chequing account. It seems that everybody in the financial services industry wants to help you manage your money.

Known as wealth management service accounts, these types of accounts offer everything under the sun. The concept behind this account is to consolidate all your financial operations into one account. In other words, a wealth management service account allows you access to all financial services from a single source. Before you determine if it is worth it, you should understand the rules.

First, a wealth management service account can be opened only through a brokerage firm. You can buy stock, sell bonds, and write a cheque to the telephone company from just one account. In addition, these types of accounts offer premium interest rates on account balances. The minimum account size ranges anywhere from $20,000 to $250,000. Some firms may allow you to combine all of your accounts to reach these minimum levels.

Wealth management service accounts, offered by many full-service and some discount brokerage firms, usually require a large initial deposit—between $20,000 and $250,000—from a combination of cash and/or securities. With wealth management service accounts, you can write cheques and invest in stocks, bonds, mutual funds, and other investment securities all from one account. Freebies include ABM cards, credit cards, and waived RRSP administration fees, plus you have access to a line of credit.

Fees to maintain the typical wealth management service account range from $25 to $200 a year. That's just for having the account; it doesn't include any commissions you incur for trades. Many firms offer credit cards, ABM cards, waived RRSP account administration fees, lines of credit and travellers' cheques at no charge as part of these accounts. For those of you who write a lot of cheques, wealth management accounts do offer a plus—unlimited cheque writing, although some firms require a minimum cheque size.

What about safety? All your assets in the account—cash, stocks, bonds, mutual funds, whatever—are insured up to $500,000, including

119

$60,000 in cash, by the Canadian Investor Protection Fund (CIPF). But more on this in Chapter 13.

If you have enough money to open a wealth management service account, more power to you. However, remember that fees and charges are higher with some asset management accounts than those at a bank.

Finding the Best Chequing Deals

Take your time when shopping for a chequing account, and look for the following features:

➤ Free chequing. Not all banks offer this type of account, but when they do, check it out. A free chequing account is one that has no monthly maintenance fee, no penalty fee if your balance drops below a certain level, and no transaction fee no matter how many cheques you write.

➤ Low bounced cheque fees. Even if you don't bounce any checks, there are times when you may deposit someone else's cheque and it will bounce—and you'll get hit with the $20 charge. (Trust me, I know from experience!)

➤ No ABM transaction fees. Make sure your chequing account allows you to perform ABM transactions without charging you a penny for doing so.

➤ Only buy the basic cheques offered if you have to buy them at the bank. Cheques ordered through a bank are expensive, so limit yourself to the basic blue or yellow.

➤ Avoid those chequing accounts that charge you an inactivity fee. Finding the best deal in a chequing account requires patience. You need to take time, do your homework, and read the fine print from the brochures the bankers give you.

Most of these freebies come automatically if you can maintain a minimum balance. So, make sure you know what the minimums are.

How affordable a chequing account is differs from bank to bank. Maintaining a chequing account used to be very expensive; today it's just moderately expensive—as long as you do your homework!

The Least You Need To Know

➤ Just because you have cheques left in your chequebook doesn't mean you have money left to burn in your chequing account. Make sure you balance your chequebook once a month when you receive your bank statement.

➤ Wealth management service accounts do provide fewer paperwork hassles, but they usually have required minimum deposits, which can be $20,000 and up.

➤ Do your homework when it comes to selecting a bank account. It'll save you money in the long run.

➤ I know I sound like a broken record, but watch those fees and charges, especially if you bank at a foreign ABM station or bounce a cheque. Foreign ABM transactions run around $1.00 per transaction within Canada and then double or more outside Canada.

Success isn't permanent and failure isn't fatal.

—Mike Ditka

WORLD OF STOCK TRADES

WORLD OF GICS AND BONDS

WORLD OF MUTUAL FUNDS

Chapter 12

The World of GICs and Bonds

In this chapter
➤ Fitting GICs and bonds into your investment plan
➤ Where to buy GICs and bonds
➤ Picking the best deals on GICs and bonds

Most people have heard of GICs and most of you have probably invested in a GIC at some point in your life. With a GIC you know what interest rate you are earning, when you will receive the interest payment, and when the principal amount of your investment matures. For example, you might find a GIC at your bank that has a maturity five years out and pays 5% (that's right, only about 5%). So if you invest $10,000 in this GIC, you will receive $500 a year and at the end of five years you get your $10,000 back.

Everyone should have a portion of their portfolio allocated to conservative fixed-income products like GICs or maybe Government of Canada bonds. When I say fixed income, that means investments which generate a fixed stream of interest or dividend income, such as bonds and GICs. When I say conservative bond, it usually means one

Fixed Income Investments: Investments that generate a predictable stream of interest or dividend income, such as bonds, GICs or T-bills.

that is backed by the Canadian government or maybe a high quality provincial or municipal government. When investing in any type of bond you should always check what each bond is rated. For the most conservative rating on a bond product you would see a rating of AAA (the highest credit rating given), the next rating down would be AA, and so on. For a relatively conservative product you would not want to go much below AA. (For a comprehensive list of bond ratings, check out the section on Bonds in Chapter 21.)

How Do I Pick One?

When investing in fixed income products—whether it be GICs or bonds—you always want to look for the highest rate of interest without assuming any additional risk. That is, you don't want to get a higher rate of return on a bond if the bond is going to be very risky (the rating might be BBB). You want to compare apples with apples and oranges with oranges. So if you want a conservative five-year fixed-income product, only look at conservative five year products.

Bonds may offer you a higher rate of return t han a GIC without taking on any more risk.

Especially in today's low interest environment it is important to get as much yield on your fixed-income products as possible. That is why I strongly suggest that you look at bonds and compare them to rates on GICs. Often it is the case that the bond will give you a higher rate of return (not always but most of the time) without taking on any more risk. Also, with bonds you have the added liquidity factor. Anytime you want to, you can sell a bond before it matures. In most cases you are locked into a GIC until it matures. GICs are neither redeemable nor cashable before maturity. With bonds, be careful when you sell them before maturity because if you sell them

Remember: most GICs are not redeemable nor cashable before maturity, whereas bonds can be sold in the open market at that day's price.

at the going rate, there is no guarantee that you will get a certain price (to see how bond prices work, refer to Chapter 21).

In addition to the added liquidity bonds offer over GICs, you can find some specialized bond-like products. For example, you can find an AAA rated bond (called an MBS or mortgage-backed security) that pays its income on a monthly basis. As well, there are bonds that pay interest based on the inflation rate. You have bonds that pay interest once a year. What I am trying to say here is that if you are looking to invest in GICs, then you should also consider a bond as a possibility as well.

The Inflation Sting

Although GICs and bonds are safe investments, inflation inevitably plays a part in reducing your purchasing power. In fact, your after-tax, after-inflation return could leave you with less than what you started with. Your goal is to earn an interest rate higher than inflation—and taxes if possible—when you're deciding how to allocate the nest egg portion of your investment portfolio. Table 12.1 shows how inflation can harm this nest egg investment.

To chase higher yielding GIC or bond rates, ask your broker or banker on the available products that are suited to your needs.

Table 12.1   The Effects of Inflation on an Investment Yield

	3% inflation	4% inflation
Initial investment (one-year GIC)	$10,000	$10,000
Interest earned (at 5%)	500	500
Total investment at maturity	$10,500	$10,500
Taxes paid (at 28%)	140	140
Total after taxes	$10,360	$10,360
Less inflation	311	414
Purchasing power at maturity	$10,049	$ 9,946

If You Have $100k, Here's How To Play

Once you have worked hard enough to accumulate $100,000, you have more options available to you, including Bankers' Acceptances (BA) and Commercial Paper. Both of these options have maturities of less than one year. In either case, you will earn higher yields on these investments than GICs or Government of Canada treasury bills (T-Bills). (Government of Canada T-Bills are bonds with a maturity of less than one year).

Bankers' acceptances are bank-guaranteed notes that offer good security. Commercial Paper provides superior yields to both GICs, Bankers' Acceptances, and most other money market products. This is because Commercial Paper is issued by corporations and is not guaranteed by the bank (remember, as you increase your risk tolerance, your return increases). The terms to maturity on both BAs and Commercial Paper are much shorter than GICs and bonds: they come in 30, 60, 90, and 180 day maturities. There is also Government Guaranteed Commercial Paper, but the yields here are slightly lower than regular Commercial Paper.

The Timing Factor

How long do you lock your money up when it comes to investing in fixed-income products? No one knows the direction of interest rates for sure, so no one really knows exactly how long to lock up your money in a fixed income type of product. If you think interest rates are going to rise, you will want to invest with short-term maturities in order to have the investment maturing shortly so that you can take advantage of the increase in rates when it happens. If you think interest rates are going to decline, you will want to take advantage of the rates now before they go lower, and invest in longer maturities.

Some experts suggest a laddering approach when deciding on the amount of time you should lock up money in a fixed-income product.

One very popular strategy for investing in bonds is called laddering. This occurs when you select a combination of maturities to invest in. For example, suppose you have $50,000. You can choose to invest it in a five-year Government of Canada bond. This means that when the bond matures you are then stuck re-investing it at whatever the rates are in five years. However, if you ladder you investments across five different maturities then you diversify your re-investment risk. Say, for example, you invest $10,000 in a 1-year, 3-year, 5-year, 7-year and 10-year bond for a total investment of $50,000. This way if rates go up in the short-term or in the long-term—you will have money maturing that will be able to be re-invested at higher rates.

The Least you Need to Know

➤ When you are investing in a GIC or bond you are locking your money in at a specific rate for a specific time period.

➤ Consider bonds along with GICs, as bonds may be able to offer you higher returns.

➤ For investments of $100,000 or more, Bankers' Acceptances and Commercial Paper offer better rates for timeframes of less than one year.

**I had plastic surgery last week.
I cut up my credit cards.**

—Henry Youngman

Chapter 13

What About Safety?

In this chapter

➤ How bank deposits are insured

➤ How other investments are insured—if at all

➤ Where to find out how strong—and safe—your bank is

Have you ever thought about what would happen if you lost your home to a fire or smashed up your car in an accident?

When you buy a home, mortgage lenders require you to protect it and your belongings from damage. The answer? The right homeowners' insurance policy. And if you think about it, your chances of being in a car accident these days are growing. That's why automobile insurance is expensive—because the risks are so great. In case of tragedy or accident, most people proclaim: "Oh, the insurance will cover it." But you have to *have* insurance to protect yourself from these types of losses.

Financial catastrophes have blown many investment plans to smithereens. To avoid this, you should have some type of insurance to cover your deposits and investments. This chapter explains how you can ensure that your bank deposits are safe.

And for Your Protection

You're at your local bank ready to make a deposit. As you stand in the line for the teller window, you notice a sign out of the corner of your eye that says, "Deposits Insured Up To $60,000." "So, what?" you say to yourself. You hand your deposit to the teller and feel confident that nothing can go wrong. Your money will be there when you need it. Plus, it's backed by the government, so you assume your money is safe. Or is it?

For your protection, the Canada Deposit Insurance Corporation (CDIC) was created. The CDIC is a federal Crown corporation that was established in 1967 to protect the money you deposit in financial institutions that are CDIC members, in the event of their failure. The CDIC insures your deposits if a member institution becomes insolvent. This insurance is subject to eligibility and maximum coverage (which will be explained shortly). All you need to understand are the limitations on the insurance coverage for your bank accounts.

 CDIC stands for Canada Deposit Insurance Corporation. This federal Crown corporation was created in 1967 to protect the money you deposit in member financial institutions.

The maximum basic protection you can have with one member institution is $60,000, including principal and interest. The $60,000 maximum includes all the insurable deposits you have with the same CDIC member. Deposits at different branches of the same member institution are not insured separately. Not all financial institutions are members of the CDIC; membership is limited to banks, trust and loan companies.

You do not apply for deposit insurance. Eligible deposits held with CDIC member institutions are automatically protected. To be eligible for CDIC deposit insurance protection, monies held must be:

➤ in Canadian currency, payable in Canada;

➤ repayable on demand, or no later than five years from the date of deposit;

➤ insurable "deposits", rather than other types of uninsurable investments; and

➤ placed at a financial institution that is a CDIC member.

Insurable deposits include: savings and chequing accounts, term

130

deposits of no more than five years (e.g. GICs), money orders, drafts, and travellers' cheques issued by member institutions. Some of the common investments that the CDIC does NOT insure are: foreign currency deposits (e.g. accounts in U.S. dollars), term deposits that mature more than five years after the date of deposit, bonds issued by governments and corporations, T-bills, mutual funds, stocks, and investments in mortgages.

The CDIC insures joint deposits separately from any deposits held by the individual owners in their own right. The maximum protection for all deposits held by the same joint owners with each CDIC member is $60,000, including principal and interest. This $60,000 maximum applies to the joint owners collectively, NOT to each individual. The account holdings must meet the same eligibility requirements as stated above.

For RRSPs, eligible deposits are insured separately from other deposits held in your name at the same CDIC member institution. The maximum coverage for your RRSP deposits at one member institution is $60,000, including principal and interest. Remember: the CDIC does not insure some types of investments that you may hold in your RRSP, including foreign currency deposits, mutual funds, stocks, bonds, and T-bills.

To protect money you invest in any financial institution, you need to follow these guidelines:

➤ Make sure you bank at a federally insured institution. Look for the CDIC seal shown below or ask your customer service representative whether the institution is an CDIC member.

➤ Keep in mind that depositors, not the accounts, are insured up to $60,000 including interest and principal. If you have three accounts at one bank worth $60,000 each for a total of $180,000, you are only insured up to $60,000—not the full $180,000.

Bet You Didn't Know

You can obtain a listing of CDIC members by obtaining a pamphlet, usually at your local bank. Or you can call the CDIC directly at 1-800-461-CDIC.

➤ If you have an RRSP at a bank, eligible deposits in your RRSP are insured separately from your other accounts, to the maximum $60,000

➤ If you invest in mutual funds, stocks or bonds, understand that they are not (and I repeat NOT) covered by CDIC insurance. Many customers mistakenly think that some of these investments are backed by the CDIC because they're sold by banks. Not true. Make sure you know the difference between insured deposits and uninsured investments.

CIPF stands for the Canadian Investor Protection Fund. It was established in 1969 and is financed entirely by the members of the securities industry, such as the stock exchanges and member brokerages.

A Word About Brokerage Accounts

Now that we've covered deposit insurance protection at your local bank, let's turn to your brokerage account. And yes, brokerage accounts are insured as well. However, they are covered by a different act, with different coverage protection rules. It is called the Canadian Investor Protection Fund (CIPF). CIPF is not a provincial government or even a federal agency. The group that funds it is made up of dealer members, such as brokerage firms.

As a member of CIPF, your brokerage account is covered up to $500,000 per customer, including $60,000 in cash. Accounts held at brokerage firms, mutual funds companies, banks and other firms that are members are covered. Check with your broker to ensure CIPF membership.

All accounts of a client, such as cash, margin, options, futures, and foreign currency are combined and treated as one general account and are entitled to the maximum coverage. Separate accounts are each entitled to the maximum coverage of $500,000 per account. Some examples of separate accounts include: RRSPs, RRIFs, RESPs, and Joint Accounts.

CIPF does not cover any losses that you incur because of a bad investment decision. If you invest in a stock and it hits the skids, that's your loss.

CIPF insures your brokerage account in the event a brokerage firm fails. If a firm does fail, your accounts are usually transferred to another brokerage firm or your investment certificates (such as stock or bond certificates) are sent directly to you. Speak with your broker or an investment representative to clarify the nitty gritty details of how the coverage works.

The Least You Need To Know

➤ The Canadian Deposit Insurance Corporation (CDIC) insures customer deposits of up to $60,000 in the same institution, whether it be a bank, trust or loan company. Any amount over $60,000 is not covered by CDIC insurance in the event of a bank failure. Check to see if your financial institution is a member of the CDIC.

➤ The insurance that protects customer accounts at member brokerage firms is the Canadian Investor Protection Fund (CIPF) insurance. The coverage limit is $500,000, which may include $60,000 cash.

In spite of the cost of living, it's still popular.

—Kathleen Norris

Part 3
Stocks—The Grandaddy of All Markets

If you think about the stock market, what types of images do you conjure up? A ticker tape running across a screen with numbers and fractions? Anxious traders flailing their arms, making hand gestures (all kinds, I'm sure), screaming at each other, and trying to buy or sell shares of stock in the pits of a financial exchange?

Is it financial wizardry in the making? Not really. There's nothing mysterious about the stock market. Trading dates back to the times when people used to barter their goods. Farmers would stand in the middle of their fields, bickering about how many cows one farmer would get in exchange for the other farmer's chickens.

Today, with five major financial exchanges in Canada and the computer whizbang trading programs, you can find many opportunities to make money in the stock market. This part explains how you can get in on the stock market action and gives you basic strategies for maximizing your stock market profits.

Chapter 14

Stock Market 101

In this chapter

➤ Stock market jargon that will WOW your friends

➤ What life is like in the pits

➤ How to buy and sell stock

Investing in stocks seems scary, right? Your grandparents' or parents' conversations about how they lost all of their money during the Great Crash of '29 remain vivid in your brain. Even the four-hundred point plunge in the TSE 300 Composite Index (and the 500 point drop on the Dow Jones Industrial Average) on October 19, 1987 frightened regular, average Joe people like you and me into thinking that the stock market is a dangerous, hectic, and volatile place.

The reality is that the stock market can be dangerous if you don't know what you're doing and you rush into it. Just imagine how confused you would be if you tried to program your VCR to record "Traders" every Thursday night and didn't read any directions. Or if you went skydiving for the first time and ignored the instructor. Ouch!

Do your homework and look at the returns, though, if you're going to invest in the stock market for the long haul. From 1926

Another name for an investment product is **security**. You'll see the terms security, investment security, and investment product used interchangeably in this book.

Common stock shares are securities which represent an ownership interest in a company.

through 1992, the average annual return on common stocks was around 10.4%. A $1,000 investment ten years ago in a stock performing as well as the TSE 300 index would have grown to $2,674—an average annual return of 8.8%. The same $1,000 invested in the S&P 500 index ten years ago would have grown to $4,809. This tallies to an 15.1% average annual return. If you invested $1,000 in the S&P 500 back in 1924, it would be worth a whopping $4 million today!

This chapter explains how you can get on the road to being a successful stock investor. If you stay in the stock market for a longer period of time, you lower your chance of losing money. That's why financial gurus promote the "buy-and-hold" strategy. You can make money investing in stocks if you give the stock market—and yourself—enough time! After you pass Stock Market 101, you'll know what a stock is and how to buy and sell one.

Before we're off to the races, let's just review some terms you should know. Money talks and here's how. You were introduced to a few terms in the first chapter, such as "investment product." Many times in the investment world, investment product will be used interchangeably with investment security, financial security, financial product, investments and financial instrument. You also learned that one of the trade secrets to making money on the stock markets is to buy low and sell high. But let's take the next step...into the stock market.

Bulls, Bears, and Such

Now here's a few more terms to get you going. You hear about these "bulls and bears" in the stock markets. What are they?

1. Animals from the city zoo.
2. Investors dressed up in costumes running up and down the streets of Toronto.
3. Animal crackers from a cookie box.
4. Names for market watchers.

I sure hope you picked number 4. There are two animals in the markets—two four-legged ones, that is. The bulls and the bears. When industry experts claim: "Oh yes! We're heading toward a bull market!" do you know what that means?

A bull is a pretty ferocious animal that stomps its hoof on the ground several times when it's ready to CHARGE. A bull in the financial markets means the same thing: "full steam ahead!" If prices on many investment securities are rising and the general consensus is that they're going to continue upward, it is a bull market. A bull market pushes its way up and takes prices with it.

If you think prices on different investment products are going up and you are optimistic about the general direction of the financial markets, you are said to be "bullish."

On the flip side are the bears. Bears meander through the wilderness and fish for salmon in cold streams. They are huge and sometimes awkward and clumsy. They don't charge forward, but once they get moving, boy, they can really hustle. Also, they at times catch people by surprise.

In financial terms, bear markets react the same way. A bear market brings prices down. Party poopers and prophets of doom rejoice. These market watchers tend to be big-time pessimists. If you think prices on different investment products are going down and you are pessimistic about the direction of the financial markets, you are said to be "bearish." Keep in mind that whether it's a bull market or a bear market, you can make a profit. You'll learn how later on.

Taking Stock of Stocks

When you hear of the word "investing," most people think about stocks. Buying low and selling high is a strategy that works best here. When you hear the word "stock," most of you will think of common stock. Common stock is a security that represents ownership in a corporation or company. A share of common stock represents a proportion of ownership in a particular corporation. For example, if I own a corporation called Cracker Slops Inc., with a total of one hundred thousand shares of stock, and you own one hundred of those shares, you own one one-hundredth of my company.

For you to own a share of common stock, a company has to offer common stock to the public, which they do in an *Initial Public Offering*

(IPO). At the point the company sells stock to the public, the company becomes a *publicly-traded company.* (If it were a privately-held company, no shares of any type of stock would be issued to anybody).

In Canada, extensive legislation and regulation exists to protect investors and ensure high ethical standards. The Toronto, Vancouver, Montreal and Alberta exchanges, along with the Investment Dealers Association of Canada, are *self-regulatory organizations (SROs).* As self-regulatory organizations, they are responsible for overseeing their members' operations. The SROs, along with provincial security legislators and administrators, regulate the securities industry. No federal regulatory body for the securities industry exists in Canada, unlike the U.S., where the Securities and Exchange Commission (SEC) regulates the U.S. markets on a national level.

The Investment Dealers Association (IDA) is the Canadian investment industry's national trade association. Its mission is "to foster efficient capital markets by encouraging participation in the savings and investment process and by ensuring the integrity of the marketplace." The IDA represents approximately 160 member securities firms, and monitors activities of member firms across Canada.

Understanding how the ownership part of common stock comes about is important. For example, if I own a telephone company called Bells and Whistles and need to raise more money, one way in which I could do this would be to issue shares of ownership—common stock—to the public. Why would I want to do this? To raise more money for business operations. If you wanted to invest in my company, then you would buy these shares from a brokerage firm that is associated with the offering.

The raising of money for my company is done through an initial stock offering, or what is more commonly referred to as an *initial public offering (IPO).* The company would then hire several brokerage firms to handle this stock offering, and you, the investor, would buy the shares from one of these brokerage firms in this initial sale. The money that's raised goes to the company. When the company sells these shares to the public through the initial public offering, it is said to be offered in the *primary market.* Once the initial offering is completed, the company doesn't receive any additional monies (unless it has another stock offering, which would then be called a *secondary offering).*

Here's a basic idea of how the initial public offering process works:

1. All the initial investors who purchased the stock at the initial offering own the stock at the price they bought it. For example, let's say the initial offering was to sell one million shares of Rhino Shoehorns company stock at $10 a share so the company could raise $10,000,000. The offering was successful, and all one million shares were sold.

2. You, as the investor, bought one hundred shares for $10 each. You control $1,000 worth of Rhino Shoehorns stock until the stock starts trading in the financial markets. When it does that, the stock is said to be trading in the secondary market, when the price will rise and fall.

> An **initial stock offering** (more often called an initial public offering (IPO)) is the first time a company issues its stock. A **secondary offering** is any stock offering made after the initial offering—be it the second offering, the third, or the tenth.

3. When a stock trades in the secondary market, it is bought and sold by other investors. Typically, the transaction (the buy or the sell) takes place on the floor of an exchange.

When you participate in an initial public offering, you don't pay any commissions. The price at which you buy the shares is determined by one thing—the company. After the initial stock offering, the company has the money it raised and needed. The company doesn't receive anything from any trades afterwards. Even if all one million shares were bought and sold by other investors in one day, the company does not receive a dime.

> Declared by a company's board of directors, **dividends** are quarterly cash payments made to stockholders. It's a way for a company to share its profits with you. Think of it as a profit distribution.

Whether the price of the stock (and therefore its value) rises or falls depends on the supply and demand for the stock in the marketplace which, in turn, can depend on what the company does internally. If, for example, the Rhino Shoehorns company used the $10 million

Bet You Didn't Know

Often, you'll see "tombstone ads" in newspapers like *The Financial Post* or *The Globe and Mail* advertising a company's initial stock offering. The reason they're called "tombstone ads" is because there are no frills in the advertising, just information about the who, what, where, and when—like a tombstone.

Capital gains is a profit from the sale of an asset. If you buy low and sell high, you'll make a profit, which is reported to Revenue Canada as your capital gains. Three-quarters of your capital gains is taxed at your full marginal tax rate. If you were to have a loss, it would be called a capital loss. You can apply a capital loss against any future capital gains.

to increase the production of their goods and services, then the value of the stock may increase because if production is up and sales are increasing, the company may have a profit at the end of the year. In this case, the company will sometimes pay *dividends* to its stockholders (usually on a quarterly basis).

Why buy common stock? One reason is to receive dividends. Investors who buy common stock are hoping the company will generate profits so these profits can be distributed to the shareholders.

A second reason is because of the potential of *capital gains*, which is the profit you receive when you buy low and sell high. The difference in price at which you buy and sell the stock, expressed as a percentage, is your *return*. All investors hope that a company's sales and earnings will grow so they can sell their shares for more than they bought them.

Last but not least, the tax benefit comes into play. You do not incur a tax situation until you sell the stock. For example, even if you bought one hundred shares of the Fantastic Gaskets Company at $10 a share and the current trading price is $50 a share, you don't have a profit (or a tax situation to report to Revenue Canada on your tax return) until you sell it. Until you do so, it is known as a *paper profit*. Obviously, tax issues do not apply when you are dealing with tax-sheltered accounts like RRSPs or RRIFs.

What happens if I didn't raise enough money for my company the first time around? I would then conduct a secondary offering by issuing more shares. More shares of my company stock would be outstanding, and that would reduce the proportion of ownership (or *equity*) you have in my company. For example, if you own one hundred shares of Bells and Whistles when there are ten thousand shares outstanding and I sell ten thousand more shares, a total of twenty thousand shares are outstanding. Your ownership is reduced by 50%. This dilution in ownership may be offset by the benefits the company gets from the proceeds of the secondary offer.

> A **return** on a stock is expressed as the percentage increase (or decrease) in the price of the security since purchase. For example, if you bought one hundred shares of stock at $10 a share and sold all of your shares five years down the road for $20 a share, your return would be 100%.

People invest in common stock for many different reasons. If you're a risk-taker you might want to make a large return on an initial investment, in which case you'd look for stocks that appreciate in price. Or you may want to keep a steady, safe flow of income, in which case you'd go after dividend-paying stocks because they provide income. Either way, you can get both forms of income return from investing in common stock, as explained in the next few sections.

Mo' Money through Dividends

As a shareholder (or part owner of my company), you might receive a dividend, which comes from my company's *earnings*. Companies report their earnings in an earnings report table on a quarterly basis. However, my company doesn't always have to declare a dividend. In fact, if my company falls on hard times and the earnings drop, the first thing to go will usually be the dividends that are paid to shareholders.

When discussing company earnings, you should be familiar with the following terms:

➤ **Revenues.** The total gross sales figure of a company before any expenses are deducted.

➤ **Net Income.** The amount of profit earned during the time

 The interest or value which you have in an investment is your **equity**. For example, owning one one-hundredth of my company is your equity in my company. Stocks are sometimes synonymously called *equities*.

reported (a quarter). Many times companies will compare their net income figures on a quarter-by-quarter basis.

➤ **Earnings per share.** Indicates how much of the profit from net income is attributed to each common share of stock that is outstanding.

After reviewing their earnings, corporations make dividend payments to common stock shareholders on a quarterly basis. The following four dates determine who gets paid and when in this process:

Declaration date. This is the day that the board of directors announces the dividend, how much it's going to be, and when it'll be paid to common stock shareholders.

Record date. On this day, the company examines its list of shareholders. To receive the dividend, you must be on the list on this day. You are on this list if you own the stock on this day, i.e., you bought it before the ex-dividend date. If not (alas, my friend) you don't get the dividend!

Ex-dividend date. This day comes two business days before the record date. Investors who buy the stock aren't entitled to receive the dividend if they purchase the stock on or after this date because it takes three days to settle (finalize) the trade. This trading procedure is known as normal (three-day) settlement. The ex-dividend date is the first day you can purchase the stock without the dividend. Hang in there. This'll make more sense in a minute.

Bet You Didn't Know

When you buy or sell a stock, it takes three business days from the initial transaction date for the trade to settle. This is known as normal settlement. For example, if you were to sell one hundred shares of stock at $10 on Tuesday, you'd receive $1,000 less commissions (your net proceeds), but not until three business days later on the Friday.

Payment date. This is the day when the company actually cuts the dividend cheques. Usually, it's about two weeks after the record date.

Using an illustration will help. By looking at the following figure, you can determine when you should buy the stock in time to receive the dividend.

October						
Sunday	**Monday**	**Tuesday**	**Wednesday**	**Thursday**	**Friday**	**Saturday**
	1	2	3	4	5	6
7	8	9	10 Declaration date	11	12	13
14	15 Ex-dividend date	16	17 Record date	18	19	20
21	22	23	24	25 Payment date	26	27
28	29	30	31			

An example of key dates leading up to the payment of a common stock dividend.

The board of directors declares a $0.50 dividend on Wednesday, October 10th. This dividend will be paid to the owners of record as of October 17th, and the company will mail out the cheques on October 25th. For you to receive this dividend, you need to be on the list as a shareholder as of October 17th. That means the last day you can purchase the stock, get on the company's list, and be eligible to receive the dividend is October 12th. If you purchase the stock on or after October 15th (the ex-dividend date), you won't be entitled to the dividend. On the other hand, if you own the stock and sell it on or after the ex-dividend date you will receive the dividend because you were on the shareholders' list as of the record date.

Take the dividend that was paid to you, and add it to the rise in price of your stock. Now divide that by your beginning price, and you have the **total return** on your investment, which includes your dividend income and price appreciation.

145

How much are dividend payments? Whatever the board of directors say they are. To determine the amount of dividend you'll receive, multiply the number of shares you own by the amount of the dividend. For example, if you own two hundred shares of a stock and the dividend is $0.75, your dividend payment will be $150. Keep in mind that a company doesn't have to declare a dividend and that the amount of the dividend is not fixed. One quarter it can be fifty cents, for example, and the next quarter it can be ten cents.

Go Figure!

Canadian stock prices trade in five-cent intervals. U.S. stocks usually trade in increments of one-eighths, although sometimes you will see price intervals of one-sixteenths or one-thirty-secondths. When a stock price starts to rise, it'll move up in varying increments. If the current price is $50 a share, it may trade at $50.50, $50.25, $50.75, etc. It the stock is rising rather quickly, it may trade from $50.25 and jump to $51, for a rise in price of $0.75. To determine the market value of your stock, you'd multiply the number of shares that you own by the current price of the stock. If you own one hundred shares and the stock is at $50.50, your market value is $5,050. Got it?

Let's get your noggin working. Pop quiz! Get your pencils ready. If you own one hundred shares of the Zany Zipper Company and the current price is $20, the market value of this stock is $2,000. Let's say the price jumps to $21.55. What is the new market value of your stock portfolio?

a. $2050.50

b. $2155.00

c. $2100.00

d. I don't know because I'm watching my favourite "Beachcombers" rerun.

If you did the math, the correct answer is b. How'd you get it? Multiply the amount of shares you own (one hundred shares) by the current price of the stock ($21.55), and your answer is $2,155.00.

As you learned in Chapter 5, many newspapers have daily stock listings in which you can check pricing and other facts about a particular stock. An example of a stock listing can be seen in the following figure.

52-week high	low Stock	Sym	Div	High	Low	Close	Chg	Vol (100s)	Yield	P/E ratio
13.60	8.20 Chai-Na-Ta	CC		8.40	8.40	8.40	+0.10	12		5.2
2.65	1.15 Channel	CHU		1.25	1.15	1.15	-0.10	78		38.3
18.75	14.40 Chapters	CHP		17.25	17.25	17.25	+0.15	24		21.0
4.83	0.69 Chase Res	COS		0.80	0.80	0.80		22		
8.60	5.15 Chatea sv	CTU A	0.30	8.50	8.50	8.50	-0.10	30	3.5	14.9
21.50	9.75 Chauvco	CHA		18.70	18.50	18.60	-0.10	98		23.8
0.89	0.49 Cheni Res	CHB		0.57	0.55	0.55	-0.05	90		
36.00	25.00 Chieftain	CID		29.80	29.80	29.80	-0.65	5		31.9
49.25	36.90 Chrysler	C	a 1.60	45.95	45.45	45.80	+0.30	12	4.9	6.7
25.00	17.00 CHUM nv	CHM B	0.08	24.25	23.80	24.25	+0.25	9	0.3	26.1
43.00	27.00 ✦ Cinar Film	CIF.A		43.00	43.00	43.00	+2.50	5		51.8
43.00	26.00 ✦ Cinar sv	CIF.B		43.00	43.00	43.00	+2.00	1		51.8
3.10	1.76 Cineplex	CPX		2.54	2.45	2.46		491		
40.50	27.00 ✦ Cinram	CRW	0.16	37.00	36.50	36.60		212	0.4	27.1
1.45	0.51 Cmtech Tel	CTM		0.55	0.55	0.55		5		
1.85	0.05 Circuit Wrl	CCW		0.07	0.06	0.07		120		
7.95	6.15 Clarivest	CVG	0.10	7.60	7.45	7.45	-0.15	8	1.3	
3.10	1.61 Claude Res	CRJ		2.00	1.95	2.00		38		25.0
24.80	10.00 ✦ Clearnt	NET.A		17.00	15.85	16.75	+0.85	1773		
13.00	9.40 Club Mona	CMI		12.50	12.25	12.25		22		
12.00	6.55 ✦ Clublink	LNK		11.55	11.25	11.40	-0.15	145		40.7
25.30	18.75 Co Steel	CEI	0.40	22.55	22.25	22.55	+0.05	159	1.8	
25.75	25.05 Co-op	CCS PR A		25.75	25.65	25.75	+0.15	59		
5.00	2.50 Cobre Min	CBU		3.60	3.55	3.55	-0.20	43		
20.55	9.95 Coca Cola	KOC		19.85	19.75	19.80	+0.05	231		50.8
11.35	8.00 Cogeco sv	CCA	0.24	11.25	11.15	11.25		28	2.1	10.9
53.50	25.00 Cognos	CSN		49.00	43.50	44.00	-3.00	894		39.4
9.25	1.00 Colony Pa j	CYX		1.40	1.00	1.10	-0.40	580		
25.90	8.15 Com Dev	CDV		24.50	23.50	24.20	-0.50	124		41.7
5.00	2.25 Comaplex	CMF		2.50	2.25	2.35	-0.05	191		
41.50	26.65 ✦ Cominco	CLT	0.30	36.70	36.25	36.25	-0.25	979	0.8	21.2
3.10	1.60 Communic	CSY		1.80	1.60	1.80	-0.20	10		
2.75	1.30 Compas	CMN		2.50	2.41	2.50	-0.10	1310		8.3
1.39	0.65 Compton	CMT		1.30	1.25	1.28	+0.03	3192		64.0
19.50	10.75 Computalg	CGH		18.90	18.50	18.90	+0.30	350		15.2
3.50	1.75 Computer	CPU		2.10	2.10	2.10	+0.25	501		

A typical stock listing found in the newspaper.

What Should I Do?

Investors should always plan on investing in stocks for the long-term. Gurus who predict that the stock market is going to plunge or soar don't really know. In fact, no one really knows how high or low stocks will go in a relatively short timeframe. Whether you're investing in stocks for growth and appreciation or just to receive the dividend income, thinking and planning for the long-term is a strategy that wins hands down.

The proof is in the pudding. If you had invested $10,000 in the TSE 300 ten years ago in 1987, you would have almost tripled your money to $27,000 today.

What if you only have $1,000 to invest? Is choosing growth and appreciation over dividend income better? Which approach works best for you? It all depends on your financial goals. If you have time on your

It isn't that difficult to read a stock quote. Just keep in mind that you need to know the company name or ticker symbol to first locate your quote. Some basics? The HIGH, LOW, and CLOSE represent the highest and lowest prices the stock hit during one trading day, and the price at which it closed.

Don't get caught up in the wave of investor euphoria or gloom and doom and base your decision to buy and sell on what the crowd is doing. When stock prices are going up, your gut instinct is to buy more, just as when stock prices are dropping, your heart tells you to sell. Don't let that happen. Think long-term.

side, such as ten to fifteen years before Junior starts university, you need your money to grow rather than concern yourself with earning income along the way. Stick with the price appreciation focus. It could be considered the buy low and sell high approach, although remember you're doing this over a long period of time. If you are looking to realize large capital gains, this strategy should be your main focus. This may be one of the areas where a full-service broker or Investment Advisor will be able to help choose the right investment selection for you.

If you're looking to maximize growth potential from a stock over the long-term, you can start off with $1,000, depending on which stock you buy. You might not be able to purchase one hundred shares (a round lot) at first, but you can purchase an odd lot (less than one hundred shares) and just keep purchasing additional shares over the long-term.

Those investors who seek income from these stocks typically just buy and hold the stock. They don't necessarily focus on the potential for price appreciation; rather, these investors want to earn income from their stock investment. You can invest your $1,000 here, too, but in order to increase your income (larger dividend payments) you are going to have to increase the number of shares you own.

What Else Do I Get?

You may be wondering what other perks you get for owning part of a company in the form of stock. Unlike a bond, which has a maturity date, the life of a stock is infinite. Common stock never has a maturity date and can continue paying dividends and growing in value forever and ever. Plus, stock investors can't lose more than one hundred percent of their investment (assuming the stock was fully paid for and not purchased on margin). No matter how much money my company loses, as a shareholder you are not liable for anything.

Guess what? You also get voting privileges on important corporate matters, such as who to elect for a board of directors. Most companies are run as a "one-share/one-vote rule." If you have one hundred shares then you get one hundred votes. Easy enough.

But I Prefer Preferred Stock

There is another type of stock that exists—*preferred stock*. Preferred stock is similar to common stock in that it reflects ownership in a company. Preferred stock owners do not get voting rights as common stockholders do, but they are entitled to receive their dividends before common stock shareholders. Plus, if the company is liquidated—that is, if it goes belly up—claims from preferred stockholders are satisfied before those claims from common stockholders.

Preferred stocks are securities or shares representing an ownership interest in a company and have "preference" over the common stock shares. Most buyers of preferred stock are large corporations and institutional buyers.

The other difference between common and preferred stock is the value of the dividend. Preferred shares are usually entitled to a fixed dividend expressed as either a percentage of the par or stated value, or as a stated amount of dollars and cents. However, dividends are not obligatory; the board of directors elects whether or not to issue a dividend. In practice, dividends are paid if justified by earnings.

Life in the Pits

Most investors think of the Toronto Stock Exchange (TSE) when they think about trading securities. And it's true, many of both common and preferred stocks, and some bonds, issued by Canada's largest companies trade at the TSE. Bay Street is one of the most recognized and most powerful streets in history because of the Toronto Stock Exchange.

But what exactly is the TSE? If you've ever been in the visitor's gallery that overlooks a major financial exchange's trading floor, it might seem like the building's been overrun by a bunch of Neanderthal men and women screaming at each other. The correct definition of a stock exchange is a place where buyers and sellers come together to transact business. These financial wizards trade securities by agreeing on a fair price based on the supply and demand for these securities.

The TSE floor itself does not exist anymore. The traders that previously worked on the floor are now sitting at their company desks. This is a result of technological advancements in the markets, which allow your orders to be executed more quickly and more efficiently.

The trading hours for most financial exchanges are 9:30 a.m. EST to 4:00 p.m. EST.

The volume on over-the-counter (OTC) markets for debt securities is roughly 35 times larger than the stock markets.

The total number of the major financial exchanges in Canada is five. For a list of these financial exchanges, check the appendix in the back of the book.

In 1996, more than 22 billion shares of stock were traded on the Toronto Stock Exchange. This was a banner year for the markets, and unprecedented records of heavy trading volume continue to be set.

Additionally, you should understand a second major type of market on which securities trade: the dealer or *over-the-counter market (OTC)*. The OTC represents a network of dealers who trade with each other over the phone or computer network, with no central market. The OTC market is not a physical exchange like the Toronto Stock Exchange, but rather a computerized system that provides brokers and dealers with price quotations for stocks traded over the counter. Almost all bonds are traded on the OTC. As well, there is an organized over-the-counter stock market known as the Canadian Dealing Network Inc. You can tell if a stock is traded on the OTC by the number of letters in the ticker symbol. Typically all other exchange-listed stocks have one, two or three letters in their ticker symbols; OTC-listed stocks have four.

May I Take Your Order, Please?

When you order your favourite sandwich in the local greasy spoon, you have certain particulars that need to be met. Ketchup, mustard, hold the mayo, no onions, and lettuce and tomato on the side, please. These days, not only do you have to worry about the order coming out right, but also about the price. Have you seen how much a turkey club sandwich can go for these days?

Knowing how to trade stock won't make you an elitist, but it will put you ahead of the game. You see, when you buy or sell a stock, you are making a trade. When you buy shares of stock through an initial stock offering, your money is going to the company. When you buy or sell the shares in the secondary market through the brokerage firm, your money doesn't go to the company but to the seller. In a trade, there always needs to be a buyer and a seller.

The seller could be anyone. You don't see that person. It could be me. It could be Aunt Gert. Or the little old man with the big ears and cigar hangin' from his mouth that lives down the street. Maybe it's Jim Carrey or Lloyd Robertson. The seller is someone who has also called up his or her broker and put in an order to sell a certain number of shares.

Where do the buyer and seller meet to make the trade and close the transaction? They used to meet on the floor of a stock exchange, but due to automation, the transactions now take place between the computer terminals of brokerage firms and stock exchanges. Remember, for every share you decide to buy, there's another investor on the other end who has decided to sell.

Here's a list of the most common types of orders you execute through your broker to either buy or sell shares of stock. These orders are placed over the phone with your broker; you don't need to be there for him or her to write the ticket or electronically send in the order. Once the order is executed, you'll receive a confirmation in the mail detailing all of the information.

GTC

GTC stands for *good-till-cancelled*. You tell your broker that you want to buy shares of stock at a particular price, and the broker won't trade until

If you ever use a GTC order, follow the stock price closely so you can cancel the order if you think the stock price will fall below your order price. If you place the order and never follow the stock price, your order could get filled and you wouldn't know it until the trade confirmation arrived in the mailbox.

that price is met. However, your order remains "good-till-cancelled": it doesn't expire until you cancel it. For example, if you wanted to buy five hundred shares of Motorcycle Mama Company stock which is currently at $30 a share but you think the stock is worth $28, you would put in a GTC order for two hundred shares at $28. Until you cancel that order, it remains in effect. Therefore, you don't pay for the GTC order until it is executed.

What if the price never comes down to $28? Don't ever say never when it comes to trading stocks. The price could drop, but it also could be a long time before it does. Meanwhile, you lose the opportunity to have your investment appreciating in a stock.

Another drawback to a GTC order occurs when the stock falls below your order price immediately after your broker executes the order. If the stock trades at $30, then $29.25, and then continues to slide to $27, you'll still buy one hundred shares of stock at $28, even though the stock has already slipped to $27. Your portfolio is now down $100.

The **bid** is the highest quoted price that any prospective buyer will pay for a security at a specific moment in time.

The **ask** value is the lowest quoted price that any prospective seller will sell a security at a specific moment in time.

Market Maven

Imagine telling your broker that you want to sell all three hundred shares of your TechnoTweak Computer Company stock at whatever price it is trading. That's known as a *market order*. This type of order is the most common order used by investors. You buy or sell a specified number of shares immediately at the best available price. Here's how it works.

If the last trade was at $29.50 and you enter a market order to sell, you'll probably get the price close to $29.50 a share. However, the actual price could be higher or lower if the price of the stock changes before the order is entered into the system and executed. You will get a price that the market determines at the precise time that your order is received. Most of the time, brokerage firms handle market orders rather quickly. If the price of stock changes dramatically by the time the order is received at the trading post, you're stuck with it, whether it's favourable or not.

When you place a market order, be sure to ask your broker for the *bid price*, *ask price*, and *last trade price* of the stock you want to buy. A broker gets this data from his or her computer terminal or ticker machine, and it looks similar to this:

TCC	29.50	29.25 B	29.75 A	30,700 V
(Symbol)	(last trade)	(bid)	(ask)	(volume)

The last trade is the price at which the last trade was transacted. The bid is the price you would get if you sold the stock right now and the ask price is what you buy the stock at if you bought it immediately. The volume represents the number of shares that have currently exchanged hands or traded so far that day. Using the preceding example, if you were to put in a market order to sell your shares, you would get a price of $29.25 (the bid) or close to it.

Limit Up or Down

This one's a little more tricky. A *limit order* is an order to buy or sell shares of stock, but only if you can get it at the price you want or better. This order can be a day order (it expires at the end of the trading day if not executed) or a GTC order. An example? If you want to sell five hundred shares of a certain stock but only at a price of $18 or better, you would enter a limit order stated as "sell 100 shares limit $18." If a buyer is willing to pay $18.25, your broker would sell your stock at $18.25— remember, it is at the price you want or better. If the best price available is $18, then your order is executed. However, if the highest bid is only $17.75, then your order is not executed and your shares are not sold.

Stop Right There!

Using a *stop order* is tricky as well. With this type of order you buy a stock above or sell a stock below its current market price. Wait, this sounds like the opposite of buying low and selling high, right? In order to understand it, let's compare it first to a limit order. A limit order is an order to buy or sell shares of a stock at the price you want or better, right? A stop order is similar: it's an order to buy or sell shares of a stock when its price hits the price you specify. However, once the specified price is reached, your order then becomes a market order and will be executed at the best available price.

A stop order has a few useful purposes. If you bought stock at $20 a share and over a period of two years the stock price appreciated to $50 a share, you have a very nice profit. Still, you feel that the stock can go even higher, but you don't want to lose the enormous profit you built up. You end up torn between selling the stock that you have and hanging onto it for a little longer aiming for a higher price.

Here's how a stop order can help alleviate your problem. If you enter a "stop loss order at $48," then if and only if the market value of the stock drops to $48 does your stop loss order become a market order to sell. Your shares would then be automatically sold at market, at about $48 a share. Mazel tov! You have protected your profits. If the stock price doesn't fall to $48, the order is not executed.

If you have placed a sell stop order or a buy stop order and the current trading price gets further and further away from the stop order price, you may want to change your stop order price to one that is closer. For example, if the stock is at $50 a share and you bought it at $40 a share, but are afraid the price is going to drop, you could put in a "stop order at $48" to ensure a profit in case the stock price does drop.

There's another type of stop order you should know about, the *stop limit order*. You would use a stop limit order as a way of overcoming the uncertainty of not knowing what the execution price will be after the order becomes a market order.

Break it down into two parts using a hypothetical example. A stop order is an order that is treated as a market order once the specified price has been traded (reached). For example, if you put in a "buy stop order at $23," that indicates that you want to buy the stock once its price hits $23 a share. Once that $23 price has been reached, your order becomes a market order and you get the best prevailing price. (It isn't necessarily $23 but as close to it as possible, unless the stock price is volatile.)

Here's the second part. The limit order is

an order that you place when you want to buy or sell a stock at the exact price indicated. If the price isn't reached then it isn't executed. Combining the two together forms a stop limit order. It allows you to specify the limit price, either trying to get the maximum price you'll pay if you were to place a stop limit to buy, or the minimum price you'll accept if you place a stop limit to sell.

Stay with me, folks. A stop limit order to buy is executed as soon as the stop price (or higher) is reached, and then an attempt is made to buy up to the limit price. Therefore the order does not become a market order. If the attempt is uneventful and you don't get the limit price, the order isn't executed. A stop limit order to sell is executed as soon as the stop price (or lower) is reached, and then an attempt is made to sell at the limit or at a better price. Therefore this order also does not become a market order. Again, the order is not executed if you don't get at least the limit price.

The Least You Need To Know

➤ Buying stock represents ownership in a company. For example, if you bought one hundred shares of a company's stock and there are one hundred thousand total shares outstanding, you would own one one-hundredth of the company.

➤ When a company announces that it is making company stock— either common or preferred—available to the public, it makes an initial public offering (IPO). Any time after this that the company announces the availability of additional stock, it is known as a secondary offering.

➤ When you invest in stock, you are making a trade through a broker. In the world of stock trading, there is always a buyer and a seller.

➤ Know the different types of orders you can place when you make stock trades. They include a market order, a limit order, good-till-cancelled, day order, a stop order, and stop limit order. The most commonly-used order is a market order.

➤ When you want to make a profit on a stock trade, you must buy the stock at a lower price than what you sell it for. BUY LOW AND SELL HIGH is the fundamental rule in investing!

"The stock doesn't know you own it."

**—George "Adam Smith" Goodman,
Money Game**

Chapter 15

Tricks of the Trade

In this chapter

➤ The most commonly asked question in trading—and its answer!

➤ How to pick the winners

➤ A few financial tidbits to help you along the way

The easiest concept to learn about making money on the stock markets is to "Buy Low and Sell High." Without doing any mathematical formulas, you know that trick of the trade will earn you a profit. But that isn't the only concept you should base your investment decisions on. Sure, you can buy a stock at a low price and sell it at a high price, but how do you know if it's the right price? How do you know if it's even the right stock for you? This chapter introduces a few ways you can compare stock prices and what the different types of stock are that you can invest in.

What Did the Market Do Today?

When you ask someone how the market did today, what does the question really mean? Technically, you are referring to the TSE 300 or the

The reason an index is a useful tool for investors is that it gives a good indication of the performance of that particular market sector, such as utility stocks or small company stocks. Therefore, use an index as a means to gauge how your stock is doing by comparing one to the other. You shouldn't necessarily base your sell decision on whether an index is performing 5%, 10%, or even 20% better as a whole compared to your stock. Rather, use it as a guideline.

TSE 35 Composite Index (or the Dow Jones Industrial Average (DJIA) in the U.S.) that everyone—market watchers, the media, and consumers—follows. The TSE 300 and the TSE 35 are used as indicators of how well or how poorly the entire stock market did that day.

The TSE 300 comprises 300 Canadian stocks, including BCE Inc., The Toronto-Dominion Bank, Alcan Aluminum, and Northern Telecom. The 300 stocks are classified by industry so that 14 major group indices and 40 subgroups are tracked. The TSE 35 was introduced in 1987 and includes 35 of the most widely traded stocks on the Toronto Stock Exchange.

In Chapter 14, you learned how to read a daily stock quote to find out current data about a particular stock. If you were to take a bundle of stocks of all different types and lump them together, with a few financial formulas you could have an "average" or an index. All these averages or indices give you an idea of where a stock is going. Today, there are dozens of indices you can follow. They are always listed in the financial sections of the national newspapers.

The TSE 300 and the TSE 35 are the two most widely used indices in Canada, and the DJIA is the most common index in the U.S. Another is the Standard & Poor's 500, which is calculated from five hundred American stocks (including the DJIA's thirty blue-chip stocks).

An investor uses one of these averages or indices as a benchmark to gauge how his or her portfolio is doing by comparing returns from these benchmarks to his or her personal investment portfolio. For example, if your portfolio were to be heavily weighted in gold, you would follow the gold index. Similarly, if you held a lot of bank stocks, you would track the banking stock index.

Another reason these benchmarks are used is because of the historical data that they can provide. If you want to find out how utility stocks performed during a recession or how blue-chip stocks fared during inflation, these indices and market averages can tell you. Using these benchmarks enable you to determine which stocks would be wise to buy or sell given a specific economic environment.

No matter which index you choose to follow, you should do the following:

1. **Understand the components in each index.** The stocks that make up the TSE 300 are obviously different from those that make up the Dow Jones Industrial Average. Once you know which stocks are in each index, you'll be able to choose which one to follow.

2. **Check to see if the index is made up of smaller indices.** This is just for informational purposes. Many times, a large index, such as the Wilshire 5000, which consists of five thousand different types of stocks, will represent a broader measure of stocks. Because a larger, broader index covers a greater percentage of the market activity of all stock issues traded, larger indices are good benchmarks for gauging how your investments are doing. If the indices continue to increase by a large margin and your investment portfolio as a whole is going nowhere, consider re-allocating some of your stock positions.

3. **Research how the major market indices performed during inflationary periods and recessions.** Investigating the performance during those past economic periods will let you know which stocks to choose during certain economic timeframes. For example, let's say you're interested in the banking industry, and you look into the historical performance of the banking stock index to see how banking stocks perform during recessionary periods. If the index's performance was down during the last recession and all previous recessions, and economists are currently forecasting another recession, don't consider purchasing banking stocks for your investment portfolio.

Following an index sometimes turns into "beating the index" (or at least trying to). Many professional money managers use the big indices, such as the TSE 300 or S&P's 500, as benchmarks that they have to "beat." It's a difficult feat to accomplish, and most professional money managers just try to equal the market.

Picking the Winners

Knowing when it's the right time to be in the stock market shouldn't be difficult. It's always the right time if you do your research, buy quality stocks, and learn to be patient. An overnight success really takes a lot of time. Investing and patience go hand in hand. They do a little jig, and you could win big. Before any secrets are revealed, know the different types of stocks that exist; when buying a stock, choose one that has objectives consistent with your investment goals, as described next:

Blue Chip Stocks

These stocks represent solid, large, established companies with stable earnings and superior management. They usually pay dividends (so they provide steady income) and are the more conservative among stock picks. Examples of blue chips include: BCE, Bombardier, and Laidlaw.

Growth Stocks

Investing in growth stocks is one of the most popular ways to make money over the long-term. Why? Because the companies that issue them are built for growth. The long-term buy and hold approach works best here. Growth stock companies are those that exhibit faster-than-average gains in earnings and profits over the last few years and are expected to continue doing so. Growth stocks can give you exposure to good returns over the long-term. There may be some rough bumps along the way, but you must remember to think long-term.

The idea of investing in growth stocks is to buy and hold the security. It is the easiest way to make money in stocks over the long-term.

Investors lap up these company stocks like thirsty dogs on an August afternoon. This pushes the stock prices even higher. Then something happens, like a change in management, and the stock value sinks. Be careful when investing in these volatile stocks.

Growth stocks usually include *small-caps* (smaller companies), *mid-caps* (medium-sized companies), and *large-caps* (larger companies). Agressive growth stocks include mainly small- and mid-cap companies. They typically do not offer dividend payments to shareholders. Some examples of company growth stocks are in the sectors of computers,

> ## Bet You Didn't Know
>
> Small-cap stocks are the most risky growth stocks because they aren't as well established in the marketplace as some of the bigger competitors. However, there is more growth potential in a small-cap stock.

biotechnology, health maintenance organizations, and retailing stocks—companies such as Newbridge Networks, Hummingbird Communications, Biochem Pharma, and Extendicare Inc.

Investors in search of high returns from growth companies get too excited about the potential growth and forget the price. One of the ways to determine if you are paying too high a price for a growth stock is by looking at the company's *P/E ratio*. This stands for the price/earnings ratio. Technically, the figure is derived from taking the price of the stock divided by company earnings. Many analysts use this ratio as a yard stick to measure companies in the same field. It may indicate if the price of the stock is overvalued.

You also need to look for the company's *earnings growth rate*, which tells you the rate at which company profits increase on a year-to-year basis. If there is a high earnings growth rate, typically there is a high P/E ratio. It would be an ideal investment if you found a growth stock with a high earnings growth rate with a lower P/E ratio. For example, if Cuckoo Clocks Incorporated's profits are growing at 20% a year and its price/earnings ratio wasn't growing as much, the stock would be a bargain because it hasn't realized its true value yet. Be careful though—there may be a reason for a below 20% price/earnings growth, e.g., lawsuit, anticipated increased regulation.

P/E Ratio stands for price-earnings ratio. This number is derived from taking the current price of the stock and dividing that number by company earnings.

Income Stocks

You can get capital appreciation and steady income from income stocks. A stock with solid dividend increases can actually pay more over time

Income stock prices are greatly affected by the general direction of interest rates because when interest rates fall, the stock prices on income stocks tend to rise. This makes the dividend income you can earn just as competitive as other income-producing investments, such as bonds.

Try and find companies that are consistently raising their dividends and don't carry a lot of bad debt when searching for a good income-producing stock.

than if you were to invest in bonds. Preferred shares are income stocks. Examples of income-producing stocks include electric, gas, and telephone companies, banks, along with blue chip stocks.

Income stocks tend to be less volatile, and they are an appropriate choice for those investors who can't afford to take on a lot of risk. In the past, the typical stereotype of income stock shareholders were widows and orphans because they both need the income without a lot of risk. Today, income stocks offer high yields for those investors who are seeking more income out of their investments rather than price appreciation.

Cyclical Stocks

Get your motors running and head out on the highway! Cyclical stocks ride the economic highway. Companies that are closely tied to the ups and downs of our economy are cyclicals. Careful, though, because to profit handsomely, you have to time your buys and sells.

Examples of cyclical company stocks include automobile manufacturing companies, steel companies, and paper companies. The reason these types of companies are cyclical in nature is that they incur a lot of costs to run their manufacturing plants. When the economy is growing and production is up, and consumers are utilizing the products these companies produce (increased demand), cyclical companies can meet these high costs and even pocket a profit. But, if the economy isn't doing well and consumer demand is down for these goods and services, company earnings can drop. See why learning about the economy is so important?

Because cyclical stock prices are so volatile, it's a little difficult to time your investing. Keep the following in mind:

➤ Buy cyclical stocks when their well has just about run dry, and their situation can't get any worse.

➤ Sell cyclical stocks when they are enjoying record profits and everything seems hunky-dory.

Initial Public Offerings (IPOs)

One of the more interesting opportunities in the stock market is the IPO. You learned in Chapter 14 that when a privately-held company goes public, an initial public offering is held for investors to buy stock (ownership) in the company. True, an IPO stock can soar to two or three times its value in just one day, but over the long-term, IPOs can be extremely sensitive to the general direction of the stock market.

These are also called *new issues*. Stock prices on new issues may soar right after the offering because of all the hoopla that surrounds it. Be careful, though, because new issues are not guaranteed to go up in price.

Penny Stocks

A company that offers penny stocks typically does not have any substantial products or services. The company is usually still in the development stage, which is why they always need to raise more money.

Examples of penny stocks might include junior exploration firms such as mining companies, or maybe companies in bankruptcy that are trying to make a big comeback. The reason they are so risky is that they are not as stable as other companies. As an investor, be prepared to lose all of your money because of the risks involved. Typically, these stocks trade for less than $5 per share.

Investing in the stock market can work for or against you depending on how much research you do. Research your investment choices carefully. Don't act on a hot stock tip from your neighbour. Find out what type of business the company does, if it has a lot of debt, and what the competition is doing. If you are still not comfortable basing your investment decision on this information, this is where your broker can add value. Once you invest, then you'll want to continue monitoring company business. Has the business changed? Is it providing a level of service above and beyond the competition? Is debt increasing?

Remember when considering investing in the stock market that one of the best sources of information about a company is its annual report. This information gives the company's current financial status and changes in the business operations.

One of the best ways to learn how to pick winning stocks comes from observation. Look around you. Many times a good stock choice will come from paying attention to your surroundings. If, for example, everyone is (still!) drinking Slurp-N-Burp soda, and it looks like it's not just a fad but a habit that's here to stay, see what type of information you can find out about the company.

Also worth mentioning is that you shouldn't necessarily focus on the price of a stock. Why? If you expect to double your money over the long haul, price should be a concern but not the driving force behind your decision to pick a winner.

Plan to invest for the long-term. Even if you hear a story of a stock purchase that made your brother-in-law Billy a financial windfall overnight, don't put your life savings in it with the hopes of becoming a quick millionaire. Instead, remember all of the work that you did at the beginning of this book. You know your financial goals by now and are working on getting there. But you could destroy all of your goals just like that (snap your fingers) if you give in to temptation.

Which Comes First? The Market or the Stock Price?

When making a stock purchase decision, it's important to know if the market is considered to be temporarily overvalued. A market is overvalued when a number of stocks are trading at a price that's higher than what they're truly worth. They're "rich," like a huge slice of double-double chocolate fudge marble-glazed cocoa cake.

Figuring out if the market is overvalued requires complex financial formulas and ratios (and what seems to be the equivalent of an accounting degree), but the way to get around that is ask your broker. Of course, you can break out the abacus and start figuring it out on your own, but that's what your broker's there for—to tell you things like whether the market is overvalued or undervalued.

Once you know this, you'll get a better idea of whether you should buy the stock you're interested in. If the stock is trading for much less than it's worth, that's like buying a $20 stock for only $10. That's a bargain and known as value investing. However, if the stock is overvalued, give it a second thought before you buy it. Would you want to pay $40 for a $30 stock?

Also, you can compare your broker's information to the TSE 300 Composite Index. This is another reason why studying an index is so important. It tells you when the entire market is undervalued or overvalued. When the TSE 300 earnings are higher than your stock's earnings (P/E ratio), consider the stock to be a good value and a good buy. However, if the situation were reversed and the stock's earnings were higher than the market's earnings, your stock may be trading for more than what it's worth.

There are many variables to consider when trying to decide if a stock is trading at good value or not. Make sure you consider all of them, e.g., competition, management, etc. And, don't forget, have a selling target price in mind even before you purchase the stock. Don't just buy a stock and then plan on it going through the roof. Pick your target point and stay with it. You'll learn more about when to sell a stock in the next chapter.

Borrowing From Your Broker

Guess what, folks? You don't always have to fully pay for stocks that you purchase, and there is no time limit in paying the money back. Your brokerage firm can loan it to you. Here's how it works.

As an investor, you can pay part of the purchase price for a stock trade and borrow the remaining balance from your brokerage firm. This service isn't free, though. The brokerage firm charges you interest. Before you can do this, you need to set up a margin account and sign a margin agreement. Once this account has been established, the money you pay for the trade is the *margin* and the money that you borrowed is your *debit balance*. That's what you owe the firm (eventually). The stocks that you buy, provided they are marginable, serve as collateral for the loan.

Your broker can tell you if a stock is marginable, and how much margin you have to put up for the purchase. There are different margin

Bet You Didn't Know

Securities are usually registered in the street name, unless either of the following occur:

➤ The stock certificates are sent to your house and then registered in your name.

➤ The certificates are registered in your name but held by the brokerage firm in its safe (in safekeeping).

rates, depending on the price range the stock falls into. Because the firm loaned you the money, the stocks are registered in *street name*, which means they are registered in the name of the brokerage firm. They get their money back when you sell your securities.

You may be asking yourself why anyone would want to borrow money to buy stocks. Because you expect the price of the securities to rise at a faster rate than the amount of interest you'll pay to borrow the funds. It gives you leverage.

Table 15.1 Maximum Loan Values for Margin Accounts

(use this as a guide—most brokerage firms have more conservative loan values)

On listed securities selling:	Maximum Loan Values
Option Eligible Securities	70% of market value
at $2.00 and over	50% of market value
at $1.75 to $1.99	40% of market value
at $1.50 to $1.74	20% of market value
under $1.50	No loan value

Here's how leverage works in a stock trade. Assume that you have been watching Rubberware Tire Company trade at $20 a share and expect the price of the stock to double within the next year or so. You can afford to invest $2,000 for one hundred shares. You could, of course, buy one hundred shares for $20 a share, pay $2,000 (plus commissions), let them appreciate to $40 next year, and sell them for $4,000, making a $2,000 profit. You've doubled your money—100% profit.

What happens if you margin the securities? You would put up fifty percent of the purchase price, according to the maximum loan values the exchanges set, as listed above. (Assume Rubberware is not an option eligible security.) Because the amount of margin you have to put up is dependent on the stock (i.e. market value, option-eligibility), be sure to confirm this amount with your broker.

In this case, you would still invest $2,000 of your money, but you would also borrow $2,000 of the firm's money and buy two hundred shares. Now you've invested a total of $4,000. Assuming that the stock did double in value, you would be able to sell your shares for $8,000. Of course, you have to pay back the $2,000 plus interest that you borrowed. This interest is known as the *broker loan rate*. The broker loan rate ranges anywhere from the prime rate to prime plus one or two percentage points tacked on.

Bet You Didn't Know

Prior to the 1930s, there was no minimum restriction on the amount of margin investors had to post. That's why so many people lost money during the stock market crash of '29— because many investors had margined their securities and they couldn't come up with the money required to pay back the margin loan.

Let's assume the rate was 5%. For a $2,000 loan, 5% would equal $100 for a year. After you repay the loan and interest, here's how your profit would sum up:

$8,000 (sale of stock) – ($2,000 (paying back the loan)

+ $100 (interest on the loan)) = $5,900.

$5,900 - $2,000 (your money) = $3,900 (your net profit).

Therefore the return on your investment is close to 200%, much, much greater than 100%! You've almost doubled your money.

Bet You Didn't Know

While using margin to buy securities sounds great, there are times to avoid it. First of all, just as stocks go up, they can also fall. Therefore, you could suffer a loss if the price of the stock drops. Second, not all securities are marginable, and depending on the rules, some securities require more than thirty percent to be margined. Third, even if the price of the security doesn't move at all, you still lose because of the amount of interest you pay for borrowing the money.

If you have margined some of your securities and the price falls, the brokerage firm will require you to deposit additional money into the margin account to bring it up to the required minimum level. This additional deposit is required because the stocks are the collateral for the loan. As collateral, if they drop in value, you need to make up the difference. Therefore, the present value of the stocks you bought on margin must equal the loan amount (in the previous example, 50%).

Who Has Short Shorts?

Another type of trade that must be done in a margin account is a *short sale*. A short sale is when you sell a stock that you don't own, but instead borrowed from the brokerage firm. When the price of the stock falls, then you would buy the stock back at the lower price and keep the difference as profit.

Remember all that "buy low and sell high" stuff? Well, here you're "selling high and then buying low" to make a profit. Imagine that. An exception to the rule. Here's an example of why you'd do this. Zany Zipper Company is trading at $10 a share. Bad news is leaking out and you think the stock is going to go into the toilet. In your margin account, you would profit from the stock's decline by borrowing one hundred shares from your broker (known as *shorting the stock*), selling it short at $10 a share, waiting for the price to drop to $2 a share (or whatever your target price is), buying one hundred shares back at $2 a share, and then returning the shares to your broker. This gives you a gross profit for yourself of $800. Not bad.

Let's see how this looks mathematically.

Zany Zipper Company stock	
current market price:	$10 per share
You borrow one hundred shares:	100s (s = short)
Total value or your investment:	$1,000s (s = short)
Price drops to $2. Current value	
of your investment:	$200
You buy back the shares at $2 a share:	$200

$1,000 (short sale of stock) – $200 (bought stock back) = $800 profit (less commissions, of course).

There's a risk, though. The market value of the security could go up. Then you would be selling short and buying the stock back at a higher price (because you have to return the stock you borrowed from your broker). This situation is extremely risky because your maximum loss is unlimited, as the stock could theoretically go to infinity and your loss would be infinite. (However, stocks don't go to infinity).

And you are at risk of a possible *short squeeze*. This means the borrowed stock needs to be returned to the rightful owner. When this happens you may be forced to buy the stock back in the open market even though it may not be at a favourable price. You are stuck with the loss. Bottom line: short selling is very risky.

The Least You Need To Know

➤ When you invest in the stock market, plan to invest over the long-term. The average long-term time period is about five years. Don't expect to make a killing overnight in the stock market. You'll only lose your shirt—and then some.

➤ Market indices and averages like the TSE 300 give investors an idea of the general direction of the stock market. Use them as a benchmark (guide) to see how your investment portfolio is doing.

➤ When you choose to invest in a stock, keep in mind your investment objectives. Decide whether you want to invest for growth potential (price appreciation) or income (dividends).

➤ You can borrow money to purchase securities (buying on margin) or borrow stocks to sell (selling short) from your broker by opening up a margin account. However, trading stocks on margin is quite risky if the market value of your stocks drops dramatically. Selling short can also be risky if the value of the stock rises.

➤ That's right! I'm going to say it again. BUY LOW AND SELL HIGH!!!

Chapter 16

Know When to Hold 'Em, Know When To Fold 'Em

In this chapter

➤ How fear and greed can cloud your decision to sell

➤ When to take your profits

➤ The best time to cut your losses

When Kenny Rogers sings "You got to know when to hold 'em. Know when to fold 'em. Know when to walk away. Know when to run. You never count your money while you're sittin' at the table. There'll be time enough for countin' when the dealin's done," he may have been talking about love, but the lesson can conveniently be applied to your investments. (Thanks, Kenny!)

As this chapter explains, buying and selling securities requires you to know when to hold 'em and when to fold 'em. Think of the best price at which to buy a security, but determine a target price at which to sell it, too. Don't buy a stock, a bond, or even a mutual fund just because it's a "good buy." That's only half the battle.

One of the best ways to determine a target price is to reflect on your financial goals again. What are you saving and investing your money for? Is there a specific amount? If you need $20,000 for your son Billy to go to university in ten years, at some point you are going to have to sell your investment to get the cash to pay for tuition, room, and board. Deciding what you need the money for aids in targeting a selling price.

Don't Let Fear and Greed Get to You

Earlier in this book, I noted that statistics show that seventy percent of all investors lose money in the stock market because of fear and greed. These same investors buy poor quality stocks at too high a price, thinking they're going to get rich overnight, only to find their hard-earned savings cut in half. Sometimes these investors get greedy and want more, more, more! Others ignore even the most obvious market signals and sell their stocks for a loss.

 Don't sell in a haphazard fashion to cut your losses. Take the time to review company news and see if there has been any bad publicity. Check to see if a number of investors dumped several large blocks of stock. Also investigate the possibility that the stock has been declining for some period of time.

Don't believe your stock price will always rise, just as you should believe that it won't always fall. There are always two sides of the coin in trading stocks. Just make sure you're not flipping the coin of greed and fear.

Take this hypothetical example—but whatever you do, don't try this at home!

Mr. and Mrs. Jones just had a baby girl. Because the Joneses have already started their financial planning (having read Chapter 3 of this book!), one of their biggest financial goals and priorities is to pay for their daughter's university education. Because they have eighteen years until she starts university, the Joneses decided to invest in a growth stock for the long term.

Each year, Mr. and Mrs. Jones plan to invest $1,000 in a stable growth stock that has had good earnings over the past ten years. The Joneses want this criteria and have all the necessary information at their fingertips because they did their homework.

Now the daughter is six years old and wants a Shetland pony (I said this was hypothetical). Mr. Jones, of course, cannot deny his daughter a pony. He needs cash fast—she's in earnest and her birthday is right around the corner. So he takes out $3,000 (or whatever the going rate is for a four-legged mammal) and expects to double his money from a stock tip he overheard in the barber shop.

The $3,000 is then invested in a penny stock trading at $3 a share. Mr. Jones buys one thousand shares and waits for it to double. (Meanwhile, the university investment account is cut in half because he took this money out.) Guess what happens? The stock price goes to $5. Mr. Jones isn't satisfied—he wants to double his money. The stock price goes to $5.50. Still, Mr. Jones sweats it out and waits. Then news of company bankruptcy comes out and the stock price drops to $1.50. Mr. Jones, well, he sold all one thousand shares at a loss.

Greed, friends. This is a good example of how greed can get the best of you. Somehow, Mr. and Mrs. Jones will now have to invest even more money for their daughter's college fund.

The bull market of the early 1990s created some awesome increases in stock prices. The problem is that those investors who bought low and saw their stocks move up quickly also watched their stock prices fall because they wanted to squeeze out as much as possible from the rise in price. Guess what? They didn't take their profits and sell their stock. Investors cried "Oh, they'll rise again." But greed clouded their decision about when to sell.

This is a common mistake that investors make. When stock prices move up quickly, people think that since it only took a little while for the stock to move up significantly, it'll do even better over the next few months. So they tend to hang on.

The bottom line is that you need to stick with your investment objectives or you'll never reach your financial goals. Make up a list of rules before you start buying stock, e.g., sell half the position and take some profit when the stock reaches price X. If you must have some "greed" money, allocate $20 to $30 a month for you just to do whatever you want with it. I don't recommend this, however; your first priority should be to meet your financial goals.

Now let's take a look at how fear can cloud your investment decision. The Smiths, who live next door to the Joneses, are very conservative and frugal people. They don't live beyond their means. In fact, they buy the basic necessities and save all the rest of their money.

Eeeek! They save their money! Where? In a low-interest bearing savings account earning a 2% annual yield. The Smiths think they're smart, because they've identified all of their investment objectives and their financial goals. However, they were too afraid to risk any of their principal, so they opted for the safety of a bank savings account.

Very respectable, but not very smart. If the Smiths are die-hard conservatives, a portion of their money can be kept in a money market deposit account. However, they won't reach their financial goals in the time required. The fear of losing their money is too overwhelming for them. This is how fear clouds your investment decision to buy.

You can also have fear about selling a stock. Some investors, for example, might be losing sleep over their first stock purchase. They are so fearful of having the stock drop from $20 a share, let's say, to $5 a share overnight that they decide to sell all of their shares the next trading day at the current price of $21 a share. Sure, they can sleep better at night, but the stock is now trading at $29 a share. Fear can cloud your decision as to when to sell if you are not keeping up with the current events and information about the company, its earnings, its financial reports, and the general direction of the financial market and industry.

Fear Not—It's Stop Loss to the Rescue

Stop loss orders can help you be a little bit greedy and protect you from losing your profits. Remember, a stop loss order is when you tell your broker to sell your stock when it drops to a certain share price. Here's how to be smart when using stop loss orders:

➤ Don't put the stop loss price too close to the current stock price. If the current trading price dips just a hair before it rises again, your stop loss order would be executed and you might miss out on further profit potential.

➤ Investment analysts and a few technicians use the following rule when entering stop loss orders: set the stop order price at ten percent below the current stock market price.

➤ Remember not to confuse a stop loss order with a stop limit order. A stop loss order protects your profits by selling your shares of stock should it fall in price to the price that you set. Unless a limit is set for the stop loss order, the order becomes a market sell order (shares sold at best available market price). A *stop limit order* gives the investor the advantage of specifying the limit price, meaning the maximum price you'll accept in the case of a stop limit to sell.

But remember: if the price drops below the limit you set, the stock will not be sold, regardless of how low the stock goes.

Take the Money and Run

Every investor wants to make a lot of money. The promise of a stock price rising is invigorating. Growth potential is a very important consideration in buying stocks, bonds, mutual funds, options— you name it! Ultimately, you want to choose a stock that has great profit potential. Of course, the only way to reap a great profit is to buy AND SELL the stock. Otherwise, the only profit you will see is a paper profit. Typically, this type of approach is a bit more aggressive than if you were to invest in a dividend-paying stock, where you usually buy and hold it. Remember, though, that you should invest for the long-term.

Recognize how easy it can be to become greedy when trading stocks. You can protect your profits and give greed a swift kick by placing a **stop loss order** (see Chapter 14). Your broker will sell the stock if the price drops to a specific point, but remember to raise the stop loss order if the stock price continues to rise.

I won't lie to you. It is very difficult to know when to sell a stock. Sure, you have access to research reports. Comments from your broker might tell you to watch the stock one more day or maybe wait until the next market rally comes around. Realize that you can't control the ups and downs of the stock market or whether or not your stock appreciates in value. However, you can control when you want to sell the stock and learn to identify situations when you should sell.

It's Better to Sell Out Than To Fade Away

As you become an educated investor, there is one thing (among many) to look for when evaluating the best time to sell your stock. It's an easy thing to spot and requires only a little more observation than usual. It's a fad gone bad.

If you bought stock in ABC Toy Company right before their Danger Ranger toys were literally swept off the shelves by eager consumers, you probably would have witnessed a substantial rise in the stock price. Lately, though, your observations tell you that Danger Rangers are out.

Kids are going crazy for the Grover Rover's Megablast Machines manu-
factured by a competing company. You may notice your ABC Toy
Company stock trying to rally to a new high, but the price starts dropping. You're trying to decide whether to sell your shares and realize
your profits.

At this point, you should use a stop loss order and tell your broker
to sell the stock automatically when it drops below the stop price. This
way you protect your profit—even if the stock price rises. In fact, every
time the stock price advances, cancel the old stop loss order and enter a
new one with a higher selling price.

Merger Mania

Another time to realize your profits is when a company merger is anticipated. Waiting with bated breath, investors pounce on rumours of company mergers. Typically, the stock price will jump sky high with the
high hopes of the pending merger, only to drop when the merger actually takes place. What happens is that the interest created by rumours
flying brings in new investors, pushing up the stock price. When the
merger mania subsides, the interest in the company drops, and so does
the stock price. It brings to mind an old adage that some investors follow: Buy on rumour, sell on news. Regard it as just that—an old adage.

Patience, Patience

After choosing the stocks you want to buy, it's equally important to
choose when you want to sell. Another rule is patience. The average investor has no patience. Patience and discipline can pay off when you
are trying to realize your profits. Many times, I have followed a stock for
a year or more before it hits the right mark—a good quality stock with a
low price. Discipline helps you buy the right price, and patience enables
you to sell at the right price, too.

Cutting Your Losses

No one—not even wise old Uncle Merle—knows the highest price your
stock will hit before it tanks. Understand, though, that if you don't realize your profits, you may have to cut your losses. "Cutting your losses"
is a favourite phrase among stock traders. It means you haven't realized
your profits, usually because the stock price has dipped and hung below

your purchase price. Set a loss limit before you buy the stock and sell the stock if it gets there. For example, a sell rule might be: if the stock falls 10% from your purchase price, then you sell it.

It is difficult to pinpoint exactly when you should cut your losses, but if your stock is trading well below the price you bought it at, consider selling. For example, if you bought one hundred shares of a stock at $40 a share, and now it's trading at $20 a share, your market value dropped fifty percent. Your stock would have to double in price—GAIN ONE HUNDRED PERCENT—just for you to be back where you started.

As a rule, keep the following guidelines in mind:

➤ Take the time to review company news. Has there been any negative publicity that caused the price of the stock to drop? Might it blow over quickly? Make sure you keep abreast of all company information. Contact the shareholder services department if you have questions. Call your broker for more information. Finally, make sure you continue to follow the financial reports that are sent to you.

➤ Is the drop in price a big drop that occurred in just one day or has it been steadily declining? If it is a big price drop that has occurred in just one day, take a step back and review the situation. Why the drop? Is it bad news that'll just have a temporary effect or is it the shape of things to come? If it's a temporary situation, you don't have to sell your stock. However, if the price has been steadily declining for a while, review all of your research information and consider cutting your losses.

The Least You Need To Know

In this chapter, you learned how to best decide when to buy or sell stocks. The following are determinants in that decision process:

➤ Making a profit requires you to buy the stock low and sell it higher. If you buy the stock at a low price and it is trading up from where you bought it, there's no profit until you sell it—although the price appreciation does look good on paper!

➤ Realizing your profits is the ultimate motive for investing. However, if you let the two negative emotions—fear and greed—get in your way, your profit potential might be reduced. Watch out for that trap! Make your decision based on your original investment goal.

➤ Only you can make the decision about when to sell your stock. Watch for key indicators, such as a decline in a fad product, an anticipated merger, or if a bad rumour is circulating. Establish your "sell" rules well ahead of time, before buying the stock.

Chapter 17

The DRIP—
A New Way
To Play

In this chapter

➤ You can begin with as little as $10

➤ Why dollar cost averaging is important

➤ Available resources

When you think of the word "drip," the irritating trickle of water that keeps you awake at night comes to mind, or perhaps the class geek. A drip is really steady droplets of falling water. As they fall, the droplets begin to collect and the water begins to rise.

Now apply this to investing. If you steadily and consistently drop a little bit of money into an investment program—with no commissions charged—what do you get? A dividend reinvestment plan (DRIP). This chapter tells you how investing in DRIPs can add up to an ocean of net worth.

The DRIP Concept

In the past, the strongest emphasis of dividend reinvestment plans was placed on purchasing a few shares of stock at a time instead of receiving a

The major advantage of DRIPs is that no commissions are charged.

cash dividend. For example, as you learned in Chapter 13, a company can offer a dividend to its shareholders in the form of cash or stock. So instead of receiving a dividend cheque in the mail for a measly $1.50, you invest that dollar and a half back into the company. A DRIP enables its shareholders to accumulate a growing number of shares of a company's stock without paying commissions.

Today, DRIPs are offered by over sixty Canadian companies. DRIPs build wealth slowly through accumulating small shares of the stock and enabling you to bypass commissions, because you purchase the shares directly from the company. In fact, some of these companies offer investors the advantage of purchasing company stock at discounts of usually about 5% below the current market price of the stock.

Some DRIPs permit investors to send in an optional cash investment. Those who do may require a minimum dollar amount and similarly, may set a maximum dollar amount you can buy. This cash investment option enables you to purchase additional shares. For example, if a company stock was trading around $50 and you sent in only $25, you would receive a fraction of a share—in this case, half a share. These fractional shares continue to build and you receive that fractional part of the dividend.

Keep in mind that when you send in additional payments, your account isn't usually credited immediately. Many companies invest these payments once a month or every quarter. That's why it's important to time your purchases. If a company makes its investment date on the 25th of each month and you send in your payment on the 1st of each

Bet You Didn't Know

Companies must pay dividends to offer a DRIP program. That's why the DRIP offering list of Canadian companies leans towards established, blue-chip stocks.

month, your cash sits there for twenty-four days earning no interest. The company is just holding onto it until the investment date.

Let's look at an example of how a DRIP works. Suppose your kids and their friends are gobbling up Chief Beef Lunchmeat, produced by Premier Meat Company. You do your investment research and find out that the company has a pretty solid background, and the stock currently trades at around $42 a share. You can purchase one hundred shares at $42 a share or whatever the current market price is and pay $4,200 plus commissions. If you don't have enough money for one hundred shares but want to invest because Chief Beef Lunchmeat is a good product, you can participate in their dividend reinvestment program if they offer one.

> Start early with a DRIP program. It doesn't require a lot of money to invest and is a great way to meet your long-term investment goals.

Going on the Record

Here's where a slight drawback arises. Not all companies that are publicly traded offer DRIPs. With those that do offer them, in most cases, you have to become a shareholder of record to enroll. Check to see if your brokerage firm offers a DRIP program. If not, here's what you do: Buy at least one share of stock from your broker that is registered in your name. This share of stock can't be registered in a brokerage or "street" name.

Once you purchase the share, make sure that you tell the broker you want the stock certificate sent to you. Make sure the spelling of your name and your current address appear on the front of the stock certificate. So, now that you have the stock registered in your name, where do you keep it? Well, you can either hold it in safekeeping at your brokerage firm, or put it in your safe deposit box, if you have one. Be sure to check the safekeeping fees.

Once you have become the shareholder of record as a result of registering the stock in your own name, notify the company that you want a DRIP application and a prospectus. Make sure you read the prospectus

Be careful, companies may cancel their DRIP programs at any time. So, don't purchase stocks just because they offer DRIP programs.

to determine whether there are any fees or charges, what the minimum and maximum optional cash payments are, and when they make their purchases. Fill out the application and send it in. After you sign up for a DRIP through the company you will have the dividends automatically reinvested for you.

Other DRIP Features

Tired of buying your grandchildren toys for Christmas which they quickly toss aside, having become mesmerized by the box the toy came in? Through DRIP programs, some companies make it easy for you to give a stock as a gift. Plus, the stock can appreciate, whereas the toy usually winds up on the "Under $2" table at your next garage sale. All you do is contact investor services at the company and open an account in the recipient's name. The company sends a gift certificate representing the shares to the recipient.

Dollar Cost Averaging

Making regular investments of a fixed amount of money on a periodic basis helps you take advantage of dollar cost averaging, one of the market's biggest secrets to investment success. By empowering yourself with this investment strategy, you avoid making initial purchases at the top. Making money on the Canadian stock market begins with our favourite rule, folks—buy low and sell high. With dollar cost averaging, you'll never buy all your investments at the top—perhaps some of them, but not all. That's the beauty of this strategy. With the same amount of dollars each month (or however often you choose to invest), you buy more shares of an investment when the market is low than when prices are high.

Here's how it works. With the Sky's the Limit Stock, let's say you want to invest $200 a month for the next twelve months. Currently, the stock is trading at $10 a share, so your initial $200 investment purchases twenty shares. Table 17.1 shows what happens when the market price changes.

Table 17.1 How Dollar Cost Averaging Works for You!

Month	Dollars Invested	Share Price	Shares Purchased	Total Shares to Date
January	$200	$10.00	20.00	20.00
February	$200	$12.50	16.00	36.00
March	$200	$14.00	14.29	50.29
April	$200	$13.00	15.38	65.67
May	$200	$13.00	15.38	81.05
June	$200	$9.00	22.22	103.27
July	$200	$10.00	20.00	123.27
August	$200	$11.25	17.78	141.05
September	$200	$13.50	14.81	155.86
October	$200	$15.00	13.33	169.19
November	$200	$14.50	13.79	182.98
December	$200	$14.00	14.29	197.27

Total Number of Shares: 197.27

Total Investment: $2,400.00

Total Value of Portfolio: $2,761.78

Net Profit: $361.78

When you invest in a dividend reinvestment program or a direct purchase plan, you are practicing dollar cost averaging. It can't guarantee you a profit, nor can it protect you against loss, but it does enable you to buy more shares in a mutual fund or stock as prices are declining and buy fewer shares as prices rise. However, if the financial markets keep dropping, at the end of the twelve-month period you'll have a loss. That's why you need to use this strategy over a period of several years. (Mutual funds are the biggest source of dollar cost averaging investing. You'll see how it works in Chapter 27.)

Even though it only takes a few bucks to start investing in a DRIP, you still need to do your homework on the company. This isn't a "buy and hold forever" investment. You can do that, but you also need to keep on top of the quality of the company's financial position and its strength in its respective industry. See Chapter 6 to learn how to get information about a company's performance.

Where Can You Sign Up?

We know that investing in stock is not for rich folks only. Even small investors can participate in the stock market through DRIPs. You can start with investing as little as $25 in some of Canada's best companies and accumulate shares over a period of time using dollar cost averaging. Check to see if your brokerage firm offers a DRIP service—you can sign up through your broker.

The Least You Need To Know

➤ Investing in the stock market isn't just a rich man's game. Small investors can buy stock with as little as $25 in a dividend reinvestment program.

➤ By using dollar cost averaging, you'll never make all your purchases at the top of the market, which catches many investors. Instead, you'll be able to buy more shares when the market price drops than when the price rises.

➤ Companies must pay dividends to offer a DRIP program; therefore the list of Canadian companies offering DRIPs leans toward established, blue-chip stocks. Companies may cancel their DRIP program at any time, so don't purchase these stocks solely for the DRIP. Don't forget to do your homework.

Chapter 18

Trading with the Trends... And Other Pitfalls

In this chapter

➤ Why you shouldn't follow the crowd

➤ How to avoid an investment scam

➤ Other words of wisdom

Trading stocks or bonds has its inherent risks. Volatility (rapid change) in the stock market can take even the strongest-stomached investors for a wild ride. The possibility of not being able to reinvest your money at the same rate of return is apparent in a down market. Plus, there's always the possibility that you won't have access to your money as quickly as you need it.

One example of what I consider to be risky is making your investment decisions based on what other people are saying or doing. While it's true that words of wisdom come from elders and those who are more experienced, one of the best ways you'll learn about investing is by making your own mistakes. Obviously, you want to avoid making as many mistakes as possible, and this chapter gives you some solid advice, rather than old maxims, that can help you become a successful investor.

Don't Follow John Q. Public

There really isn't a John Q. Public, for those of you who want to know. All those people with 2.5 kids, a dog, a white picket fence, a station wagon, and a house in the suburbs make up John Q. Public. You should only invest in a security when you have done all your homework—not when the John Q. down the street says the market is ready to rally.

Here are some tips to keep in mind:

1. You can listen to your friend's stock tips, but don't blindly invest in the stock without doing your own research. This includes getting a company's annual report, its prospectus (if it's a new offering) and research reports. You need to make sure your friend's advice is credible.

2. Many times, investors get their stock recommendations from the market gurus who promote their latest "sure thing" stock choice on financial television programs. While this information may be coming from a professional, such as a portfolio manager or notable stock trader, wait before you contact your broker to place that order. You need to do your research here, too.

3. Pay attention to any special information that's reported in the media. This information includes but is not limited to the following:

    ➤ Company layoffs, hiring freezes or even hiring booms.

    ➤ New products or services coming out into the market and/or new contracts that have been awarded to the company.

    ➤ Any existing products or services being recalled or taken off of the shelves.

    ➤ Whether a company did not report profits this year even though it usually does have a profit.

    ➤ Whether a company reported its first-time profit.

    ➤ The company's competitors: how are they performing?

Listening to the recommendations of the media—whose members consider themselves the experts about what John Q. Public is doing or should be doing—doesn't always work when it comes to investing. In fact, you can achieve investment success by not following the crowd. Instead, you should do your homework and challenge the masses!

What happens when you invest in a way that's contrary to what everybody else is doing? You may come out ahead. Suppose you're investigating a stock as a potential investment. You've been following the stock price for awhile, hoping to pick up on a potential profit opportunity. Only a few people are investing in the stock, and you haven't heard any solicitations from any brokers about the company. After you do your homework to make sure this is a good quality stock, you buy it. Not many investors are demanding shares for this stock, so the price is low.

As luck might (hypothetically) have it, the company announces pretty favourable news and the stock price takes off. Investors are now clamouring to buy the stock on their brokers' recommendations. This increase in demand may push the price up. Other investors are buying this stock at much higher prices than what you paid for it. You can now sell it and make a tidy little profit.

While the above sounds like an impossible dream, it isn't. True, there'll be times during your investing lifetime when all of your investments won't act favourably. But, as you become an educated investor, whether you deal with a full service or a discount broker, you can make intelligent investment decisions on your own without following the crowd.

Ignore the Fads

Investing in fad stocks is another way you can be misled by John Q. Public. A fad stock is nothing more than a relatively short-term, popular stock. Think of a fad stock this way: How long did bell-bottoms last? (I don't care what the fashion world says).

Investors jump on the bandwagon and buy up whatever stock is hot right now. It could be a computer stock, a retail stock or even a gaming stock (like the riverboat casinos). The price moves up so fast, word gets out on the street, and the price moves up more. Investors pour money into this stock even as the price rises, but in this case, the overinflated stock price is not a true measure of the company's worth.

Make sure you understand the difference between a fad stock and a company that produces fad products. A company that makes fad products, such as popular diet drinks and clothing, can be a solid growth company that's here to stay.

Don't buy a fad stock just because it is in the public limelight. Remember, the secret to making money on the markets is buying low and selling high. Investing in a fad stock will only be profitable if you catch it before it becomes a fad.

Looking for a Broker?

Choosing a broker is like choosing a doctor or a dentist. Think about it. You are entrusting this professional with your finances (in the case of the broker). So it makes sense to do your homework before you invest. Ask friends and colleagues for referrals. Even better, go to your family bank branch and ask them who they recommend.

Compile a list of qualities that you are looking for in a broker, along with your own financial goals and objectives. What type of experience does the broker have? Is his/her investment philosophy in tune with your own? Book appointments with the top three or four brokers that you have selected and go and "interview" them. Above all, you should feel comfortable with the broker you choose.

The Right Stocks

One way to learn how to buy the right stocks is to determine which investments you should avoid. Beware if any of the following occurs:

Don't believe that you'll make a fortune overnight from someone claiming that you can...especially if it's over the telephone. Making a good fortune takes time and patience. To protect yourself and your money, ask the solicitor for written information. If you receive some type of information and it appears to be fishy, either contact the Investment Dealers Association of Canada, relay the information to your provincial Securities Commission, or line your bird cage with it.

Be wary of callers you don't know who promise sky-high investment returns. If you are consistently receiving high-pressure sales calls from someone you don't even know, you may want to check up on the company he or she works for.

Don't buy any type of investment from someone who says it's inside information. Even if this person is promising that his hot stock tip will double your money, trading stocks based on inside information is illegal. And the regulators will do something about it.

(There are a number of high profile people sitting in jail because greed got the better of them.)

On a final note, I would like to share with you one phrase that stuck in my head from my consumer economics class in high school: if it sounds too good to be true, it probably is.

The Least You Need To Know

➤ If you follow what everyone else is doing in the investing arena, make sure you do your homework first before you buy.

➤ Take the time to select a broker who you are comfortable with and who meets your objectives. Ask friends for referrals. Or call up your bank and ask for a referral. Set up appointment times and interview your top choices.

➤ If it sounds too good to be true, it probably is.

"Don't try to buy at the bottom and sell at the top. This can't be done, except by liars."

—Bernard Baruch

YES, GIMME A HUNDRED—
YOU GOT IT,— NO, NO,
LET THOSE GO
CHEAP— HELLO,
YEAH, SELL THOSE—

Chapter 19

Specialty Equity Products

In this chapter

➤ Real Estate Investment Trusts (REITs)
➤ Royalty Income Trusts
➤ Convertibles

And if you thought there weren't enough investment products on the bond and stock markets—there are some specialty equity products available to you. Some of these are relatively "new" to the market, and have become very popular among Canadian investors. So, to keep you up-to-date with the investment lingo, here are a few more products for your reading pleasure.

Remember, "equities" refers to ownership of property; you can have equity in your home, for example, or by owning stocks.

WHAT?

REITs

REIT stands for real estate investment trust. As the name suggests, this is an equity product that invests in real estate.

Some people make the mistake of assuming that REITs are fixed income products. A REIT differs from your typical equity product because it is a closed-end mutual fund trust which trades like stocks do on the stock exchange. (The term closed-end means that there is a limited and fixed number of shares issued.)

The mutual fund part comes in because, essentially, REITs securitize different commercial real estate assets into a pool and sell interest in these pools as units of a trust. The return an investor (called the unitholder) receives from the trust will be made up of rental income from tenants in existing properties, as well as the returns on any acquisitions of property that the trust may partake in.

Bet You Didn't Know

Because REITs are high-yielding securities that typically yield 9% to 11% in today's environment, they have become very popular among investors.

One of the major advantages of REITs over your typical equity product is that REITs are tax-advantaged. The income from the REIT properties flows through to the unitholders along with the Capital Cost Allowance (CCA) which reduces the tax liability to the unitholder. What this really means is that the income flow from the rent paid by the tenants to the REIT is not treated like income but as a reduction in the cost of the security, which means a deferral of taxes. Did you get that? It sounds pretty confusing, I know, but the bottom line is that REITs are taxed differently and at a preferred rate to equity products (i.e., stocks) if held over the long-term.

Why Invest in Real Estate?

For starters, diversification. You want your portfolio to be spread across various asset classes to reduce risk. Most REITs represent pools of diversified real estate assets across different real estate sectors and regions. You'll also find some REITs with a more narrow focus, such as REITs that invest solely in apartment buildings.

Secondly, REITs are not as volatile as stocks. Commercial real estate values don't fluctuate widely, as the price of an individual stock can. Historically, REITs have shown consistent growth. Finally, because REITs are traded on the stock markets, they're liquid.

This explanation of REITs is meant only as an introduction. As with any investment, there are risks—please consult with your broker to see if REITs make sense in your portfolio.

Royalty Income Trusts

The majority of royalty income trusts are oil and gas ventures.

Like a REIT, royalty income trusts area currently a high-return equity product. A royalty trust is another closed-end fund that is designed to pass on the income and certain tax benefits from natural resource extraction to unitholders. The most popular royalty trusts are oil and gas royalty funds, but similar ventures are also available for mining and iron ore production.

It works like this. For example, with oil and gas trusts, the operators acquire interests in producing oil and gas wells, passing on the income to unitholders on a monthly or quarterly basis. The operator purchases oil and gas assets, and in turn, sells a 99% royalty to the trust. The sale of the royalty in combination with some debt financing, represents the capital used by the operating company for the purchase of the oil and gas assets. The trust then sells trust units to the public in order to raise funds for the purchase of the royalty.

One of the main differences between REITs and royalty trusts is that the underlying asset is a depleting one for royalty trusts (unless the trust acquires property in the future). There are two general categories that the assets of a royalty trust fall into based on the expected lifespan of the asset. If the asset is expected to deplete over ten to fifteen years, the royalty trust is classified as having a depleting reserve base. If the assets are expected to have a life that exceeds thirty years, the royalty trust is classified as a long-lived royalty trust.

As mentioned earlier, royalty trusts, like REITs, are tax advantaged. The income flow generated by the royalty trust may partially be a "return of capital" to the unitholder. Because this is a return of capital and not income, it is not taxed like income. Remember, income is taxed at the highest rate relative to dividends and capital gains. For this and other reasons, you can defer taxes on this income. Taxes may eventually need to be paid upon the sale of the units.

Both REITs and royalty trusts provide reliable income and tax advantages, but are also complex investments that should be thoroughly researched before you invest. You can contact your broker for a prospectus on a particular fund, or for investment advice.

Debenture
A certificate of indebtedness of a government or company backed only by the general credit of an issuer. Debentures, unlike bonds, are unsecured by any assets. They are considered riskier than bonds.

Convertible
A bond, debenture or preferred share which may be exchanged by the owner, usually for the common stock of the same company.

Convertibles

No, we're not talking cars here. Convertibles are not similar to REITs or royalty trusts other than they are considered equity investments. A convertible is issued by a corporation and may be a bond, debenture or preferred share which may be exchanged by the owner, usually for the common stock of the same company. They are ideal for investors wanting steady income but who also want to participate in the growth of a company.

Convertibles are similar to corporate or government bonds in that they pay a fixed rate of interest over their term. Like bonds, convertibles may be purchased and sold after they've been issued. They are priced in the market based on their interest rate and the risk sensitivity.

What makes convertibles different from bonds is the holder's ability to convert the bond, preferred share or debenture into common shares of the company at a set price. It is this feature that is attractive to investors. In fact, investors are usually willing to accept a lower yield for the opportunity for capital appreciation in holding common shares. In this way, convertibles are looked upon as "two-way securities."

When you are looking to invest in a convertible, some things to consider include the interest rate, conversion price, maturity date, credit risk, and the details of the terms of the conversion. Lower yields on convertibles typically mean that the conversion would probably result in capital gains. On the other hand, higher yields usually indicate a greater financial risk associated with the company.

Convertibles offer the advantage of having predetermined income flow from interest payments plus the option to participate in the company's growth through share conversion.

Perhaps an example would help. Let's say the ABC convertible debenture (it could be a bond or preferred shares) matures in five years. It pays 4% each year until maturity. The debenture is convertible to ABC stock at a stock price of $35. The terms for this particular debenture state: For every $1,000 face value worth of the debenture, you will receive 100 shares on conversion. That means it will be in the investor's best interest to convert the debenture to stock if the stock rises above $35. Otherwise, the investor will continue to receive the 4% interest if he or she holds on to the debenture. If the debenture is held until maturity, the investor will receive the par value for it, just like any other bond. (This example will work for convertible preferred shares as well as convertible bonds.)

Are you still with me? If you're not, don't panic. The purpose of this chapter was to introduce you to these products, to get your feet wet. Deciding whether or not to invest in them—that's up to you. And your broker is there to help. Don't be shy—just ask.

The Least You Need to Know

➤ REITs and royalty trusts can offer you income with significant tax advantages. But there are risks. Research before you invest.

➤ Convertibles offer you the opportunity to convert you bonds, debentures or preferred shares into the common stock of the same company. Make sure you understand the terms of conversion before you invest.

"Buy on the rumour, sell on the news."

—Market maxim

SO HE SAID TO INVEST IN JELL-O THAT TASTED LIKE MEAT PRODUCTS. I SAY, "IS THAT SO? JELL-O THAT TASTES—

SOAP BOX

·tAP·
·tAP·

Chapter 20

News You Can Use

> ### In this chapter
> ➤ Getting your hands on stock research reports
> ➤ How each of them can help you with your investment planning
> ➤ Don't forget your broker as a resource

You know what the products are. Good. You learned that buying low and selling high is a good financial strategy. Great! But what's low and what's high? Obviously, that depends on price. Many times, when the price is right, you can make a bundle. So toss aside those Plinko chips and hold onto your showcases. Here's a few more terms that will help you learn what's low and what's high.

Technical Versus Fundamental Analysis

Many times, prices of investments rise and fall, and rise and fall, eventually creating a pattern. Investors who base their buying and selling decisions on these patterns—known as price patterns—are referred to as technicians. These are the market wizards with dozens of coloured pencils and reams of graph paper. They don't care if a company makes widgets, gadgets, or gizmos. They just look at the charts they've created and determine the target price at which to either buy or sell an investment. They often look at past price history (past performance) to aid in their decision. This function is known as *technical analysis*.

What about those financial geniuses who place more emphasis on the value of an investment than its price? These intellectuals analyze the financial conditions of companies and markets and buy when the price of the investment has not realized its real value and sell when it is considered to be overvalued. These value-oriented investors are known as *fundamentalists* and the function they perform is *fundamental analysis*. They crunch numbers from a company's annual report and try to make sense out of them. They also investigate why a particular security is out-of-favour among market watchers. Or they may study why a security is so hot that everyone seems to be lapping it up.

Ask anybody for advice about investing in stocks, bonds, mutual funds, or any type of investment. Believe me, whoever you ask (your father-in-law or Grandma Betty's neighbour) will drag out the soap box and give you their advice...for free. Each individual has a story to tell of how his stockbroker made him a fortune. For every story like this, however, you can count on a hundred stories of how bad investments wiped somebody out.

Asking for advice is okay, but you can't believe everything you hear. Reading about investment advice is even better, but don't believe everything you read, either. This chapter explains how to find additional resources for reliable stock investment information.

Read All About It!

There are available newsletters that give stock advice. And that's just about stocks! Most of these investment newsletters reflect the personality of the writer. If the writer is having a good day, well then, she might be bullish on specific investments. But if the writer got up on the wrong side of the bed, gloom and doom might be the day's headline. That might sound a little farfetched, but most investment newsletters reflect the interests of the author.

Subscribing to a financial newsletter is one way to get investment advice. A multitude of different types of newsletters exist, and each covers just about every different type of investment strategy available. Some letters use technical analysis and are chock full of charts and graphs—it's up to you to decipher them! Other letters use fundamental analysis and discuss the value of a company and the potential for earnings growth. Still others provide information about initial public offerings, hostile takeovers, inside company scoops, foreign information, and our current economic situation and what impact it has on investments. You name it, it's probably being published in a newsletter somewhere.

DON'T buy an investment newsletter until you see a sample copy, especially if the subscription price is several hundred dollars. Instead, ask for a trial subscription to check out the style, writing, and advice found in the newsletter. Happy reading.

Is any of this advice rewarding? Some newsletters give solid advice and justify their positions. These newsletters can be a real plus in picking out the right investments. Others do not give good advice and often mislead subscribers. It's a shame because many of these financial newsletters are costly and could cost you hundreds of dollars each year. To make matters worse, sometimes the subscription department refuses to send out sample copies unless you have a paid subscription. But it doesn't cost anything to ask!

The Good, the Bad, and the Ugly

Okay, where do you start? How can you tell the best from the rest? For quick stock research, just let your fingers do the dialing. *The Financial Post* offers what's called Facts On Demand, which is a fax service offering reports on almost 5000 North American companies. Each report provides investment recommendations including buy/sell or hold, recent developments, material changes, latest financial results, comparative data, and more. The great features of this service are: it's available twenty-four hours a day, seven days a week; it's same day service; and you don't have to subscribe to a whole year's worth of reports—you can buy just one. However, you can only receive these reports by fax at this time. The reports cost $3.50 per unit; or you can save money by subscribing to one of their discount packages. To speak to a customer service representative, call (800) 661-7678. To order, call toll-free at (800) 340-2039 (ask for Operator 7).

If you don't have a fax machine, don't worry, because there are

Bet You Didn't Know

There are more financial newsletters that cover the stock market and investing in stocks than any other investment product.

many other investment newsletters on the market today. One service that tracks several investment newsletters is MPL Communications, based in Toronto. You can order the following reports, and more, through them by calling their customer service line collect at (416) 869-1177. Here are some highlights:

➤ ***Investment Reporter.*** Named one of the top five advisories in the world over the past ten years, the *Investment Reporter's* key stock recommendations have proved consistently solid. This report includes an investment planning guide with model portfolios, an index of 100 "Key Stocks," and a telephone hotline service. A one year subscription costs $279 (plus applicable taxes).

Please, please, please, keep in mind that I'm not telling you to go and sink all of your money into a subscription service. Rather, consider these newsletters recommended reading to further your knowledge about the financial markets.

➤ ***Blue Book of Stock Reports.*** Established in 1941, the *Blue Book* keeps more than 245 Canadian companies under continuous review and provides a regularly updated, fact-filled stock report for each company. Each report gives buy/sell or hold advice, along with risk assessment and the portfolio type it is suited to. A one year subscription costs $279.

➤ ***Investor's Digest.*** Published bi-weekly, readers get buy/sell recommendations, summaries of brokers' research reports and interviews with professional money managers. A one-year subscription costs $137.

➤ ***Money Reporter.*** For people who are interested in earning more interest, this bi-weekly publication tracks the latest developments in income investments. Preferred shares, DRIPs, and strip bonds are covered. The report advises you on how to earn high and safe income from your investments. For a one-year subscription price of $179 plus taxes, you get income-producing model portfolios, monthly fact-sheets and a telephone hotline service.

➤ ***Best U.S. Stocks for Canadian Investors.*** This report is written specifically for Canadians who want to add diversity and security to their portfolios with profitable U.S. stocks. The bi-weekly publication includes recommended stocks and stock portfolios, tax laws, and forecasts of the U.S. economy and stock market. A one-year subscription is $157 (plus applicable taxes).

For those of you who don't have the budget to buy the research, much less the time to analyze these reports, your broker can help. In fact, full-service brokers have access to all this information, plus access to top analysts and up-to-the minute information on their computer links.

The Least You Need To Know

➤ Investment newsletters are to be used as a guide to learn more about the financial markets. Don't treat them as the cure-all to your investment plan. Do other research to confirm that the investment's a good idea.

➤ Your broker is an excellent source for stock research if you don't have the time and energy to muddle through the investment newsletters, not to mention the budget!

There may be a recession in stock prices, but not anything in the nature of a crash.

**—Irving Fisher, economist,
six weeks before the 1929 crash**

Part 4
IOU—Learning the Basics of Bonds

A bond, no matter what type, is an IOU. A junk bond? An IOU. Municipal bonds? Still IOUs. Corporate bonds? Again, bonds are IOUs from the issuer, promising two things—to pay a set rate of interest and to repay your original investment at a later date.

Making money on bonds used to be the most simple, safe investment around: invest your money in a bond at a fixed rate of return, wait a spell, and boom, there's your income. But the bond world has changed over the past several decades. The rise and fall of interest rates has caused both glory days and mayhem for bond investors. New and different types of bonds flourished in the markets during the early 1980s. It's trickier now, but you can still make a tidy sum in the bond market, as this part of the book explains. So gear up and let's go!

Chapter 21

Getting a Grip on the Bond Market

> ## In this chapter
> ➤ What is a bond?
> ➤ Risks involved in investing in bonds
> ➤ A financial strategy for conservative investors

A bond is basically an IOU. Taking this one step further, a bond is a certificate that stands for a loan from the investors buying the bonds to the government (federal, provincial, or municipal) or company that issued them. Think of it this way: an issuer of a bond, like the Canadian government, is a borrower of monies. You, the investor, are a purchaser and a lender of monies. In other words, you lend the Canadian government money, and you are the purchaser of their debt.

Here's an example. You own a company named Elastic Plastic which makes the little plastic rings on the outside of

A bond, by definition, provides a fixed stream of income (the interest payments) as well as full repayment of principal at a stated maturity date.

shoelaces. Your product is selling like hot cakes, and you need to increase production to make more little plastic rings. But you have no money left. To raise more money (also known as capital), you "take out a loan" by issuing a bond certificate to me. In return for me loaning you my money for a specific period of time, you promise to pay me a fixed amount of interest every six months. At the end of the specified period, I receive the amount I loaned to you.

These debt instruments pay you interest in exchange for your "loan." In this chapter, you will learn about the ins and outs of bond investing, how following the direction of interest rates plays a role in your bond portfolio, and what type of fixed-income strategy works best for you.

How Much Do We Owe?

In the bond market, buyers and sellers figuratively meet to agree upon a price to buy or sell bond securities. Bonds are not typically traded on a financial exchange (they trade on the over-the-counter market, as discussed in Chapter 14) with the exception of a few corporate bonds (those are traded on the Toronto Stock Exchange).

In Chapter 14, you learned that stock represents ownership in a company. If you bought one hundred shares of XYZ Toy Company and there were one hundred thousand shares outstanding, you would own one one-hundredth of the company. Bonds do not work this way. As a bond investor, you are lending your money to the government or corporation. This "loan" requires the bond issuer (the government or corporation borrowing your money) to pay you the amount borrowed plus interest over a period of time. Therefore, you are a lender, not an owner.

Traditionally, a bond issued in Canada specifies the following things:

➤ A fixed date when the amount borrowed must be paid back. This date is the *maturity date.* Although there is a stated maturity date, this doesn't mean that you have to hold the bond until it has matured. You can sell it at any time prior to its maturity date. (By the way, this is something that GICs, for the most part, do not allow you to do.)

➤ A coupon rate. Most bonds also pay you interest. The amount of interest that is paid reflects the *coupon rate* that is stated on the bond. The coupon rate can be either a *fixed rate* that pays you the same amount of interest every year (this is by far the most common method), or a *floating rate* where the amount of interest is adjusted periodically based on some pre-determined index, like the Consumer Price Index (CPI), which tracks inflation.

➤ The *face value*, also known as the *par value*, is the amount of the original investment, or principal. This amount is equal to the amount which you agreed to lend to the borrower and is the amount that will be repaid upon maturity.

Here's what a typical bond trade would look and "sound" like: "I bought $1,000 worth of an 8% bond due on September 18, 2000." This means that you invested in a bond with a $1,000 face value, an 8% coupon rate, and a maturity date of September 18, 2000. Therefore, you have lent the issuer $1,000 until Sept 18, 2000 (however, you can sell the bond prior to maturity if you like). The issuer will pay you 8% a year to borrow that money from you. The $1,000 principal amount will be paid back to you on the maturity date, on top of the interest payments.

Bond Prices and Interest Rates

The following principle is the cardinal rule to know if you want to understand bond investing.

As interest rates go up, bond prices go down. And when interest rates go down, bond prices go up. This is why it is said that interest rates have an inverse relationship with the bond prices. Just remember, they move in opposite directions of each other. Repeat to yourself: If interest rates rise, bond prices go down.

Suppose you own thousands of dollars' worth of government bonds that were issued in the early 1980s with coupon rates between 12% and 15%. These bonds are still earning that interest even today, and you can't earn that kind of interest on government securities now. As of June 1997, the average coupon rate

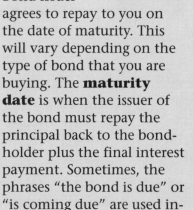

The **principal/face value** is the amount of money the bond issuer agrees to repay to you on the date of maturity. This will vary depending on the type of bond that you are buying. The **maturity date** is when the issuer of the bond must repay the principal back to the bondholder plus the final interest payment. Sometimes, the phrases "the bond is due" or "is coming due" are used interchangeably with the date of maturity.

on long-term government bonds (maturity greater than ten years) was roughly 6.60%. Ouch.

So what do you think investors are willing to pay you for your 12%–15% coupon bonds? Because today people are only able to buy government bonds at an average 6.60%, some investors are more than willing to pay you a higher price for your high coupon bond. If, for example, you originally lent the government $1,000 back in the early eighties, you'd be receiving, say, 12% or $120 a year worth of interest payments. In today's market, if an investor wanted to lend the government $1,000 with the same terms, the investor might receive $66 a year in interest payments which equates to a 6.60% yield. The difference accounts for the fall in interest rates.

Now if you own this bond that pays a whopping $120 worth of interest a year, why would you even think of selling it in the open market before maturity? Well, what happens if Jim Bob offered you, say $1,050, $1,150, even $1,200 for the bond that you originally paid $1,000 for? Now, you might think about selling the bond. Keep in mind that Jim Bob would receive the same $120 a year of interest on a bond he paid $1,200 for. That would be a return of less than 12%, (i.e. $120 of $1,200 is 10%!) While you were holding the $1,000 bond, you earned that full 12%.

The amount of money Jim Bob is willing to pay above par (above the $1,000 in this case) is known as a *premium*. This premium would make the interest rate and term to maturity equal (or almost equal) to the yield of that government bond that pays you $66 on your $1,000 investment.

In other words, if Jim Bob holds the bond to maturity, he would only receive the face or par value of $1,000 back—a loss of $200. So, if you were to calculate it, for a five-year term on his bond purchase, he is earning close to the $66 on that original $1,000 government bond. (While the numbers in this example don't work out exactly, the important thing is to understand why there would b a premium on the bond.)

Do you see the relationship between interest rates and bond prices? When interest rates fall, bond prices will rise. In this case, bonds will trade at a premium to their par value, e.g. $1,200 versus $1,000. On the other hand, when interest rates rise, bond prices will fall. In this case, bonds will trade at a discount to par, e.g. $900 versus $1,000.

And you thought investing in bonds was simple. Not to worry. Bonds trading at discounts and premiums and the like apply to the investor who is active in the bond market, i.e., the investor who buys and sells bonds. If you're like the average bondholder, you'll purchase the bond and hold it to maturity and not bother with this buying and selling business.

Crash Course in Current Yields

Do not confuse the *coupon rate* with the *current yield*. Remember, the coupon rate is the stated rate on the bond and does not change. The current yield is the coupon rate divided by the market price of the bond. Because the market price of the bond fluctuates throughout the day, week or month, the current yield is constantly changing.

For example, let's say you bought a bond with a 10% coupon rate at a price of 90. The price of 90 means that you have paid ninety percent of the face value of the bond. Because the bond has a face value of $1,000, the total market value is equal to $900 ($1,000 x .90 = $900). The annual interest paid on this bond is equal to the coupon rate multiplied by the face value. In this case, it would equal $100.

The current yield at the time you bought this bond was 11%. You can determine the current yield of the bond by dividing the annual interest payment by the dollar price you paid for the bond (or the current market value if the price has changed), and then multiplying the result by 100 to get a percentage, as the following figure illustrates.

$$\left(\frac{\text{Annual Interest Payment of the Bond}}{\text{Total Market Value of the Bond}}\right) \times 100 = \text{Current Yield}$$

$$\left(\frac{\$100}{\$900}\right) \times 100 = 11.11\%$$

How to determine the current yield of a bond.

What About the Yield to Maturity?

Earlier you learned that every bond has a maturity date, and you may wonder what it has to do with how much interest you will earn over the life of a bond. This is easy. You receive an interest payment at least annually, if not semi-annually, every year until the bond matures. Therefore, if you have a bond that matures in ten years, you will receive interest payments for the next ten years. These interest payments are only a portion of the total return on a bond.

The *yield to maturity* is a measure of the total return that you can expect to earn if you hold the bond till maturity. Sometimes known as YTM, this amount takes into account the coupon rate, the bond's current market price, and the years left until the bond matures. The YTM is the standard figure used in the industry, unlike the current yield, which is rarely used. The calculation for the YTM is a pretty difficult calculation, but your broker can tell you what it is. Just know that the result represents the estimated return you can expect to receive if you hold the bond until maturity.

Buy Bonds at Your Own Risk

If you follow the direction of interest rates, you can determine the price movements in the overall bond market. Before you invest, you need to understand that price swings can mean significant profits or terrible losses to bond buyers.

Typically, the longer the length of maturity of the bond, the higher the rate you will earn. If you are lending your money to the Canadian government or a corporation for a longer period of time, you'll want a higher rate for doing so, right?

In exchange for lending your money out for a longer period of time, you should expect to receive a higher rate—but you also incur more risk, which includes price risk. Keep the following risks in mind when you are investing in any bond, and make sure your broker supplies you with enough information about a bond to comfortably evaluate these risk factors:

➤ Ask yourself if the borrower—such as a municipal government, provincial government, corporation, or even the federal government—will be able to pay back the amount borrowed from you plus the interest promised at regular, semi-annual intervals. This is known as *credit risk*. Answering this question will require you to understand the concept of how bonds are rated. Just as you used to get grades on tests in school, bonds are rated on the credit risk and assigned a rating by two rating agencies: the Canadian Bond Rating

Service (CBRS) and the Dominion Bond Rating Service (DBRS) (More about this later in the chapter).

➤ Inflation will creep up and the money you get back in the long run will be intrinsically worth less. The risk involved here is known as *purchasing power risk*, which we discussed in Chapter 5. As you follow the economy and the business cycle, pay attention to any inflationary trends that might push interest rates above the coupon rate of the bonds you own. You may want to sell your bond before interest rates exceed the coupon rate, because you don't want your money locked up in an investment that cannot even keep up with the pace of inflation. However, you have to make the decision to sell quickly. Why? Because as inflation rises, the purchasing power of the interest payments you receive gets smaller and smaller. In addition, rising inflation leads to higher interest rates, which will cause bond prices to fall.

Among bonds that have the same coupon rate, those with a longer maturity have greater price sensitivity. This means that their prices will fluctuate more for a given change in interest rates. Among bonds with the same maturity date, those with the lower coupon rate have a greater price sensitivity. Knowing this should help you better anticipate how much the value of the bonds you own will change in response to fluctuations in interest rates.

➤ As with any type of investing, there is always reinvestment risk. When your bond matures or if you decide to sell it before maturity (hopefully for a profit), you don't know what the investment climate will be at that time. You can't count on it being the same as when you bought the bond, especially if you bought a longer term bond. If you sell the bond before maturity and interest rates are lower than when you bought it, you are forced to accept a lower yield on a new investment. This scenario is known as *reinvestment risk.*

➤ If interest rates drop after you buy your bond, and you decide to sell it before maturity, you will get a higher price than what you paid. However, you can't always count on the interest rates dropping. If you need to sell your bond and interest rates are higher than when you purchased it, you're going to have to accept a lower price than what you paid. This is known as *interest rate risk.*

➤ Keep in mind that if you buy a bond and hold it to maturity the value of the bond may change along the way, but that doesn't matter if you don't have to sell the bond before maturity. At maturity you will receive the full principal amount back.

Rate That Risk

Bond securities do receive grades, just as schoolchildren do after taking a math test. In fact, before buying any bond, you should find out its investment grade, or *rating*. Companies like the Canadian Bond Rating Service (CBRS) and Dominion Bond Rating Service (DBRS) grade most bond securities. Each of these services uses a different rating scale, taking into account different risk factors.

Here's an example of what a rating scale might look like.

Canadian	Dominion	What Does It Mean?
A++	AAA	Highest quality
A+	AA	Very Good quality or Superior Credit quality
A	A	Good quality or Upper Medium grade
B++	BBB	Medium quality
B+	BB	Lower Medium grade
B	B	Poor quality
C	CCC	Speculative grade
D	CC	In default
Suspended	C	Lowest standing
ZZZ	ZZZ	You're sleeping….Wake up!

Bonds with lower investment grade ratings will usually offer higher coupon rates than bonds with higher ratings. If the coupon rate were the same no matter what the rating, who would buy the lower rated (riskier) bond? In exchange for loaning your money when there's a higher investment grade risk, you receive a higher interest rate. This is where trading risk for reward comes into play.

It's also important to note that even when the ratings for bonds are equal, interest rates for short-term bonds (that is, bonds with closer maturity rates) are typically lower than interest rates on long-term bonds (bonds that mature further in the future). For example, if you invest in short-term government bonds (which have maturities of one year or less), you will receive a lower rate of interest than if you parked your money in a long-term government bond with the same credit rating.

Never buy an unrated bond. If the issuer does not apply for and receive ratings on its bonds, the bonds will be harder to resell to any investor, institutional or regular Joe. Don't take a chance on a bond that hasn't been rated.

If you buy a bond that is rated "not desirable," you will receive a higher yield; however, there is a lot more credit risk involved than if you were to invest in a high grade bond. This is part of the risk-reward scenario in investing.

WHAT?

Whoa, Throw Me a Curve!

The following figure represents a normal yield curve. This graph represents the fluctuations in interest rates that occur over time and affect bonds of the same quality with varying lengths of maturity.

The result looks like a curve, which is exactly what it is, a yield curve. The vertical axis shows the yield, and the horizontal axis shows

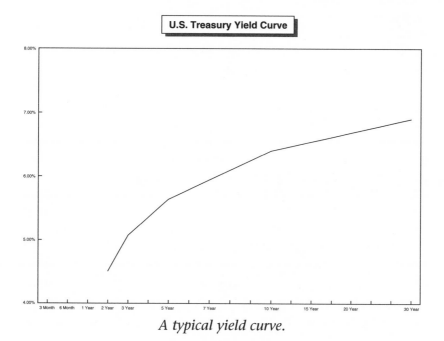

A typical yield curve.

the term. The curve tells you if short-term interest rates are higher or lower than long-term rates.

➤ If short-term rates are lower than long-term rates, the yield curve is a *positive yield curve* or normal yield curve.

➤ If short-term rates are higher than long-term rates, the yield curve is a *negative yield curve* or an inverted yield curve.

➤ If there is little difference between the two, the yield curve is *flat*.

 For the most part, the only thing you need to understand about the yield curve is that it is typically positive, which is upward sloping. It is typically positive because investors who are willing to tie up their money for longer periods of time are usually compensated for the extra risk with higher yields.

Think of it this way. If I borrow money from you for ten years instead of one, you are going to charge me more interest for borrowing it for a longer period of time because you won't be able to use your money at all during those ten years.

So why study the yield curve? It isn't that difficult. You can even plot the points on the graph and make your own curve. If you understand how easily the yield curve works, you can make your own judgments about the direction of both long-term and short-term interest rates based on the shape of the yield curve. This can assist you in making a decision about when to buy and sell bonds.

An upward-sloping yield curve implies that interest rates are expected to rise in the future. Because of the inverse relationship between bond prices and interest rates, you would expect bond prices to fall. On the other hand, a downward-sloping yield curve indicates that interest rates are expected to fall. Therefore, bond prices will rise.

What If Interest Rates Flip Flop?

If, after a bond is issued, interest rates should rise or fall, the market value of the bond drops or rises. Here's what happens next.

➤ **If interest rates rise and I'm a saver.** You don't have to worry about keeping a portion of your money in savings, a money market account, or even a Guaranteed Investment Certificate because rates are going up. That means you'll earn more money on your money.

➤ **If interest rates rise and I'm a borrower.** Don't panic. Shop for the best rates around, whether you are borrowing the money for a new car, new house, or new whatever! But don't take too much time doing so if rates keep going up.

➤ **If interest rates rise and I'm an investor.** You may want to look into short-term investments with maturities of two years or fewer (a short-term government bond, for example). Longer term investments, such as a thirty-year bond, might not be a wise move if rates are going to keep rising. Why? Because you could lose out on earning a higher interest rate, thus foregoing a larger amount of semi-annual interest payments.

As an example, let's say I issue a twenty-year, 9% government bond, and you want to buy one (interest payments would be $90 a year on a $1,000 bond). That means that you are buying a bond, issued by the government, that will mature twenty years from now. Over the next twenty years, the bond will pay you 9% in interest every year.

Let's say the bond in our example is for $1,000, and five years down the road you can't wait till maturity and want to sell, but there are still fifteen years to go. The bonds that have a maturity of fifteen years (you have to compare apples to apples) offer a better yield: 11% because interest rates have gone up. If you try to sell your 9% corporate bond for its full face value, you will have a hard time doing so. After all, who would want to buy a fifteen-year bond yielding 9% a year (that's $90 a year in interest income) when you could buy a fifteen-year bond yielding 11% (that's $110 a year in interest income). You might have to sell your bond for less than its face value (at a discount). (This is an example of interest rates rising and bond prices falling.)

If you are looking into buying a house, you may want to check out a fixed-rate mortgage instead of an adjustable-rate mortgage. The rate you receive on your mortgage is fixed and cannot change. However, the adjustable-rate mortgage, although a few percentage points lower than a fixed rate, will rise as long as rates keep going up! up! up!

➤ **If interest rates fall and I'm a saver.** You'll want to find the best-paying money market deposit accounts around to keep a portion of your cash liquid (not really liquid, like Kool-Aid, but "available").

➤ **If interest rates fall and I'm a borrower.** Just as we saw the wave of refinancings in 1993 when mortgage rates bottomed out, you'll play the "should I/shouldn't I" game of wondering if rates have hit their lowest point before you borrow money to build a new house, to refinance a house, or to buy a new car.

➤ **If interest rates fall and I'm an investor.** If you invest in the stock market—through stocks, DRIPs, or stock mutual funds—you'll probably be in for a good upwardly mobile ride. Typically when interest rates fall, the stock market reacts favourably. Bond prices rise, too. Before you figure out your strategy with your bond investing, you need to consider a few important factors.

If you are a current bondholder, you need to determine why you are holding the bond. For example, are you holding it for income (meaning that, as a bond investor, you are more interested in getting as much of an interest payment yield as you can with a specific level of risk)? Are you holding it for reasons of capital appreciation (meaning you are buying the bond at a low price and a high yield and selling it at a high price and low yield to make a profit)? As long as you identify which type of bond investor you are, you will know what to do in a changing economic environment.

Using our previous example, if after five years you want to sell your bond and interest rates are falling, prices on bonds would be going up. Therefore, you can sell your bond that yields $90 a year in interest income at a higher price, or premium, because the current market rates are much lower. (This means that bond prices have risen.)

The Ladder to Successful Bond Investing

Snakes and Ladders is an all-time favourite for many children. You roll the dice and move the corresponding number of spaces. If you plan your strategy well (and with a little luck), you'll move up the ladder. The faster you move up the ladder, the closer you come to winning the game. But there's a little more risk involved at the top of the board. The possibility of landing on a snake increases, and if you land on a snake, you sail back down and have to start all over again. Structuring a ladder (no snakes, though) to accommodate your bond portfolio is a worthwhile strategy for some folks. Unlike the game, a bond ladder involves more time and patience, but the rewards are much greater!

A bond ladder is not an actual physical device, but a strategy of investing your money in bonds. When you create a ladder, you invest in bonds with maturity dates scheduled consecutively over a number of years. A laddered portfolio includes a range of securities with varying maturities.

Here's how it works. If you want to invest $100,000 of your investment portfolio in bonds, you could choose to divide the money into a number of parts rather than sink all $100,000 into just one bond. Let's say it's January 3, 1999, and you are strategically planning out your bond portfolio. You decide the best strategy is to ladder your bond portfolio with government bonds.

You may want to divide up your money into ten parts of $10,000 each. You would buy government bonds that mature year after year starting in 2000. Therefore, the longest maturity date would be the year 2009. After you construct your laddered portfolio, the idea is to hold on to the bond securities until maturity. As the bonds mature, you would reinvest the proceeds at the end of your ladder. For example, in 2000, when your first bond matures, you would reinvest the proceeds in a bond that has a maturity date of 2010.

Your laddered portfolio would look like this:

Bond 1	$10,000	Invest in 1-yr. Government of Canada (GOC) bond @ 4.67 yield	Matures next year (year 2000)
Bond 2	$10,000	Invest in 2-yr. GOC bond @ 5.22 yield	Matures in 2001
Bond 3	$10,000	Invest in 3-yr. GOC bond @ 5.57 yield	Matures in 2002
Bond 4	$10,000	Invest in 4-yr. GOC bond @ 5.76 yield	Matures in 2003
Bond 5	$10,000	Invest in 5-yr. GOC bond @ 5.94 yield	Matures in 2004
Bond 6	$10,000	Invest in 6-yr. GOC bond @ 6.14 yield	Matures in 2005
Bond 7	$10,000	Invest in 7-yr. GOC bond @ 6.25 yield	Matures in 2006

Bond 8	$10,000	Invest in 8-yr. GOC bond @ 6.40 yield	Matures in 2007
Bond 9	$10,000	Invest in 9-yr. GOC bond @ 6.51 yield	Matures in 2008
Bond 10	$10,000	Invest in 10-yr. GOC bond @ 6.72 yield	Matures in 2009

A bond ladder is a financial-planning tool that defines a simple way to increase yields without taking on much more risk. You increase your yields because, by extending maturities, you take advantage of the higher rates paid on longer-term bonds. There's your answer to the $64,000 question.

Plus, if rates move even higher, you will always have a bond security coming due (maturing) that year to take advantage of any other higher-yielding investment. Remember, though, this investment strategy only works if you hold these bonds until maturity. If you follow through with this system, you will always be able to take advantage of the most recent interest rates with the monies that are maturing. Even if rates are going lower, keep in mind that you don't have to worry about having all of your money locked into a lower rate since you alternated your maturity periods. What a way to ride the rates!

You can protect some of your liquidity by scheduling your shorter-term securities on your bond ladder to mature at times when you know you need the funds. For example, if you are planning to buy a house next year or if your granddaughter Brittney will be starting private school, you can stagger the maturities on the securities to come due when you need the money. You are in control!

The Least You Need To Know

➤ A bond is nothing more than an IOU from its issuer. The issuer could be the Canadian government, a foreign government, a city, a province, or a corporation. Regardless of who it is, the issuer is the borrower, and you are the lender. Because you lent them your money for a certain amount of time, the issuer promises to pay you back in full on a certain date, plus pay a set amount of interest (the coupon rate).

➤ There is an inverse relationship between interest rates and bond prices. When interest rates go up, bond prices go down. When interest rates go down, bond prices go up.

➤ Even though bonds were once thought to be the investment for safety, they do not escape all risks. Most risks can be avoided if you buy a bond and hold it to maturity. Look at the investment pyramid in Chapter 5 to see where they fit into the scheme of things.

➤ Creating a laddered portfolio by investing in bonds with staggered maturities can reduce some risk and increase yields.

➤ If you follow the yield curve, you can pretty much figure out the direction of both short-term and long-term interest rates. If you figure out the direction of interest rates, you can pattern your investment decisions about buying and selling bonds accordingly.

➤ Unfortunately, no one can accurately predict future interest rates. So no one can predict future bond prices, either.

The safest way to double your money is to fold it over once and put it in your pocket.

—Kin Hubbard

Investing with the Government

When you think of the Canadian government, what images come to mind? The Prime Minister? Hefty tax bills? The House of Commons? What about investments?

The Canadian government is one of the most common and safest places you can invest your money. Why? Because the Canadian government puts its full faith and credit on all of its securities. As you read this chapter, you'll learn what types of government securities exist and how you can make money from them.

We Want You!

A rather reputable trader named Bernard Baruch used to say: "I'm not as concerned about the return on my money as I am about the return *of* my money!" Investors in government securities have followed this old maxim to the letter.

There are different types of government issuers for debt. They range from the federal government to the provincial governments to the municipal governments, each with their own credit rating.

Credit risk shows the financial soundness of the company that is borrowing money through issuing fixed-income securities. Companies with a strong financial position, good income prospects, and a low level of outstanding debt probably will receive a high credit rating.

Why would the government need to borrow money? The government issues debt instruments (securities) in the form of Treasury bills, government bonds and savings bonds to finance its deficit spending.

The Canadian government had more than $574 billion in debt as of the 1995–96 fiscal year. This debt is the money that the government has borrowed over the years, and it keeps growing. Therefore, when you invest with the government, you are loaning the government your money to help finance its deficit spending.

One of the biggest reasons people invest in federal government securities is because anyone who invests in them will receive their money back when promised. There really isn't any credit risk when you invest in government securities.

Traditionally, federal government securities have the reputation of being safe investments. They are backed by the full faith and credit of the Canadian government. Not too many other bond investments can make this claim. Due to the safety factor, however, the interest rates paid on government bonds are lower than that of comparable bonds of different issuers.

The introduction of new fixed-income products in the early 1980s, and the wide swings in interest rates in the past few decades, have caused government securities to rise and fall more frequently than in the past. Fixed-income securities do experience a lot of price volatility. When interest rates rise, bond prices fall. That means that the value of your bonds fluctuates either higher or lower than the original purchase price, depending upon the general direction of interest rates.

The value of government securities also rises and falls along with that of other fixed-income securities, but the Canadian government's claim to fame of being a creditworthy borrower keeps government bond investors sleeping soundly at night, knowing that when they wake up their principal will be safe.

Investing in securities with high credit quality is usually most apparent during economic downturns. During an economic slowdown or even a recession, investors usually make a shift to quality. Why? During these hard times, companies with a lower credit rating may have difficulties in meeting the interest payments and/or principal obligations of their outstanding debt. You are more likely to see companies file for bankruptcy during hard times versus prosperous times. As a result, investors will move toward those investments that hold a high credit rating during poor economic conditions.

If the economy is experiencing a slowdown or a recession, consider looking into better fixed-income investments, such as government securities.

Three Ways to Security

The three main classes of government securities are the following: Treasury bills (T-bills), government bonds, and government strip bonds. Each is backed by the full faith and credit of the Canadian government. The differences lie in the minimum investment amount and the length of available maturities.

Interestingly, market watchers view government securities as benchmarks to the interest rate world. The Canadian Treasury bill is widely quoted and compared to other investments. In fact, big-time investors and financial gurus will speak of how well or how poorly an investment did compared to a similar government security.

Government bonds are *coupon* securities, and government strip bonds are *zero-coupon* securities (the coupon has been "stripped" from the bond). Treasury bills and strip bonds are considered *discount* securities. The difference is that discount securities, such as T-bills and strip bonds, don't pay any interest. You purchase the security at a "discount" from its face value, and at maturity you receive the full face value. The difference between the discount price and the face value received at maturity is the "interest" earned on the investment. Strip bonds act like T-bills, but have a term to maturity of more than a year. Coupon securities (bonds), on the other hand, pay interest semi-annually and the face value at maturity. The interest payments that you receive are fully taxable in the year that you receive them.

T-Bill, Oh What a Thrill!

Commonly referred to as T-bills, these securities are issued with varying maturity dates: three-month, six-month, and one-year maturities. The minimum purchase is $5,000 and they are sold in increments as small as $1,000 thereafter.

T-Bills are short-term securities of less than one year that are purchased at a discount and then mature at face value.

A T-bill differs (as do strip bonds) from the other government securities in the way the interest payments are calculated. There is no specified interest rate at all. Investing in a T-bill would work as follows. Typically, you would buy a T-bill at less than its $1,000 face value. For example, if you bought one six-month T-bill, you would not pay $1,000 for it but rather an amount that is less, perhaps $950. Because you are buying the T-bill for less than its true value, you are buying it at a discount from its face value.

It's math time. If you bought a $1,000 six-month T-bill for $950 and held it until maturity (when you would receive the face amount of $1000 back), you would receive $1,000 on the maturity date. The return on this investment is $50.

$$\$1,000 - \$950 = \$50$$

The difference between the price you bought it at and the price you sell it at is your interest. In this scenario, you earned 5.26% over six months on your investment ($50/$950). (Annually, your return would be 10.52%.)

Government Bonds

The length of maturity for government bonds, both federal and provincial, is longer than T-bills—in one year intervals from one year to thirty years out. The federal government is the largest single issuer in the Canadian bond market, having about $234.1 billion of debt outstanding at the end of 1994 (excluding T-bills).

Unlike T-bills or strip bonds, government bonds carry a definite interest rate on the face value of the security and pay interest every six months. Plus, you do not need as much money up front to buy a government bond. The minimum investment for a government bond is $1,000. Government bonds trade in increments of $1,000. When a government bond is trading below $1,000, which is known as par, it is said to be trading at a discount. This is why government bonds are considered to be priced at a *discount to yield*. If it is trading at $1,000, it is trading at par. If the government bond is trading above $1,000, it is priced over par at a premium.

As mentioned earlier, when you read a bond quote in a newspaper you will see a dollar price and a *yield-to-maturity (YTM)*. This yield-to-maturity represents the approximate return on your investment if you were to purchase the security at the quoted ask/offer price and hold the security to maturity.

There are a few assumptions made when calculating the yield-to-maturity. First, all interest payments can be reinvested at the yield-to-maturity. Second, you must reinvest all of your interest payments. This means that if you purchase a note or a bond that is quoted as having a 7.00% YTM, you take all of your semi-annual interest payments and reinvest those proceeds at a rate equal to 7.00%. The reality is that it is highly unlikely that you'll be able to reinvest all proceeds at that rate.

One more thing. When you purchase a government bond, you will receive a full six months' worth of interest on the next scheduled coupon payment date no matter if you held the security for the full six months or three days. If you bought a bond three days before it pays interest, you will receive the full interest payment, which represents six months' worth of interest, or approximately 180 days. But this doesn't seem fair to the person who sold you the bond. To compensate the seller, there is what is called *accrued interest*. In this case, the seller would receive accrued interest to compensate him or her for holding the bond up to three days before interest is paid. So the total cost to you will be the dollar price plus any accrued interest. The prices that you see in the newspapers are only the dollar price and do not include any accrued interest.

For example, if you bought a $10,000 face value 8% bond on February 15, and interest payments are made on January 1 and July 1 of every year, it has been forty-six days since the last payment. Take forty-six and divide it by the actual number of days between January 1 and

July 1. Get out your calendars! Assuming February has twenty-eight days, the total actual number of days should be one hundred and eighty-one. (Add up the first six months of the year.)

So now the whole calculation looks like this:

Accrued interest = principal x rate x time

= $10,000 x 0.040 (that's 4%, i.e., half of 8% because it's semi-annual) x 46/181

= $101.66

Now what about those semi-annual interest payments you receive? If you really want to be a math whiz, figure it out with this formula: accrued interest = principal x rate x time. The principal "ingredient" never changes. But the rate and time factors are different.

For example, to figure out how much interest you're going to receive on your bonds, know that you are paid semi-annually, meaning every six months. So for a $10,000 face value 8% bond, you will use half the annual rate to make your calculations. Cut the 8% in half to 4%, and plug it into the rate section of the formula. Therefore, every six months you'll receive $400.00. That's your fixed return.

Fortunately, you don't have to whip out the calculators or consult the math nerd in your son's trigonometry class. Whenever you buy a bond, the interest payments are already calculated for you. I just wanted to see if you were paying attention. Those of you who didn't follow, back up and try again. After all, it's your money!

Because bond prices move in the opposite direction of interest rates, there is more price volatility (ups and downs) in longer-term government bonds. The longer the maturity, the bigger the swings in prices as these bonds are bought and sold.

Government Strip Bonds

Government Strip Bonds (or "Strips" as they are commonly referred to) are created from the "stripping" of the coupon payments from the principal of the underlying bond. (Strips, by the way, can be created from any bond, not just government ones.) They operate very similarly to T-Bills as they sell at a discount and mature at their full face value. Strips exhibit greater price volatility than conventional bonds of equivalent term. A strip entitles the holder to a single payment at maturity with no interest in the interim. With the purchase of a strip bond, you know the maturity date, the amount you'll receive on that day, and the exact yield from your date of purchase if held to maturity. The term to maturity ranges from one to thirty years.

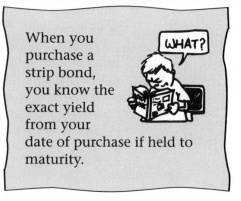

When you purchase a strip bond, you know the exact yield from your date of purchase if held to maturity.

Strip bonds do not pay any interest until maturity but you pay tax on the interest that is earned each year, as if it were paid out. The government treats the difference between what you pay and what you will receive at maturity as deemed interest. Therefore, you have to report this interest as it accumulates each year on your tax return. This is why strip bonds are so popular in RRSPs, RESPs, and RRIFs—because they are untouched by taxes.

The benefits of these zero-coupon bonds are threefold. First, if they're issued by the government, you get the backing of the Canadian government. Second, you get a slightly better yield if you buy and hold them to maturity than if you were to buy a government bond and hold it to maturity. Lastly, you can buy them at a discount with them maturing at their full face value, thereby avoiding reinvestment risk.

Buy, Sell, or Hold?

Here are some buying scenarios that can help you make decisions about buying, holding, and selling government securities.

➤ If you buy a ten-year government bond and hold it until maturity, you'll receive the face value of the bond.

➤ However, if you were to sell the bond before it matures, then you would be exposed to any swings in interest rates and the ups and downs in prices that are currently the norm in the bond market. As a result, the proceeds you receive can be different than the face value.

➤ If you bought a ten-year government bond with a face value of $1,000 at 95 ($950) with a 10% coupon rate and held it until maturity, you would get $1,000 when it matured. (You've also generated a capital gain of $50 ($1,000 – $950) which is taxable if held outside a tax-sheltered plan). Plus, over the ten years, you could collect $50 every six months in interest payments.

➤ But what if it's only four years into the life of the bond and interest rates are falling? Your ten-year bond is now worth more than what you paid for it. You know this because you understand that when interest rates fall, bond prices rise. You may sell the bond before it matures, thus following the cardinal rule of buying low and selling high. However, once you sell the bond you give up any future interest payments and just keep your profit. Keep in mind that your profit can only be invested at the new, lower rates.

Consult your broker regarding different government security offerings and their yields. He or she can make suggestions and do the buying and selling of the bonds for you.

They Make Great Presents

Canada Savings Bonds are available for sale every October.

Canada Savings Bonds (CSBs), and provincial savings bonds, like other government securities, are safe—they are backed by the full faith and credit of the Canadian government. Unlike other bonds, CSBs can be cashed by the owner at any bank in Canada at any time. CSBs do not rise and fall in price and may always be cashed at their full par value plus any accrued interest. Purchasers must be Canadian residents and the bonds cannot to transferred.

Since 1977, CSBs have been available in two forms: a regular interest bond and a compound interest bond. The regular interest bond pays annual interest on November 1 each year. The compound interest bond forgoes the receipt of annual interest to allow the unpaid interest to compound annually and therefore earn interest on the accumulated interest.

The reason Canada Savings Bonds have been so popular among Canadians is because they are available in smaller denominations. You can buy them for as little as $100 each, with other denominations of $300, $500, $1000, $5,000, and $10,000.

How do they trade? Well, you don't buy them on the open market or at auction, nor are they bought and sold on the floor of a financial exchange. Instead, you can purchase them at your local bank or brokerage firm.

Bet You Didn't Know

The government imposes a maximum purchase limit for savings bonds and sets these limits each year. The maximum purchase limit for each series has ranged from a low of $1,000 to a high of $75,000.

So why should you invest in the Canadian government? Because government securities issued are considered one of the safest investment vehicles around. Most government bonds, for example, are noncallable, which means the government cannot call your bonds in before maturity. Therefore, the re-investment risk is reduced.

Noncallable, shown as "NC" on a bond certificate or trade confirmation, means the issuer cannot "call back" and redeem your bond before the date of maturity.

The Least You Need To Know

➤ Investors purchase government securities because of their high degree of safety. They are conservative investments and provide a steady stream of income every six months if held to maturity (with the exception of Treasury bills and strip bonds which you buy at a discount and receive your interest income on the day of maturity).

➤ Government bonds trade in increments of $1,000. When a government bond is trading below $1,000, which is known as par, it is said to be trading at a discount. This is why government bonds are considered to be priced at a discount to yield. If it is trading at $1,000, it is trading at par. If the government bond is trading above $1,000, it is priced over par at a premium.

➤ Another government security is the savings bond (Canada Savings Bonds or provincial savings bonds), which can be purchased in smaller denominations with as little as $100.

The use of money is all the advantage there is in having it.

—Benjamin Franklin

MBS, Corporate, and High-Yield Bonds

In this chapter

➤ What an MBS and Corporate or High-Yield Bonds Are

➤ Bond Credit Ratings Re-visited

➤ Why you should invest in them

Now that you have a grip on the bond market and the various government bonds available, let's turn our attention to some of the other fixed-income products out there. Remember, fixed-income products are those that guarantee a fixed stream of interest or dividend income.

Mortgage-Backed Securities (MBS)

When a high-yielding investment is safe, guaranteed, and offers liquidity, it's no wonder that it would become popular with investors. An MBS, which stands for a mortgage-backed security, offers all these features. Each MBS represents a pool of mortgages. Each pool is a collection of mortgages like the mortgage you or I would have on a house. The creation of an MBS begins when a financial institution participates in the National Housing Act (NHA) MBS process by advancing a loan

WHAT? An MBS is a Mortgage-Backed Security. It represents a pool of mortgages guaranteed by the Canada Mortgage and Housing Corp.

on a residential property. The financial institution then gathers several of these mortgages and packages them into a pool, typically of $10 to $30 million in size, and becomes an MBS issuer. MBSs are then sold in minimum multiples of $5,000 and have varying terms to maturity.

Every month, the financial institution collects monthly payments of interest and principal from the homeowners and deposits them into a trust account. The Canada Mortgage and Housing Corporation (CMHC) then remits the funds in the trust account to the MBS investors. The CMHC guarantees each mortgage in the pool against default, and also provides a timely payment guarantee to the investor, so that any shortfall in the trust account will be made up by cash provided by the CMHC. The CMHC is also a federal Crown corporation, so that MBSs are therefore backed by the full faith and credit of the government of Canada.

Mortgage-Backed Securities come with specific terms and conditions. These specifics would include the term (let's say five years), the interest rate (7%) and whether or not it is an open or closed mortgage. An open mortgage allows the customer to pay off the mortgage early—in this case, before the five-year term. (Depending on the terms of the mortgage there may or may not be a small penalty associated with paying off the mortgage early.) On the other hand, a closed-end mortgage does not allow the customer to pay off the mortgage early.

Now, as an investor in an MBS you want to make sure of a couple of things. The first thing you want to find out before you purchase anything is if the MBS is open or closed. In most cases you will want a closed MBS. This means you know the term of the MBS, meaning that you will know it will pay you that 7% for five years. If the MBS is open, it may be paid off before the five years are up and you will have to find another product to invest your money in—maybe at a lower rate. Essentially, the closed MBS takes the uncertainty out of investing.

One of the most attractive features of MBSs is that they pay their interest on a monthly basis. Most bonds pay interest every six months. Many investors rely on income from their portfolio to help pay the bills, so an instrument that pays on a monthly basis is very attractive. One other key feature is that MBSs are RRSP and RRIF eligible, which means your investment remains tax-sheltered while in the plan.

Corporate or High-Yield Bonds

Corporate bonds, also known as High-Yield bonds, are debt issued by corporations. They are considered high-yield debt because they tend to be rated BBB or lower (remember those bond ratings in Chapter 21?). A BBB rating indicates a medium-grade credit quality. For taking on some risk (i.e., a slightly lower bond rating) you are rewarded with a higher return, hence the name high-yield bonds.

As you know, governments issue debt. The federal government issues debt or raises money by selling products to the general public like Canada Savings Bonds (CSBs), or Government of Canada bonds, or T-Bills. Corporations, too, need to raise money as well from time to time and they do this by selling their bonds, just like the government would, to the bond market.

Corporate bonds are just like Government of Canada bonds. The major obvious difference is the issuer. Corporate bonds are backed by the corporation that issues the bond. As with government bonds, corporate bonds are rated to establish an investment quality grading on the bond. There are two independent bodies that rate bonds and attach their rating for the investor to use. The two

The Advantages of an MBS:

➤ Safety. MBSs are guaranteed by the Canada Mortgage and Housing Corp, which is a federal Crown corporation, meaning they have the backing of the government of Canada.

➤ High yields. Historically, MBS yields are higher than Government of Canada bonds of equivalent term.

➤ Liquidity. MBSs can be sold prior to maturity.

➤ Monthly income convenience.

➤ RRSP/RRIF eligibility.

Corporate Bonds, also called high-yield bonds, are debt issued by corporations.

independent bodies are Canadian Bond Rating Service (CBRS) and Dominion Bond Rating Services (DBRS). (The bond rating list is shown in Chapter 21.)

Corporate bonds are rated lower than government bonds. So, by definition, corporate bonds present a higher credit risk to the bond-holder. In other words, the risk of the issuer not paying the interest payments is greater with a corporation then it would be with the government of Canada. This means that the government bond would be rated higher than the corporate bond, say, for example, AA while the corporate bond might be rated BBB or lower. To compensate for this additional risk, you are paid a higher rate of interest. So you get more interest than you would if you owned a Government of Canada bond that matured at the same time.

Many of the corporations you see issuing debt are companies you would find in the TSE 300 index. In fact, over 70% of the companies in the TSE 300 would have their debt rated BBB or lower if they were to issue debt.

Always Check the Bond Credit Rating

Not all corporate bonds are necessarily good investments. The credit rating analysis is very important especially on the corporate bonds that are rated very low or not at all. A *credit rating analysis* basically analyzes the ability of the issuer (the corporation) to pay off their debt. The problem with this analysis is that it is an ongoing process. As a result it requires a great deal of time, not to mention expertise. Do not be discouraged. Your broker can advise you in this area.

Before you invest in any bond, check the bond credit rating.

Another option would be to look into investing in a high-yield bond mutual fund. As explained in Part V, one of the advantages of investing in mutual funds is professional money management. In this case, the fund manager performs the credit risk analysis for you on an ongoing basis. Be careful, though: just because a mutual fund has the term "high yield" in its title does not mean it only invests in corporate debt. Make sure you look into the types of investments the mutual fund holds before you put your money on the table.

Risk Versus Reward

Having said all that, corporate bonds or high-yield mutual funds may not necessarily be for you. They are riskier than Government of Canada bonds but less risky than equities. In other words, if company MNO issued bonds and stock, investing in an MNO corporate bond would have less risk than investing in the stock. Why? Can anybody tell me? The greatest risk in investing is that one of the companies you invest in will go bankrupt and close up shop. If MNO closed up shop, then any money that was left over from their operations would go to pay off the bondholders first and then—and only then—would the owners of equity (or stock) get their chance. (You guessed it: stock holders rarely see any money.)

> Assess your own risk tolerance. This will help you develop your financial strategy and decide what types of investments to hold in your portfolio. Remember, the higher your tolerance for risk, the higher the potential returns.

What does all this mean? It means that the corporate bond, although a bond, behaves differently than a Government of Canada bond. The differences are in the risk and returns. The higher your tolerance for risk, the greater the potential returns. High-yield bonds can help diversify the investments in your portfolio. If you can deal with the added risk and volatility, certainly look to some exposure to high-yield bonds.

If you have put together your financial battle plan, and assessed your risk tolerance as outlined in Chapters 3 and 5 (very important chapters to make notes from, by the way), you should know what type of investments you'll be comfortable with, and whether corporate bonds fit in there. If you haven't set your financial goals yet—what are you waiting for? Make your money work for you; the earlier you start, the bigger the payoff will be.

The Least You Need To Know

➤ Mortgage-backed securities, or MBSs, represent pools of mortgages that offer safety, liquidity, and high yields.

➤ Corporate bonds, also known as high-yield bonds, are debt issued by corporations offering high yields due to medium grade (or below) bond credit ratings.

➤ Before you buy any bond, make sure to check the bond credit rating.

Part 5
Mutual Fund Mania

A mutual fund is an organization whose only business is investing your money. They don't make widgets or gizmos. They invest everyone's money by "pooling" it together to buy or sell stocks, bonds, or a combination of the two. You can choose from different types of mutual funds based on your investment objective.

So, if you're like most people who don't have a million bucks or even $100,000, your near-perfect answer is a mutual fund. As you read through this section on mutual funds, you will discover one of the biggest secrets on the stock and bond markets that may help you realize many of your financial dreams, such as a child's university education, a new home, or retirement. The secret? It is…well, I can't reveal that on the first page now, can I? But you'll find out.

EENY, MEENIE, MINY, MO,...

Chapter 24

The Wide World of Mutual Funds

In this chapter

➤ One of the biggest money-making strategies on the stock and bond markets

➤ What is a mutual fund?

➤ How to select mutual funds that are the best for you

Imagine an investment that doesn't require a large initial investment, allows you access to your money all the time, and is as safe or as risky as you want it to be. It sounds too perfect, right? You're probably asking yourself, "So what's the catch?" Guess what, folks. There really isn't one. Keep reading this chapter to learn how mutual funds are an excellent way for you to make money on the markets, no matter how old you are or how much money you have. Remember, even if you only have $250 or $500 to invest, don't believe it's impossible to make money. Why? Because you are still rich enough to buy one of the best investment products around—mutual funds.

Basic Training

In a mutual fund, many investors (whether they have a lot of money or only a little bit) pool their money into a large fund organized by investment professionals. In this pool, investors own shares, depending on how much money they put in. The more money you invest, the more shares you can buy. What do these shares represent? All kinds of stocks and bonds from some of the best-run companies in the world.

A mutual fund is as close as you can get to a perfect investment product. You can cash them in whenever you need the money; therefore, mutual funds are extremely liquid. They tend to keep your risks down, too, because they implement the strategy of diversification. Mutual funds don't completely eliminate risk, but they can bring the risks down to a comfortable level, depending on what fund you invest in and what your investment objectives are.

Those are just the basics. As you continue to develop further knowledge about making money in mutual funds, you'll find they may be a great way to get your feet wet in the investment world.

A Little Trivia

You should know by now that I love to tell stories and give pop quizzes. So, here goes. Although the very first mutual fund was created somewhere in Europe during the 1800s, the mutual fund industry hasn't even been around for a century in Canada. The first Canadian mutual fund was established more than sixty years ago. Today, mutual fund companies manage over $250 billion in assets in more than 15 million accounts. And these numbers are still on the rise; mutual funds have multiplied like rabbits. Currently, there are more than fifteen hundred mutual funds available in Canada, and the industry is booming! Mutual funds are one of the most common vehicles and best alternatives for average Canadians to own different types of securities like stocks and bonds.

Why? Well, I'll let you answer that in my—SURPRISE!!!—pop quiz!

Question #1 Why are mutual funds a good investment for all investors?

a) Because they offer diversification, and you don't have to put all of your eggs into one basket.

b) Because they offer you the advantage of professional management (without paying a high professional price for it) and they do most of the work for you.

c) Because you can get in and out of the mutual fund easily, meaning it's a liquid investment.

d) Because I said so.

e) All of the above.

The correct answer is e, of course!

Question #2 How old are you?

a) 18–34

b) 35–50

c) 51–65

d) 66–89

> **Diversification** is the concept of not putting all of your eggs in one basket, i.e., spreading the risk by purchasing several types of investments. Mutual funds offer this strategy for investors because each fund purchases so many different types of stocks or bonds.

Whatever your answer, your age is a big determinant in selecting a mutual fund. Some Investment Advisors advise that the more time you have on your side, the more aggressive you can be in your approach. For example, some will advise younger clients to invest eighty percent of their dollars in aggressive mutual funds, while advising older clients and retirees to allocate only twenty percent of their money to the same category. The longer you invest, the more you can temper risk.

How Do I Buy Mutual Fund Units?

Investing in a mutual fund is quite simple. You can purchase both *load* and *no-load* funds from your broker (or directly from some mutual fund companies). Load funds are those mutual funds that may charge you a sales fee. No-load funds do not charge their shareholders any sales fees. Which is better? You'll find out in Chapter 26.

Most if not all mutual fund companies will send you information about their families of funds at your request. In the Appendix there is a list of companies, along with their phone numbers and addresses that you can contact. Or, you can ask your broker for his or her recommendations and further information. Once you have decided which mutual funds to buy, your broker can then process the transaction for you. You can also have money automatically debited from your bank account monthly and invested in the mutual fund.

Be sure to read the fund's prospectus and performance information (refer to Chapter 6) and follow up on an ongoing basis.

Once you invest, you will receive a monthly statement detailing information about your mutual fund, including how many shares you own and how much your portfolio is worth. Plus, you'll receive a statement every single time you make a purchase or sales transaction.

How Do I Sell My Mutual Fund Shares?

Selling your mutual fund shares is known as redeeming your shares or a *redemption*. To do this, simply contact your broker and let him or her know how much money you need from your investment. It usually takes about three business days for the transaction to clear. At that point, you can request that a cheque be sent to you.

The Whole Kit 'N' Kaboodle

For those of you who are developing long-term financial plans, mutual funds offer one of the best ways to stick to those plans and reach your financial goals. If you invest in a mutual fund over the long haul, you don't have to worry about timing your investment. The guesswork is eliminated for two reasons. First, mutual funds are one of the best ways to diversify, especially if you are dealing with a small amount of money (e.g. $100 or $500). Second, you have access to professional management. Remember when I said you'll have access to the best investment advice around? The investment professionals who make all of the buy and sell decisions in the mutual fund are known as *portfolio managers*.

Are They Any Good?

Portfolio managers of some mutual funds are good, and some are not so good. How can you pick the best from the rest?

You have to know how to study their track records and style of investing and pick a good-quality fund that is in line with your investment objectives. If not, make sure you are dealing with a broker or salesperson who knows enough about mutual funds to help you choose the right one for you.

There are two major styles of investing that mutual fund managers use. The first is *top-down*. Using this approach, managers look at the bigger picture, or analyze things on a macro level. They try and decide where we are in the business cycle and then over-weight their holdings in sectors that are outperforming the market.

The second style of investing that mutual fund managers use is *bottom-up*. Bottom-up investing examines the individual company, at the micro level, and looks for value, regardless of where we might be in the business cycle.

Once you become familiar with different styles of management, some Investment Advisors would recommend you consider different styles within the same asset class. For example, if you have 40% of your portfolio in Canadian equity (i.e., stocks), you might look at splitting that 40% across both a mutual fund that uses a top-down approach to investing and one that uses a bottom-up approach. In this way, you can diversify management styles within the same asset class.

The performance of a mutual fund isn't necessarily based on the skill of its portfolio manager. True, the final decision about whether to buy or sell a stock or bond for the fund rests with the portfolio manager, but he or she has access to some of the best research reports around that you might not be able to get your hands on. In addition, portfolio managers typically have their own research staff to provide them with the information they need to make better buying and selling decisions.

> **Portfolio managers** are the people who decide what types of securities to buy and sell in a specific mutual fund, keeping in line with the fund's objectives. The fund's collection of securities, typically stocks or bonds, is known as a **portfolio.**

What Else Do They Offer?

To sum up, if you invest in a mutual fund, you benefit in several of the following ways:

➤ **Instant diversification.** When you invest in mutual funds, you are buying into a pool of funds that is already invested in numerous securities (stocks, bonds, or a combination). In this way, you share in the profit or loss of that entire pool of investments. Even if you invest as little as $100, you are diversified across many securities. On the other hand, if you turned around and invested your $100 in the stock market, you would only be able to purchase a few shares of one or two companies. You can even diversify across different investing styles!

➤ **Professional management.** Professional mutual fund managers make the day-to-day investment decisions for the fund. This means that you do not have to spend all day watching the markets trying to decide whether you should buy Company A and sell Company B.

➤ **Lower fees and charges.** Because mutual funds are made up of hundreds of different stocks and bonds, the portfolio manager pays reduced commission rates when buying the securities (as low as two cents a share). This way there are no exorbitant fees to pass on to you, the investor/shareholder. Over time, you have more of your money going to work for you instead of having fees or charges eating up your principal.

➤ **Convenience.** Unless you elect otherwise, the monies you receive from any dividends and capital gains go to buy more shares in the fund, even if they only buy a fraction of a share. Over time, reinvested dividends and capital gains work for you because they continue to buy more shares—and these fractional shares will add up!

➤ **Automatic investment plans.** When you read Chapter 27, you'll discover another advantage to buying mutual funds. You can set up a monthly purchase plan where money from your bank or brokerage account is directly deposited to your mutual fund—without lifting a finger. Convenience. I love it.

NAVPS—What Does It Mean to Me?

NAVPS stands for *Net Asset Value Per Share*. This is how a mutual fund is priced. If you can comprehend how a mutual fund is priced, you will understand one of the ways to buy a mutual fund.

Each trading day, usually in the afternoon, the total market value of the securities (stocks, bonds, and so on) the fund owns are added up. For example, if the fund owns one thousand shares of common stock of the Toronto-Dominion Bank, and it closed at $45.50 per share, the calculation is like this: 1000 x 45.50 = $45,500. The fund does this for each individual security. It then adds up the value of its other assets, such as any cash (dollars and cents) it has or that is owed to it. The entire total provides a figure from which the fund subtracts all of its liabilities, as well as any other fees it owes elsewhere.

The result is the total net assets. This figure is then divided by the number of shares outstanding (the total number of shares that you and all the other investors own in the fund), which ultimately gives the net asset value (NAVPS) for each share.

What does all this mean? When the market value of the securities goes up, the NAVPS goes up. On the other hand, when the market value of the securities goes down, so does the NAVPS. When you invest in a mutual fund, you buy it at its NAVPS. Simply put, if you have $5,000 to invest in the Sky's the Limit Mutual Fund with its NAVPS at $10, you can buy five hundred shares in the fund.

However, in the real world, if you want to invest in a mutual fund, you do so by buying new shares from the fund at the NAVPS that's calculated at the end of the day. This means you never know at *exactly* what price you will get your order, whether it's a buy or a sell. (A sell is known as a *redemption*.) This is mutual fund pricing rule number one: All orders received by the fund before the cut-off time (check with your Financial Advisor for specific times) are executed at whatever NAVPS price is calculated at the end of the day. Therefore, the execution price (the price at which you'll buy your shares) is only figured after the close.

The exception to this rule is for **money market funds**. The share price of a money market fund is usually a constant $10.00 per share, so the NAVPS is always known. In money market funds, your money is invested in safe and liquid securities, including short-term government securities.

There are different newsletters that cover the mutual fund industry. Here's a list of a few newsletters that will help get you started.

➤ *The Canadian Mutual Fund Advisor*. Devoted exclusively to mutual funds, this advisory is published bi-weekly. New funds are spotlighted and existing funds are constantly monitored and reviewed for portfolio holdings, past performance, management style and risk level. Over 1200 mutual funds are covered. New subscribers receive a one-year introductory rate of $63.50. To subscribe, you can call MPL Communications collect at (416) 869-1177.

➤ *The Financial Post* publishes the quarterly *Survey of Mutual Funds*, which contains information on more than 1400 funds, a glossary of terms that defines fund types, year-over-year percentage changes in value, rates of return and more. Each edition costs $69.95 and an annual subscription to four quarterly editions is $149.95. To order, call (800) 661-POST (ask for Operator 7).

➤ *Gordon Pape's Mutual Funds Update*. To stay on top of your funds, this newsletter gives reviews and recommendations of mutual funds in light of current economic conditions. It's published six times a year and costs $37.40 (which includes GST) per year. Call (800) 567-3800 ext. 273 to order.

➤ *All-Canadian Mutual Fund Guide*. This guide delivers solid financial advice to create awareness about the possibilities within mutual funds. It's available at newsstands for $4.50, or you can call (416) 480-9425.

One Final Note

If you're among the gazillion consumers dazzled by some of the high investment returns that mutual funds are reporting in your local and national media these days, you're not alone. Just getting your feet wet is a bit easier with a mutual fund than if you were to sink all of your cash into just stocks, or only bonds. Building an investment portfolio of more than just one mutual fund is even a good investment strategy— for anyone. If you're hot on a trail of last year's winner and blindly decide to write a cheque, well, that's not a smart money move at all. Here are some hints for getting started in mutual fund investing.

➤ **If you're just starting out in mutual funds, pick a mutual fund company that offers a variety of different types of funds, such as various stock and bond funds.** This way, you can learn as much as you can about all the different types of funds in your "fund family." Another important point: Make sure that you can switch from one fund to another at no additional charge.

➤ **Keep things simple.** A conservative investor needs to start somewhere, but start slowly. Don't jump in too quickly. Start out by buying only one or two funds that are in line with your investment expectations and financial goals.

➤ **Although mutual funds offer conveniences, do not simply invest in a fund and then forget about it.** You must be able to monitor your mutual fund and your entire investment portfolio on an ongoing basis. Your risk-comfort level may change, and the financial markets may change—they usually do, don't they?

➤ **To find the right mix of what you should do, incorporate specific asset allocation strategies in your investment philosophy.** Mutual funds offer the best way to implement asset allocation. (Chapter 31 provides a good review of asset allocation strategies.) How? Because whether you have $100 or $100,000 to invest, you can help protect yourself against market fluctuations and economic uncertainties by determining the right investment mix specifically designed for you.

➤ **Proceed with caution, because if you don't do your homework, you will get burned.** True, mutual funds offer one of the best investment alternatives around. But the responsibility lies in understanding what they can and cannot do for your investment portfolio. Make sure you understand how much risk you are taking.

The Least You Need To Know

➤ Mutual funds pool all investor money into one fund that is designed to have a specific objective (which you'll learn more about in the following chapters) and continually offer new shares.

➤ Mutual funds offer many advantages, including convenience, small minimum investment requirements, diversification, and professional management.

➤ The best way to choose a mutual fund is to look at your whole investment picture and decide what you're trying to accomplish. Are you saving for retirement? A house? A month-long vacation for your golden anniversary? Ask yourself how much risk you can tolerate, and make sure you understand the relationship between risk and reward. The more exposure to risk, the more potential for reward.

➤ Your future comfort depends on how wisely you pick today. Don't blindly write out a cheque to last year's winner. Do your homework!

"In investing, the return you want should
depend on whether you want to eat well
or sleep well."

—J. Kenfield Morley

Chapter 25

What's the Name of Your Game?

In this chapter

➤ When you can begin investing in a mutual fund

➤ Different types of mutual fund objectives

➤ How to "go global" and reap the rewards of foreign investing

"Is now as good a time as any to invest?"

When people find out that I'm an Investment Advisor, that's the question they'll ask me nine times out of ten. The others usually want to know if I have a hot stock tip that will send their brokerage accounts out-of-town—to the moon! Well, you won't find any hot stock tips in this chapter, but you will learn about the different types of mutual funds you can invest in and the potential for making money in them over time.

Jumping In

Markets go up and down like two ten-year-olds on a teeter-totter, leaving small investors wondering when they should begin their investment plan. My answer? When it comes to mutual funds, as soon as you're ready.

True, stock prices tend to move in cycles, but it is difficult to pick a point in the cycle when prices are low instead of when prices are high. What about bonds? That all depends on the direction of interest rates, mainly.

You see, mutual funds often take the guesswork out of trying to time market fluctuations. You have professional portfolio managers to do that. It can be difficult for them, too, of course; if it wasn't, all mutual funds would be winners. But as long as you invest in a mutual fund, which represents a diversified portfolio of stocks and/or bonds, the movement in any one of these securities is likely to be offset by movements in the others.

Unfortunately, most investors respond to the changing market conditions precisely the way they shouldn't; they purchase securities when prices are really high because everybody and his brothers are gangbusters over the rise in prices. Then these same investors will turn around and sell near the end of a decline because they panic.

The best advice I've heard has been passed down through the years. It comes from legendary market watcher (and ultimately a millionaire) Bernard Baruch. His theory is based on the contrarian approach. "Buy straw hats in the winter time and your snowsuits in July." Think about it. How expensive is a snow suit in July? Not very. And when was the last time you needed a straw hat in the dead, cold, blustery days of winter? Probably never, unless you live in Hawaii and don't have to deal with Canada's winters. (I'm still getting the chill out of my bones.) The moral of the story: don't follow the crowd.

The best way to deal with market fluctuations is through dollar-cost averaging. Using this technique, you space your purchases out on a regular basis. You get more than an average cost here. You develop a habit of consistently making regular purchases, thus building a lifetime savings program that may ensure a rather comfortable lifestyle in the long run.

You Don't Have To Suffer from Fund Paralysis

There are more than fifteen hundred funds out there, representing hundreds of billions in assets. Short of throwing your hands up in frustration, which way do you turn?

You might already be familiar with some of the big fund families out there, such as Trimark, Templeton, and Mackenzie. Good. But what if you're not, and you don't have a clue about how to find a good fund?

When looking at the 1500 mutual funds that you can invest in, it can be intimidating. But those 1500 are broken down into three main fund categories: stock, bond, and money-market funds. The slight confusion comes from the different types of investment objectives found in each category. In the following sections, you will learn to identify the type of mutual fund you need to match up with your investment objectives and financial goals.

The Mutual Fund Mission

No matter what the fund invests in, it is classified according to the risk involved. Here's a sketch of each.

➤ **Aggressive growth.** Funds with this objective invest in companies or securities that usually achieve the greatest growth records over the longest haul. In fact, some of their long-term records are quite phenomenal, boasting as high as a 38% return over a five-year period. These funds do extremely well in bull markets. In bear markets, though, their shares are likely to suffer pretty sharp price drops. Out of all of the stock funds, these are the most risky. This kind of fund invests in mostly small-cap and some mid-cap companies.

➤ **Growth.** Go down a few levels on the investment pyramid for this one. Growth funds don't carry as much risk as aggressive growth funds do. The name of the game is the same, though: long-term growth is where it's at. Portfolio managers of growth funds tend to look into companies and securities with good, steady track records instead of putting emphasis on some fancy aggressive trading techniques. This kind of fund invests in mid-cap and large-cap companies.

➤ **Growth and income.** Growth is the key in these funds, too, but em-

Many small company stocks (which tend to be more risky) and international stocks are found in an aggressive growth fund. The risks are more intense, but the payoff is more rewarding if you can hold on for the ride.

Growth and income funds are good investment choices for older families and empty-nesters. They offer reduced risk when compared to a straight growth fund, yet they provide a steady level of income.

phasis is also put on investing in stable companies and securities that pay dividends. So you have the best of both worlds—long-term growth and dividend income. These are also sometimes referred to as "equity-income funds." An investor who is unsure about getting his feet wet and can only risk getting his big toe damp should look into a growth and income mutual fund. There is less risk involved here than with an aggressive growth or growth fund. You still get the best of both worlds with long-term growth and the potential for price appreciation and dividend income. Blue-chip stocks fall under this category.

➤ **Income.** Generally considered bond funds (you'll learn about them as you keep reading), income funds are mostly made up of bonds. These funds typically fall in the low to moderate risk level on the investment pyramid.

Stock Jocks

Stock funds (sometimes known as common stock funds) typically seek growth, usually over a long period of time through investments in the stock market. In a common stock fund, the value of your investment can fluctuate more on a month-to-month basis than in many other types of fund investments. Because of the fluctuation, you take on more risk. There are no guarantees that your investment will perform well. However, as you should already know, in exchange for more risk you have the potential to reap greater rewards.

Don't strive to constantly hit a home run with aggressive growth mutual funds. Make sure you choose a fund that will meet your investment objectives and that comes close to doing well over a longer period of time.

So why should you take these risks? Because those great rewards could mean quite a bit more money in your portfolio. That is why common stock funds typically have a growth objective. They give investors the opportunity for much greater growth than any other type of fund does. Because common stock represents ownership in a corporation (refer to Chapter 14), when the corporation makes more profits and sales, who benefits? The owners—meaning you. Thus, the value of the stock goes up, and so does the value of your mutual fund shares.

Not all stocks in a common stock fund rise at the same time, though. Many times, when a mutual fund is investing in different business sectors, one sector might be performing quite well, and the other might not be doing so hot. That's how a mutual fund provides a cushion to these bumps in the road, so to speak. Because a common stock fund offers diversification, the bumps in the road are a bit milder, therefore reducing the risk a bit.

Sectors
Specific areas that a mutual fund will concentrate on. If the fund wants to diversify, it invests in many different sectors. However, there are mutual funds—known as sector funds—that specifically invest in companies in just one industry, such as biotechnology, real estate, or gold.

Bond, James Bond

The bond securities in bond funds range from short-term to long-term, just as bond maturities do. The bond fund portfolio manager buys bonds, aiming to achieve both a high yield and stability. That is hard to do because of the see-saw of changing bond prices and interest rates

The biggest component of a bond fund is income, which is why they are often called income funds. In a bond fund, your money is used to buy bonds. Easy enough. As with bond investing, each bond in the fund carries a specific interest rate and a maturity date. The bond fund portfolio manager buys and sells bond securities that suit the investment objective of the fund. These portfolio managers have to follow the bond market and interest rate fluctuations to the letter. As interest rates rise and fall, the value of the bond securities owned by the bond fund rises and falls, causing the bond fund share prices to rise and fall.

When choosing a bond fund, you need to consider both the maturity dates of the bonds purchased by the fund (short-term, intermediate-term, and long-term bond funds) and the different kinds of bonds the fund invests in. You'll recall that Part IV describes different kinds of bonds, such as government bonds, mortgage-backed securities, and corporate bonds. There are four main categories of bond funds: government bond funds, high-yield or corporate bond funds, mortgage-backed funds, and international bond funds. Table 25.1 describes different kinds of bond funds and the bonds each kind seeks.

Table 25.1 Bond Funds and the Types of Bonds They Hold

Type	Invests in
Government Bond Funds	Long- and short-term government bonds
High-Yield/Corporate Bond Funds	Lower investment-grade corporate bonds.
Mortgage-backed	Mortgage-backed securities guaranteed by the government
International Bond Funds	IOUs from foreign corporations in the form of a bond.

Don't Overlook This One

Balanced funds split their investments equally between stocks and bonds. When one market zigs, the other zags. The main theory is to balance the two with the objective of reducing risk. Consider it diversification at its best. It's a conservative approach, and the allocation strategies in each of the funds are usually determined by which category of assets the portfolio manager thinks will do better in the current market.

Balanced funds are for those investors who need to take a conservative approach and who don't want to assume the one hundred percent risk associated with a mutual fund that invests only in stocks. Fortunately, because there are some stocks in the fund, you do get price appreciation in addition to the income you receive from the fixed-income investments (bonds, that is) in the portfolio. Returns on these funds are nothing to sneeze at, either. The five-year annual return on the average balanced mutual fund was 12%, close behind the TSE 300 with a 14% five-year average annual return.

Now for the Money Markets

When you need liquidity and preservation of your capital, look into a money market fund. Canadian money market funds must have at all times at least 95% of the assets of the fund invested in cash equivalents or short-term obligations of Canadian issuers, denominated in Canadian currency. All securities and investments held in the portfolio must mature in thirteen months (twenty-five months for government obligations) or less. The average term to maturity must not exceed 180 days. Money market mutual funds invest in highly liquid and safe securities such as T-Bills, Bankers' Acceptances (BA), and high-quality short-term corporate paper.

Many investors choose money market funds as a way to temporarily park their cash until situations change, using it as an emergency fund or as a safe haven during a rough market environment. You can also simply keep your money in money market funds until you decide which stock or bond fund investment you want.

Here's what you need to look for in a money market fund:

➤ **Convenience.** Most money market funds take one day to settle. That means you can get your money out in one business day. Make sure you find out how long it takes to get your money out, if you need it.

➤ **Minimum investment amounts.** What type of initial purchase is required? Minimum investments usually range from $500 to $1,000, although you can get started through an automatic investment plan with as little as $25 a month. You'll see how in Chapter 27.

How To Buy Five Hundred Stocks for Under $1,000

Index investing is a strategy that savvy mutual fund managers have been using for years. Obviously, you can't buy shares of every single stock in

Bet You Didn't Know

Assets managed in Canadian mutual funds surged to a record high of $258.4 billion by the end of June 1997.

the TSE 300 or the S&P 500—that would set you back hundreds of thousands of dollars! There is one way around this dilemma: index fund investing.

Each index fund maintains stocks that are chosen to mirror the index it represents. You would invest in an index fund for the long-term rewards; they maximize the potential for long-term gains. Here's a further look at some of the market indexes a mutual fund might try to mirror:

➤ **The TSE 300 (Toronto Stock Exchange 300 Index).** This index tracks three hundred Canadian stocks, classified by industry. The top three largest companies are: BCE Inc, Canadian Pacific Ltd., and Seagram.

➤ **The DJIA (Dow Jones Industrial Average).** This index tracks the movement of thirty of the largest blue-chip stocks, such as AT&T and Coca-Cola, which are traded on the New York Stock Exchange. It is most affected by movement of higher-priced shares, like IBM, for example.

➤ **The S&P 500 (Standard & Poor 500).** This index tracks five hundred blue-chip stocks, mostly traded on the NYSE. It's the benchmark to which most portfolio managers in the U.S. compare themselves. No small stocks are included.

➤ **The EAFE Index.** This is the Morgan Stanley Capital International Europe, Australia and Far East (EAFE) Index. If you want to track more than one thousand foreign stocks in twenty different countries, check this one out. It's considered the most prominent index for investing in foreign countries.

Odds are if you contact a mutual fund company and ask them if they have an index fund that mirrors any of the above-mentioned indices, they'll have one. Go for it!

Going Global

If you have a yen for investing in Japan or a strong desire to put your pesos in Latin America, you might want to invest abroad. But save that plane ticket. You can spread your investment all over the globe simply by choosing a mutual fund that invests in foreign companies.

What about the risks? Well, there are many, but the returns can pay off. In 1996, the average annual return of an international stock fund was over 12%.

Are the distance, the language barriers, and currency differences a concern for investors? Not at all. Just pick a country and read up on current events in that company (in your local paper, *The Globe & Mail* or *The Financial Post*) on an ongoing basis. For example, if you keep up on what's going on in the Far East, either through reading material or through business contacts there, you can invest in this region through a mutual fund. It's easy. You don't have to research foreign companies and run up your international calling card. Professional portfolio managers do it for you.

Investors beware. Figure out your risk tolerance before jumping into just one fund. More conservative investors might want to pick a broad-based fund (one that invests in several countries in a region like the Pacific Rim) as a way to reduce risk because foreign markets are choppy.

If you want to diversify your international mutual funds, you could, for example, pick a Japanese fund and a non-Japanese fund (those funds that eliminate Japanese investments from their portfolio) to balance the act.

For more adventurous investors, international bond funds are also available, though many financial experts scream, "Proceed with caution!" because of the currency fluctuations. This has to do with the rise and fall of a specific country's monetary unit—like our Canadian dollar, the franc in France, the Deutsche mark in Germany, and the yen in Japan. Investors interested in a bond fund should be aware that currency fluctuations (the ups and downs of the monetary unit) can affect the yield of their investment.

For example, you wouldn't want to invest in a fund that invests in German debt instruments if you thought Germany's currency would weaken, because in the end you would lose money when you switched back to the dollar. There are other ways to invest in the currency of a foreign country, but those are for the more savvy investor.

A hedging strategy is a protective maneuver that is intended to reduce the risk of loss from price fluctuations.

One question to ask when investing in foreign funds is whether the fund manager hedges the currency risk. This means: does the manager eliminate the currency risk through a hedging strategy?

Or you can play the currency game. Here's how it's played. Say you think the franc, the French currency, is going to strengthen against the Canadian dollar in the near future. Walk into any international bank and exchange your dollars for francs at the current exchange rate. Then, when the franc does strengthen, you return to the bank and turn your francs back into Canadian dollars, making a profit on the deal. Buy low and sell high, you know?

But be careful. Investors should be aware of the spread, the difference between the bid and ask prices of the currencies. For example, if the bank has an asking price of $3 per franc but a bidding price of $1 per franc, and you have to get rid of your foreign currency in a hurry, you'll wind up losing money.

Another disadvantage is that you won't be able to earn any interest on the foreign currency after the initial exchange; you can't deposit your French francs or Japanese yen into your savings account. And, of course, there's always the danger that, in the case cited, the currency will weaken.

Because many of these international funds are new, you might have a difficult time comparing one-, three-, and five-year returns because of a lack of data. Some investors might want to wait until an adequate return period is established, or seek out the mutual funds that do have a track record.

Chasing Big Returns Overseas

Another way to invest in an international mutual fund is through emerging markets funds. These funds contain billions in assets, but are a tiny part of the mutual fund universe. Some of these funds are dubbed "country funds," and returned an average of over 15% in 1996. Many investment experts say that a good way to get involved in the rapid economic growth in foreign countries is through emerging growth funds.

Emerging market funds are closed-end funds, meaning a limited and fixed number of shares is issued (unlike the vast majority of mutual funds which are open-end, meaning new shares are created all the time). They trade either above the NAVPS or below it. This is the premium or the discount, as determined by supply and demand in the marketplace. Many of these funds trade on the New York Stock Exchange (NYSE) and you can purchase them with U.S. dollars. Some examples are the Growth Fund of Spain, the Indonesia Fund, and the Korea Equity Fund.

This means that if you are interested in investing in a particular country, you might want to look at a closed-end fund. Keep in mind that closed-end funds issue a specific number of shares and trade like a stock on a stock exchange.

Another factor to consider when you invest in a country fund is whether the investment is diversified enough. Most Investment Advisors advise not to invest too heavily in one sector or one type of stock. So does investing in country funds mean less diversification and therefore more volatility? Not necessarily. A fund might invest in only one country, but it may invest in so many different business sectors that you aren't putting all of your eggs in one basket.

Reading the Fine Print

Beginning to research a mutual fund is as easy as learning to read a mutual fund quote in a newspaper. Table 25.2 lists a few mutual fund quotes.

Table 25.2   Reading the Fine Print

SKY'S THE LIMIT FUND CO.*	NAVPS	NAVPS Change
Sky Aggr Grwth Fd	26.75	+ .22
Sky Growth Fund	15.50	+ .06
Sky High Yield Bond Fund	6.75	− .11
Sky Long-Term Gov't Bd Fund	8.25	− .09
Sky Income Fund	21.00	− .10
(a)	(b)	(c)

*The above quotes are fictitious but used for example purposes.

The following list describes the columns in Table 25.2:

a) These are the different types of funds. Many of the funds are abbreviated, because there is usually not enough room in the columns of the financial section of your paper. If you don't know where to find the fund type, get the toll-free number for the fund company to call customer service and ask!

b) NAVPS stands for net asset value per share. This is the price per share you would pay if you were to invest.

c) This is a change that measures the previous day's close to this trading day's close (just like a stock quote).

Reading the fine print also entails knowing what to look for in a prospectus, which is about thirty pages of legal mumbo jumbo that contains the investment policy and guidelines of the fund. It is quite necessary to understand this document, because all portfolio managers must keep their investment practices in line with it.

Without going into too much detail (a whole book could be written on how to read a mutual fund prospectus), here's a brief list of what you should look for:

➤ Understand the management fees and fund expenses. These are the fees paid to the fund management company and are independent of any mutual fund sales charge, which is known as a *load*.

Management fees are generally the largest single expense in the fund. The prospectus will tell you how the fee is calculated. Generally, management fees range from 1% to 3% annually based on total net assets of the fund. But more on this in Chapter 26.

➤ Check out who the management is. The prospectus usually lists who the portfolio manager(s) are, their affiliations, and some general information about them.

➤ Make sure the prospectus tells you how much of an initial minimum investment is required, and how much subsequent investments must be. On the flip side, make sure you understand the redemption procedures you must follow to sell your shares.

WHAT? A **prospectus** is a legal document that contains the basic description of a mutual fund and its investment guidelines and policies. By law, the mutual fund company must send one to you before you invest.

➤ Make sure an annual prospectus or annual report will be sent to you. By law, most funds are required to send you, the shareholder, a new annual prospectus.

The Least You Need To Know

➤ When you invest in a mutual fund, you are investing for the long haul. Therefore, if you are wondering when is the best time to begin, you may want to start thinking about it today. The more time you have on your side, the better.

➤ There are three different types of mutual funds: stock funds, bond funds, and money market mutual funds. If you understand the different types of investment objectives in each, such as growth, growth and income, and income, you can pattern your investment plan accordingly.

➤ One of the best ways to invest in a growing foreign market is through investment in a mutual fund. There are international stock funds, emerging markets funds, European funds, Far East funds, international bond funds—and many more!

➤ Learning how to read a mutual fund quote in the financial section of your newspaper is easy. All you need to know is the company name and the fund(s) you have invested in, and you'll find the NAVPS or share price, and the NAVPS change, which is the change between the closing price of the previous trading day and the day listed in the paper.

If at first you don't succeed, find out if the loser gets anything.

—Bill Lyon

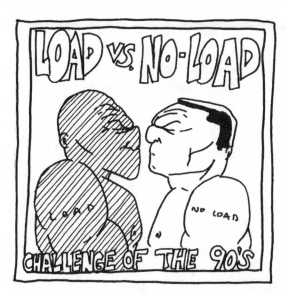

Chapter 26

How Mutual Funds are Sold

> ### In this chapter
> ➤ Load, no-load, what's the difference?
> ➤ Other fees associated with mutual funds
> ➤ How to choose among mutual funds

You know now that there are hundreds and hundreds of mutual funds that cover a wide spectrum of areas: Canadian equity, international equity, bonds, money market, emerging growth companies, index funds, etc. And now to add one more selection to your plate: loads and no-loads. As if you didn't have enough choices to make already. This chapter explains the main types of fees that mutual funds charge.

Loads, No-Loads: What's the Difference?

Mutual funds are sold either as no-load funds or load funds. When a mutual fund is sold no-load there is no charge to buy or sell the fund. Some no-load funds, however, may have a set-up fee of approximately $45.

Don't purchase a mutual fund just because it is a no-load fund. You should consider all information.

A load is the commission or sales charge associated with a mutual fund.

A back-end load fund has a fee that is charged only on the sale of the fund and this fee is charged on a declining scale (to zero if held up to six or seven years in most cases).

Load funds, on the other hand, have two options, *front-end load* and *back-end load*. Front-end load funds are sold with a charge up front. The charge will range between 0% and 5% of the amount your are investing. The amount that is charged is negotiated with your full service broker or financial planner and typically falls in the range of 1% to 3%. (Discount brokers have a set rate they charge for front-end load funds.)

When you purchase a mutual fund with a front-end load you pay a charge or commission up front but pay nothing when you sell the fund. Therefore you should consider purchasing a mutual fund with a front-end load when you have a time horizon of less than, say, five years.

On the other hand, when purchasing a load fund you have the option of purchasing it back-end load (alternately called rear-end load or a deferred sales charge (DSC)). When purchasing a fund with a back-end load, there is no charge when you purchase it, however there may be a charge when you sell it.

Here's how it works. When you purchase a back-end load fund, you pay no charge. However, depending on when you sell it, you will be charged a back-end load that applies on a *declining scale basis*. The charge for selling the fund is highest in the first year following the purchase and typically ranges from 5% to 6% in the first year and each year thereafter will decline until there is no charge at all for selling the fund. It will take anywhere from 5 to 7 years on average for a back-end load to fall to zero. It will vary from fund family to fund family. Make sure you read the prospectus for complete details on the terms of the declining fee schedule.

Usually, with funds that charge back-end loads, you are permitted to redeem up to 10% of the value of the fund each year without penalty. Also, most funds allow you to switch funds within the same family at no charge. So, if you intend to hold a fund for a while and you are investing in a solid family of funds, consider purchasing mutual funds with a back-end load. You can always switch to another fund within the family, if you wish.

> Most back-end load funds allow you to redeem up to 10% a year free of charge as well as to switch to other funds in their family of funds free of charge.

Other Fees You Should Know About

MER

One of the key items that should be looked at when purchasing a mutual fund—whether it be a load fund (front-end or back-end) or no-load—is the MER. MER stands for *management expense ratio*. It is what the mutual fund company charges the fund before any returns are paid out to the investor. The MER includes paying the manager to manage the fund and all other expenses associated with running the fund.

Although fund companies are regulated by law as to what can be charged to the MER, MERs tend to differ from fund company to fund company. MERs tend to be lower for money market and fixed-income mutual funds and higher for equity funds. If the fund is invested outside of Canada it will tend to have a higher MER. (MERs range from under 1% for money market funds to the high 2% range for high maintenance funds like international equities.)

Keep in mind that the MER can differ between mutual funds in the same asset class, (e.g. Canadian equity funds) or even differ between front-end and back-end loads of the same fund. Make sure you know and compare MERs before you purchase a mutual fund.

At first glance it might seem advantageous to purchase all your funds no-load. Be careful, though: there are many no-load funds that are good performers, but there are also many that are average or below average performers. These ill-performing funds survive because they are able to attract clients by offering no charges to get into or out of the fund. The money you're saving with a no-load fund might be wiped out by lower than expected returns!

I am a true believer that you get what you pay for. In other words, as with any investment decision, you should identify your objectives first then decide what type of fund you would like to invest in. Once you have identified the type of fund you should look at *all* the funds in that category. There are many things to consider when purchasing a mutual fund such as performance, investment style of the manager, strength of the fund family, type of load, and the MER, just to mention a few.

Trailer Fees

All mutual funds pay trailer fees. Trailer fees are paid to your broker or financial planner. (These fees are paid to your discount broker as well). Trailer fees compensate your broker or financial planner on an ongoing basis to continually monitor the mutual fund for the client. These fees are paid out before the investor receives his or her return on investment and exist on every type of mutual fund, i.e., both load and no-load. The trailer fee that is paid out will range from, say, .0025% of assets invested in a money market mutual fund to .01% of assets in an equity fund. The trailer fee is not negotiable and is paid out whether you use a full service broker, discount broker, or financial planner.

All types of mutual funds (load and no-load) pay out trailer fees.

As you can see, mutual funds need to be fully researched before any purchases are made. The load is just one variable that should be considered when you purchase a mutual fund. Make sure you do your homework before you make any purchases. Mutual fund surveys and software packages can be of enormous help here. They'll do the analysis for you. You'll be able to compare loads, MERs, and trailer fees, and much more! I've detailed some great sources for mutual fund analysis in Chapter 28.

The Least You Should Know

➤ No-load mutual funds don't carry charges to buy or sell the fund; load funds do carry these charges, either up front (front-end), or when you sell the fund (back-end).

➤ Be aware of the MER, trailer fee, and any other fees associated with purchasing the fund.

➤ Remember that while no-load funds don't charge you for buying or selling the fund, they aren't all great performers either. The money you're saving might be wiped out by lower than expected returns! Make sure to do your homework when selecting funds (whether they are load or no-load funds): look at performance history, the investment style of the manager, fees, and strength of the fund family.

**"Successful investing is anticipating the
anticipations of others."**

—John Maynard Keynes

Chapter 27

Invest with as Little as $25

In this chapter

➤ You don't need a lot of money to buy mutual fund shares

➤ Mutual funds and automatic investment plans

➤ What investment clubs are

Investing in mutual funds is the modern way to make your money grow. But what if you have a modern-day investment approach with what seems to be a caveman's savings account? Don't fret. As you'll learn in this chapter, even the largest of mutual fund families has created a plan designed specifically with you in mind. In fact ...

It's as Easy as A-B-C

Learning the alphabet was easy. It's just as easy to use this simple mutual fund investment strategy created for the small individual investor. It's the automatic investment plan.

Here's what you do. Before you even sign up to invest in the mutual fund of your choice (even before you receive a prospectus), whether you are calling or sending away for information, ask if the mutual fund company offers an automatic monthly purchase plan. If so...

➤ You have the option to invest in the fund for as little as $25 a month.

➤ Many fund families waive the $1,000, $500, or even $2,000 minimums, thereby allowing you to start with a small amount of money.

➤ You are automatically building your investment portfolio without having the added burden of writing a cheque once a month.

You can set up this type of account with your broker. You select the amount and the type of mutual fund (e.g. $25 per month into the Sky's The Limit Growth Fund). The money will automatically come out of your bank account once a month (in this case, to purchase $25 of the selected fund) and is electronically transferred to your investment account. You can change the amounts or the mutual funds, or cancel at any time.

What does this plan do? For little money to start with, you are practicing the investment strategy of dollar cost averaging.

Just as a recap, look at what dollar cost averaging can do for you. Remember that it is simply a system of making regular, fixed investments into a stock, or stock or bond mutual fund. You do this all at a predetermined time, for example on the 15th of every month (you get to pick the date). In fact, you can time it right after you receive your paycheque to ensure you will have the money in your bank account. In addition, you can make additional deposits at any time you want.

 If at all possible, do not touch the money you invest through an automatic investment plan. It's a tool to help you be disciplined, so don't give in to temptation.

Because you are doing this on a regular basis, you get to take advantage of any dips in the share price. Therefore, if the share price drops from $15 a share to $12, that same $100 monthly investment will buy more shares. And, when the share price rises after you purchase these shares, the value of your mutual fund portfolio rises as well. How can you figure this out? Simply multiply the number of shares you own by the current share price to calculate the value of your portfolio.

By implementing the dollar cost averaging strategy, you take the guesswork out of when to buy low and sell high. In other words, market timing is not an issue.

When you implement dollar cost averaging, time becomes your best friend. Just $100 a month invested over a period of ten years in a growth stock mutual fund, reinvesting all dividends and capital gains, can yield you almost $32,000.

Dollar cost averaging is a great way to save money in your RRSP or RESP. Each year, many Canadians wait until the last minute to make their contributions. Many times, those of us who don't have the cash end up taking out a loan and paying interest on the loan. Why not set up a monthly purchase plan and forgo all those interest charges? Even better, if you are lucky enough to have a Group RRSP at work, you can save on your taxes at source. Since your contribution to the Group RRSP is non-taxable, you pay less tax each paycheque.

Folks, I can't stress this enough: it is never too late to sign up and get a monthly purchase plan underway. Sure, there is always tomorrow, but you have opportunity on your side today. Make the best of it by starting a program like this one.

A Word on Investment Clubs

An investment club is a group of people—it could be as few as five or as many as thirty—who pool their money together, kind of like creating their own fund. Although all of the people decide together which stocks to buy or sell, one person usually functions as a leader. Make sure you pick someone whom you trust and who you think can be objective. Minimum investment? You pick it! Usually, though, minimums start around $100 with monthly deposits in increments of $50 each.

Everyone shares in the wealth, but not just in the profits you may make. You might learn a lot about stocks that you have never heard of before; maybe there's a financial professional in the group who has access to research reports or a doctor who knows a lot about health-care stocks. Plus, you are practicing the art of diversification and dollar cost averaging. And you might even meet your future spouse or hook up with that building contractor you needed to repair your house. For more information—consult your broker.

The Least You Need To Know

➤ Start investing in a fund's automatic monthly purchase plan as soon as you can, provided that you are comfortable with the mutual fund's investment objectives and guidelines. With as little as $100 a month, in ten years you could make up to $32,000—nearly triple your investment!

➤ Dollar cost averaging is one of the best investment strategies around. You consistently invest money into a mutual fund, for example, on a regular basis at regular intervals.

➤ Check if your company offers a Group RRSP. You can start saving taxes on your next paycheque!

➤ If you have the inkling and a few friends who want to join you, you may consider starting an investment club.

Chapter 28

The Rating Service War

In this chapter
➤ How a mutual fund rating service helps investors
➤ The top bananas available to you
➤ What to look for in a mutual fund rating service

There's a mutual fund survey war brewing, and it's up to you to pick the winner.

Now that you know what types of mutual funds exist, it's time to determine which mutual fund rating service you need to help you make better educated decisions about investing in a mutual fund.

Do you want funds that invest in companies that are poised for strong growth over the next three to five years? Maybe you want a fund that seeks out small, emerging companies that will be the mega corporations of the next century. Perhaps a fund that requires a low minimum initial investment is what you're looking for.

Whatever the case, today's mutual fund investors (and there are millions of you out there) need report-like information that will assist them in making their strategic investment decisions in mutual fund buying. This chapter helps you figure out where to turn for information.

On a Scale of 1 to 10

When I was a little boy, my mother and father would play the "On a scale of 1 to 10" game with me, my sister, and my brother. Every time we went to a restaurant for dinner, they would ask, "Okay, kids, on a scale of 1 to 10, how would you rate the food?" Whenever we saw a movie it was, "On a scale of 1 to 10, children, whaddaya think?" Even before my brother was born, when we were picking names for him, "Okay, you three, on a scale of 1 to 10, how do you like the name 'Matthew'?" My childhood was a constant rating service. I'd give it an 8 1/2.

Mutual funds are given their own version of "On a scale of 1 to 10" by more than a few contenders. The software packages available make comparing funds simple. Here's more information to help you choose the best mutual fund for you.

Separating the Best from the Rest

You can pick a fund that has a winning record today according to any of the mutual fund surveys and rating companies that exist. But that doesn't mean that same fund will be tomorrow's winner. What you can do is pick a relatively good mutual fund rating service or even subscribe to a few newsletters that cover the mutual fund industry. The advice given in most surveys and newsletters comes from financial analysts, investment advisers, or even financial planners. Remember that none of these survey reports or newsletters is predictive in nature; they just give the facts.

Here are a few ways you can get advice and cut through the murk on the fifteen hundred or so mutual funds that exist today.

One of the most informative and user-friendly surveys of mutual fund performance is *Bellcharts*. *Bellcharts* studies almost every mutual fund sold in Canada, comparing, sorting and ranking funds by performance, size, management expense ratios, volatility, and many more variables. You can select funds based on a number of criteria, including fund type, rate of return, risk/return, etc. Detailed information on each fund exists, including the fund manager, asset allocation, top ten holdings, rates of return and fees.

Bellcharts is updated on a monthly basis, and lists over fifteen hundred mutual funds and several market benchmarks. A yearly subscription with twelve monthly updates will cost you roughly $369.95 (excludes taxes). A quarterly subscription is also available at $129.95; single issues are $34.95 (plus taxes and shipping). To subscribe, you can call (416) 515-4757 in the Toronto area or visit their website at http://www.bellcharts.com to receive more information and download a free demo disk.

If you can't afford to subscribe to these rating services, find out if they offer a trial subscription. If not, they are free of charge at your local library. Check the business reference section or ask your favourite librarian for help!

PALTrak is a comprehensive guide to mutual fund performance analysis. With over sixty new fund sub-types, you can classify funds based on actual holdings. You can sort and search information by over four hundred criteria, including past performance, market value, risk/return, and asset allocation. Performance data goes as far back as fifteen years. Over fourteen hundred mutual funds are updated monthly, including dozens of market benchmarks. An annual subscription with twelve monthly updates costs $399 (plus applicable taxes). Single issues are available as well at $39 (plus taxes). You can contact *PalTrak* at (416) 489-7074 in the Toronto area. For more information and a free PalTrak demonstration, their website address is: www.pal.com.

Other less costly alternatives are the mutual fund publications offered by newspapers like *The Financial Post* and *The Globe & Mail*. Or, if you have access to the Internet, all of the major mutual fund companies have websites that you can visit for more information on their funds.

Tidbits To Keep in Mind Before Subscribing or Investing

No matter what type of service or mutual fund survey report you choose when investigating mutual funds to invest in, here are a few tips to keep in mind:

➤ Remember to remain objective. You have to have an objective source that focuses on the continuity of the mutual fund manager, and the report must evaluate that portfolio manager's performance. If the report says "This fund stinks because the portfolio manager stinks," consider choosing another service. Look for objectivity, not a cure-all.

➤ If you're coming into mutual funds for the very first time ever, look at all of the analyses out there, not just the promotional material that the mutual fund companies send to you. If you've kept all of your money either under your mattress or in a savings account, proceed with caution. Mutual fund investing is a different ball game. These reports are there to help you.

➤ Make sure you stick with tracking a fund's performance over the past one- , three- , and five-year periods. Check to see if there's even a ten-year fund history. A fund that's been around longer doesn't necessarily make a better investment, but you can see how the fund has performed during bull and bear markets.

➤ Mutual fund investors should not focus solely on which fund is really hot right now. If the Sky's the Limit Mutual Fund is gracing the front covers of all the top financial magazines, that doesn't mean you should go out and invest. Remember, past performance does not indicate future performance.

Keep in mind that those funds that haven't been around all that long obviously don't have any past performance history. Be careful when considering one of them.

➤ Do your research and don't just read a financial magazine for your bottom-line investment decisions. Understand why a fund is top banana or a rotten apple. Many magazines and newspapers report the winners, but today's winner could be tomorrow's loser-just as today's loser could be tomorrow's winner.

➤ Check out the track record of the fund's portfolio manager. Contact the fund company to find out how long the portfolio manager has been there. Why? Because each manager has his or her own trading style. Plus, if he or she has a solid history

with the fund, great. If the fund has been a winner but has a brand new manager, the same performance might not be repeated.

➤ Not only should you consider the performance ratings and the safety of the fund, but you should make sure the fund company offers other features (which should be noted on the survey). These features include fund switching, where you can switch from one fund to another with no additional service charges; monthly newsletters published by a fund family, which provide great research information and educational material for you to read on an ongoing basis; and monthly purchase plans, where you need as little as $25 a month to invest in a fund.

The Least You Need To Know

➤ On a scale of 1 to 10, subscribing to a mutual fund survey report or service scores a definite 11. Make sure you know the different types of services that are available to you, and that you are comfortable with the language in their reports.

➤ Past performance is not indicative of future performance. When you pick a mutual fund from a survey report, don't choose it just because it was last year's big cheese. It could really be sour grapes next year, and you'll be left with nothin'!

➤ Be sure to read other information sent to you by mutual fund companies, including their monthly newsletters and investment information. But don't invest based solely on this promotional material—do your homework first!

I don't know much about being a millionaire, but I'll bet I'd be darling at it.

—Dorothy Parker

Part 6
Futures and Options

The next time you are at the grocery store, look at the products on the shelves or in the freezer. You'll find some of the most common elements that make up our futures market. Orange juice, wheat (found in cereal and bread), cocoa, coffee, sugar, corn, poultry, and oats are a few examples of the types of commodities— the goods—that are bought and sold on the futures market.

The investors who wheel and deal in the futures and options markets take on the most risk any investor can. Why? Because the profits are more exponentially rewarding than any other type of investment. However, the futures and options game is not for the amateur investor. True, you can make a killing in the market and make a lot (I mean hordes) of dough. You could also lose more than you invested.

This part of the book explains how you can get in on the high-stakes game of futures and options. Definitely proceed with caution.

Chapter 29

Betting On Tomorrow

In this chapter

➤ What's a futures contract?

➤ How you can make a ton of money—and lose even more!

➤ Why futures are so risky

So what's all this hoopla about how easy it is to make money in futures? You set your sights on a few cattle or pork bellies, and overnight you're a millionaire? That's not exactly how it works.

Futures trading tempts wanna-be-rich investors with the allure of fast action, low minimums, and the potential of reaping gigantic profits. It is extremely important that you understand what a future is before you even consider investing in one. Even investors who are extremely knowledgeable and trade futures all the time have been burned. The high-stakes game of investing in futures has been known to wipe out many fortunes.

Some examples in this chapter will tell you exactly what a futures contract is. As you read on, you will see just how risky they can be.

Taking a Gamble

When you speculate in futures, you are taking a gamble. Think of it this way. When you buy stock, you have partial ownership in a company. When you invest in a bond security, it represents an IOU from the issuer to promise to pay you back in full plus interest. And mutual funds? Depending on what type of fund you invest in, you have exposure to both stocks and bonds.

Futures are a completely different story. There is no ownership, no IOUs, and no tomorrow if you lose big. I don't want to have you freak out over futures trading, but I do want you to be aware of the risks involved. First, let's take a peek and see exactly what all the hoopla has been about.

WHAT? A **forward contract** is a commitment by the seller to deliver, and by the buyer to take delivery of, a stated quantity of a commodity or security on a future date at a price determined today.

Moving Forward

Simply put, a *forward contract* (similar to a futures contract) is a contract in which a buyer and a seller agree to complete a transaction on a specific commodity at a predetermined time in the future that is based on the transaction agreed upon today. All the details are left up to the buyer and seller.

To illustrate how a forward contract works, let's say a wheat farmer is about to plant his summer crop and estimates that it will cost $2.00 per bushel to grow the wheat. He figures out that the crop will yield two hundred thousand bushels at the end of the summer. So the farmer enters into a forward contract with a buyer (like a grain or

> ### Bet You Didn't Know
>
> With a forward contract, you must make/take delivery of the commodity and settle on the delivery date.

bread company that needs the wheat) to sell the anticipated two hundred thousand bushels of wheat. The wheat will be sold at a price that represents a profit for the farmer before the wheat is even planted.

Let's add some numbers now. The buyer agrees to buy the farmer's two hundred thousand bushels of wheat for $2.50 a bushel. (Farmer's gotta make a profit, right?) The buyer agrees to buy it six months later on September 15, regardless of the market price of wheat at that time. If the farmer grows the wheat and produces two hundred thousand bushels, and it only costs him $2.00 a bushel, the farmer has a profit from the transaction. Here's the math: 200 000 bushels x ($2.50 (the sale price) – 200 000 bushels x $2.00 (his cost)) = $100,000. He gets this amount no matter what the market price of wheat is on September 15.

What happens if farmers growing wheat have poor crops, either due to poor weather or insects? A lot. Because of the laws of supply and demand, the supply of wheat is low, which pushes wheat prices higher—all the way up to $3.00 a bushel by September 15. Because of the already-agreed-upon transaction between the farmer and the buyer, the farmer must sell the wheat at the $2.50 per bushel price—and the farmer misses out on the additional profit potential. If he had waited until harvest time to sell the crop out in the market (instead of selling it in a forward contract), he could have made an additional $100,000 in profit on his two hundred thousand bushels of wheat.

On the other hand, if his crops only yielded one hundred thousand bushels, he would have to go out and buy enough wheat to honor his contract. That means he would have to buy wheat for $0.50 more per bushel than he is selling it for! (These figures in no way represent any true stories. Their purpose is to mathematically illustrate the intricacies of the commodities market.)

So what is the advantage of a forward contract? Risk is somewhat limited because both parties have limited their risk and reward. The disadvantage is that both the buyer and the seller are exclusively dependent upon each other to carry out the transaction.

Futures contract These contracts are highly standardized because the specifics (the delivery date, the quantity, and the quality) of the futures contract are determined by the financial exchange. Futures are a very aggressive type of investment. They are not recommended for the conservative investor.

I Can See the Future

Now, a futures contract is a bit different. The concept is the same: pre-selling a commodity at an agreed upon price today for delivery in the future. But the delivery dates are different because they are pre-set by a financial exchange. The months in which the contracts expire are known as the current or *spot month*.

Futures contract transactions are handled on the Toronto Futures Exchange (TFE), the Montreal Exchange, and the Winnipeg Commodity Exchange. In Canada, wheat, canola, flaxseed, oats, barley and rye have been traded on the Winnipeg Commodity Exchange for many years. A list of futures exchanges is provided in the Appendix.

In a futures contract, the transactions take place at the financial exchange and not out in a corn field or wheat field. However, the farmer and the buyer don't necessarily go to the financial exchange. The exchange brings together a number of buyers and sellers (either farmers or company reps, or even you and me) to agree upon a fair future price for a particular commodity.

In this type of contract, the buyers and sellers do not know who is on the other end of the transaction. For example, in this situation, a seller (the farmer, for example) would enter into a futures contract

Bet You Didn't Know

It is much easier to get out of a futures contract than to get out of a forward contract. How do you do it? All you have to do is take the opposite position, therefore closing out your position. This way you avoid the delivery process.

(either directly or indirectly using a broker) to sell the corn at a price he picks today. That corn is to be delivered at a pre-set time down the road that is established by the financial exchange. (For a listing of contract months, keep reading.) To sell the corn, there has to be a buyer on the other end, such as a corn product manufacturing representative. The bottom line is that sellers sell to the *clearing corporation* (the organization that "clears" the transactions—they add up all the pluses and minuses) and buyers buy from the clearing corporation.

Bet You Didn't Know

Not all futures contracts are for commodities like corn or wheat. Other futures contracts include stock index futures, Eurodollar futures, and T-bond futures.

If you were to invest in futures, you would usually do so through a full-service brokerage firm. Since your strategy is probably just to make money from the transaction (not to buy two hundred thousand bushels of soybeans), you need to make sure you constantly keep up with any changes in price of the commodity or security.

Just remember that exchange-listed futures contracts require the delivery of a specific quantity of a specific commodity (like corn or wheat) at predetermined dates.

Making or Losing Millions Overnight

When you enter into a forward contract, any profits or losses are not realized until the contract "comes due" on the predetermined date. In a futures contract, however, profits or losses are realized every day. For example, if the price of the underlying commodity, like corn or even cattle, moves away from its price agreed upon in the contract (known as the *exercise price*), the party losing as a result of that price move (whether it was up or down) must pay the one benefitting by it. Every day the money is taken out of the loser's account and deposited into the winner's account by the clearing house.

Why trade futures instead of forward contracts? Because you know exactly what you are trading in terms of the quantity, the quality, and the delivery date. The only piece of information you need to settle on is the price.

Now for the $64,000 question: How do you make money at this? First, review what you already know about commodity futures.

➤ Futures contracts are traded on financial instruments and commodities, which include various agricultural goods, and bulk products such as grain and metal.

➤ A futures contract is a contract to either buy or sell a certain amount of a commodity at a particular price within a stated period of time.

➤ That price is established on the floor of a financial exchange.

 **Exercise price** The agreed-upon price on the futures contract.

If you are going to invest in futures, you also need to understand the two types of futures traders that exist.

➤ **Speculators.** When you speculate, many people say that you are just guessing what is going to happen. In the futures market, a speculator does not own the underlying commodity (like a farmer would); that person is trying to achieve a profit from the ups and downs in the price of the contract.

➤ **Hedgers.** These traders (like the farmer, for example) own the underlying commodity. They use futures contracts to protect themselves against any changes in the price that may result in a loss for them (because they own the underlying commodity).

A futures contract requires the buyer to take delivery of, and the seller to make delivery of, the underlying commodity unless their position is closed out. How is it closed out? When one person enters into an offsetting position, opposite of his original investment.

When you buy a futures contract, it requires you to take delivery of the underlying commodity—no matter if it is wheat, gold, pork bellies, or soybeans. This is known as taking a *long position*. The advantage of entering into a futures contract is the profit potential. The disadvantage is the danger, especially when you do not "offset" your position.

Buying a futures contract doesn't require a lot of start up money. Usually, you're only obligated to put up five to ten percent of the contract's value. So, as a hypothetical example, if you wanted to buy ten soybean contracts (one contract = five thousand bushels), entering into the contract would obligate you to accept delivery of fifty thousand bushels of soybeans. If you were to follow through with your obligation, and the price of soybeans was $1.25 a bushel (hypothetically), you would have to buy all fifty thousand bushels of soybeans for $62,500.

Now we know that you aren't investing in a futures contract to end up with fifty thousand bushels of soybeans. You are probably a speculator hoping to make a profit on the change in price of soybeans. So, you put up ten percent of the contract's value, which is known as *margin* (similar to what you learned in Chapter 15 about trading on margin). You now control $62,500 worth of soybeans with only $6,250. This deposit is known as a *good-faith deposit*.

Here's how you can make or break your bank. As the price of soybeans rises and falls, your futures contract also rises and falls in value. If the price of soybeans went up from $1.25 to $1.50, the value of your futures contract would increase to $75,000. Your profit? $12,500. Not bad for a day's work.

But all trading days are not like that. You also can lose money. If soybean prices fell from $1.25 a bushel to $1.00 a bushel and kept dropping, you would stand to lose all of your deposit money if the price kept plunging. If you lost all of your money, the price kept going down, and you didn't close out your contract (get rid of it!), you might be sent a margin call, which is the maintenance requirement you must keep in your account. This covers additional losses over your ten percent deposit.

If you're a speculator and you don't close out your position before the delivery date, you must take physical delivery of the goods. (And unless you live in a mansion, it might be quite difficult to explain to your spouse how the ten thousand bushels of soybeans are going to fit in your family room.)

While you can make a lot of money trading futures, remember: you can also lose a lot of money. So don't dump your life savings into futures.

> **Bet You Didn't Know**
>
> Only about one to three percent of futures contracts traded are set-
> tled by delivery. As long as you follow the futures markets and make
> the right calls, you shouldn't have to worry about feeding the cattle
> come supper time.

What if you did not close out your contract? When the delivery
date arrived, you would have to buy $62,500 (the exercise price) worth
of soybeans, which would then be worth either more or less, depending
on the day's current price. And you could either rejoice in a profit or cry
over your losses—either one could be big!

Read All About It

How do you read a futures quote in the newspaper? Just follow me.
Futures quotations in the financial section of your newspaper are listed
alphabetically and by commodity. Table 29.1 gives a brief explanation
of how to read a futures quotation.

Table 29.1 Reading Futures Quotes for Wheat in the Paper

High	Low	Month	Open	High	Low	Settle	Change	Interest
196.4	145.0	July97	141.0	143.5	141.0	143.5	–1.5	295
171.5	149.3	Oct97	149.0	149.5	147.5	148.6	–1.2	4669
171.5	149.5	Dec97	149.0	149.8	147.8	148.8	–1.0	3505
172.0	150.0	Mar98	150.0	151.5	150.0	151.0	+1.0	1682

The following list describes the columns in Table 29.1.

➤ High, Low. This represents the all-time high and low prices at
which this particular contract ever traded.

➤ The months represent the spot month in which the contract will
expire. It is usually the third Friday of those particular months.

➤ Open, High, Low, Settle, and Change. The Open price is the price at which the futures contract opens at the beginning of the trading day. The High price is the highest price the futures contract hits that day, so the Low price is the lowest price the contract hits. The Settle price is what it "closes" out at and is the price the buyers and sellers agree to "settle" on. Change represents the change in price from the previous day's close.

➤ Interest. This is the total number of futures contracts (either the buys or the sells) that have not been offset by an opposite transaction or even fulfilled by delivery, if that were the case.

A Little Less Risk, Please

If you don't want to risk much money in this high-stakes game, there are mutual funds available, called commodity funds, that invest in futures. You could also lose money in these funds, of course, but you won't ever be subject to any margin calls.

List Some Futures for Me

Table 29.2 lists a few of the different types of futures contracts, their trading months (spot month), their minimum price fluctuation, and the exchange they are listed on.

Table 29.2 Examples of Futures Contracts

Trading Commodity	Contract Months	Size	Min. Price Change	Exchange
Canola	Feb/Apr/Jun Aug/Oct/Dec	200 tonnes	$0.0025/tonne ($5)	Winnipeg Commodity
Live Cattle	Feb/Apr/Jun Aug/Oct/Dec	20,000 lbs.	$0.0025/lb ($5)	Chicago Merc. Index Exchange

Investing in the futures market is very risky. Before you invest in futures contracts, test your theory out on paper by running through the numbers associated with buying and selling a contract. It is much less expensive that way. If this is your first time investing in the futures market, it might be a good idea to consult a full-service broker who deals with futures. There exist brokerage houses that specialize in futures.

The Least You Need To Know

➤ A futures contract is an agreement between a buyer and a seller to either buy or sell a certain amount of a commodity at a particular price on a stated date. The price of the futures contract is established at a financial exchange.

➤ The month in which the underlying commodity is to be delivered is the spot month, although only one to three percent of all underlying commodities are ever delivered. The rest of the contracts (positions) are offset (closed out, or resold) before the delivery date.

➤ Know the difference between a hedger and a speculator. A hedger owns the underlying commodity and uses futures to protect his or her position in the event of a market rise or fall. A speculator does not own the underlying commodity and benefits by entering into a futures contract to try to reap the rewards—hopefully selling the contract and making big profits.

Chapter 30

Hedging Your Bets

In this chapter

➤ What different types of options exist

➤ Why stock investors use options to protect against market fluctuations

➤ How options give you leverage

There are many strategies available to you when you trade options, depending on whether or not you feel the market will go up or down. For the purposes of this chapter, I will briefly discuss a few common strategies. These strategies include hedging a portfolio or a particular investment, getting more bang for your buck through leveraging, and a conservative strategy that allows you to generate some income when you own stocks.

I Have the Option To Do WHAT?

Imagine having the chance to buy one hundred shares of stock in a company at a fixed price for a specified time period for a small premium. By paying this premium, you get the right, but not the obliga-

Bet You Didn't Know

Triple witching happens four times a year: on the third Friday of March, June, September, and October. On this day, the corresponding months' futures, index options, and equity options all expire together.

Strike price The price at which you can buy or sell the underlying security (typically stock). For example, if you bought a BCE January 45 call, the strike price here is 45. Purchasing this option would give you the right to buy one hundred shares of BCE stock at $45 a share. If you were to buy all 100 shares it would be known as exercising your option.

tion, to own those one hundred shares of stock at a pre-determined price. Oooh, what a bargain!

And you also get to enjoy the rewards if the current trading price goes up. There's a catch, but isn't there always? As you also learned in Chapter 15, there are risks involved when using leverage. In most cases, the more leverage you use, the more risky the investment situation. Does that make options risky? It sure does, but that's why people who invest in them often realize a 100% or even 300% return on their money. On the downside, it's also how they can lose all of their money. You could incur unlimited loss in some situations.

So what are they? Options give you the right—but not the obligation—to buy or sell a certain quantity of stock or bond, stock or bond index, or futures contract. These are known as the *underlying securities*. The option enables you to buy or sell these underlying securities at a certain price, which is the *strike price*, up to a specified point in time, known as the *expiration date*.

When investing in options, you have the right to either buy or sell the underlying security. Options that give you the right to buy the underlying stock (or whatever security) are known as *calls*. On the other hand, options that give you the right to sell the underlying security are known as *puts*. When you exercise your right—known as *exercising your option*—on a call, then you "call away" the stock from the seller you bought the option from. When you exercise your right on a put, then you "put" the underlying security to the seller of the put.

So what do you want these options to do? Here is a way that may help you to remember:

➤ When you buy an option to get the right to buy the underlying security, you are buying a call. When you buy a call, you want the price of the underlying security to go up. Therefore, think of it as "call up somebody on the telephone." Call up.

➤ When you buy an option to get the right to sell the underlying security, you are buying a put. When you buy a put, you want the price of the underlying security to go down. Therefore, think of it as "put down your foot." Put down.

Expiration date Using the same example, if you bought a BCE January 45 call, the expiration date is the third Friday in January. Expiration dates occur on the third Friday of every month for stock options. Expiration dates will vary depending on the underlying security.

WHAT?

Call Somebody Up on the Telephone

To repeat, when you buy a call option, you receive the right to buy the underlying security at a set price (the strike price) for a particular period of time. Typically, this period of time is just a few months.

Options are quoted in terms of dollars, so to speak. If you bought an option that is quoted at $2, it's not really two bucks, but rather $200 because underlying securities deal in round lots, equal to one hundred shares for stock options. Other options are quoted with varying round lots.

Okay, now for a little quiz. If you wanted to buy an option for a stock that was quoted at $1.25, what would the price be? Multiply it by 100. The answer is $125.00. Try another one. What if you wanted to buy ten options for a stock at $3.75. Use the same mathematical formula. Take 3.75 and multiply it by 100 (one hundred shares of stock, for instance) to get $375.00. But hey, you wanted ten options. Multiply $375.00 by 10 to get $3,750.00 (the price you'd have to pay for ten options).

Here's an example of how calls work. Suppose you want to buy a call option and you understand that you aren't necessarily buying the underlying security—just the right to buy the underlying security at a certain price. You buy a call option for $3 with a strike price of $50, for a total cost of $300, whose underlying security is BCE (Bell Canada Enterprises) the big corporate giant. In this hypothetical example, you bought the right to buy one hundred shares of BCE stock for $50 a share until November, which is (let us say) about four months from now.

Currently, BCE stock is trading at $53. Your option tells you that you can purchase the stock at $50, but the current price is $53. Does that mean you already made a profit? No. You must remember to add in the premium, which is the price you paid for the option. Right now you are about even.

Because you own a call option, you want BCE stock price to go up in value between now and November. If, for example, BCE stock price soars to $60, your option is *in-the-money* because the current trading price ($60) is higher than your strike price ($50). Your option price could skyrocket from $3 (where you bought it at) to $10 or more, which is what you want it to do.

Now you can do one of two things:

➤ Keeping in mind that you have the right to buy the stock, you could exercise your option. That means you "cash in" your right to buy one hundred shares of BCE stock at $50 a share (those were the particulars of the options). Then you would own one hundred shares of BCE stock at $50. But wait! The current trading price is $60. What you could do is sell your one hundred shares of BCE stock at $60 (the current market value) and make a hefty profit.

It's math time.

Bought one hundred shares of BCE stock at $50 = $5,000.

Sold one hundred shares of BCE stock at $60 = $6,000.

Profit you would realize = $1,000 (less the $300 option price and not including any commissions).

Percentage profit you would realize = 233% return, which is $1,000 less $300 divided by $300.

➤ If you don't exercise your option but instead sell the option—sell your right to buy the underlying stock—you would still make a profit. You could sell the option for $10 each and receive $1,000.

Your profit will equal the $1,000 less the $300 that you paid for the option (which is the premium).

Which is the better move? The end result is the same but selling the option is less cumbersome. It's really up to the investor, although most of the time, investors don't usually exercise their options to buy the underlying security.

If BCE stock price did not rise above $50 at all, the option would be considered *out-of-the-money* and come November, your option would expire worthless…and you'd lose all $300 of your investment.

When a person buys an option, he or she pays money for it. This money is called the **premium**. When a person sells an option (a form of "shorting"), he or she receives the premium.

Why would someone buy a call option? Because of *leverage*. But why would someone want to leverage their investment? Usually, the investor doesn't want to buy thousands of dollars worth of stock and instead uses a little bit of money to control a lot of shares. It's not that he or she can't afford it—although some investors might invest in options because they can't afford to buy stock. Because of the risks involved—losing all the money you paid as a premium—I would advise you to be very careful if you do invest in options. Look at the pyramid in Chapter 5!

Put Down Your Foot and Protect Your Portfolio

Call up. Put down. Remember that, and you'll know the basics of options trading.

When you buy a put option, there are usually two reasons for doing it: if you are feeling bearish and expect to profit from falling stock prices, or to protect your investment portfolio (kind of like insurance).

If you think the markets are ready to take a tumble, you could profit by

If you buy put options to protect your portfolio from downside risk, such as when there is a steep or declining market drop, your investments won't have to make up as much ground as they would if you didn't protect your portfolio.

The terms **in--the-money** and **out-of-the-money** do not indi cate whether the buyer or the seller is making or losing money. These terms refer only to the actual relationship between the strike price of an option and the stock price.

Out-of-the-money For a call option, the stock price is less than the strike price. For a put option, the stock price is greater than the strike price.

In-the-money For a call option, the stock price is more than the strike price. For a put option, the stock price is less than the strike price.

buying an index put option. You can buy a put option on the stock markets, for example, in hopes that the price of the stock index tumbles.

Buying put options also provides you with some "insurance." For example, if you owned one hundred shares of Gillgamesh Fishing Nets stock, and you wanted to protect your position because you're worried about losing money if the price of the stock plunges, you would buy a put option that has the underlying security of Gillgamesh Fishing Nets stock.

Think of what a put option is. It is the right to sell the underlying stock at a given price. If the price of Gillgamesh Fishing Nets stock dropped, you could help cushion the blow from the loss in the one hundred shares of stock you already own.

Let's say you bought one hundred shares of ProRata Data Tech Company at $20 a share about a year ago. Today, though, you're concerned about a steep decline in the price of the stock over the next couple of months because of market news and technical indicators. You think the price drop is just short-term, so you don't want to sell your stock, but you still need to protect your shares against any decline.

Here's what you do. Let's say it's the middle of June and the current market price is $25 a share and it's starting to slip to $23. You're concerned. In order to protect your position—and keep the shares—you can buy a put option with a strike price of $20, for example, that will expire in, let's say, three months. Let's say the put option costs $175.00, which is your premium. The option quote would look something like this:

ProRata Sept 20 put 1³/₄

Buying this put option means you have the right to sell one hundred shares of ProRata Data Tech stock for $20 a share before the expiration date in September. This right allows you to sell your stock at $20 a share no matter what the current trading price is.

If the stock price keeps falling, you have the following options:

➤ You have the right to exercise your option by selling your shares of stock for $20 a share no matter what the current stock price is.

➤ You can hold onto your underlying stock and "close the position," meaning, sell your put option. If you did this, you would make a profit because your put option would be in-the-money. If the stock dropped to $10 a share and the put option has a strike price of $20 a share, the amount of the intrinsic value is $10. That's how "in-the-money" your put option is.

In this scenario, if the stock price rose, your put option would be out-of-the money and your option would expire worthless. The amount of money you paid for the option—the premium—would be lost.

The premium of an option equals its in trinsic value and its time value.
Intrinsic value is that portion of a call that represents the amount by which the market price of a security exceeds the exercise price. The **time value** is the market value of the option less the intrinsic value.

When you invest in index options, you never exercise your options. It just isn't done—it's cash settlement. That would mean you would have to buy or sell all of the underlying stock, and the commissions alone could buy you a new home!

And Your Time Is Up

When do listed stock options expire? Are you ready? On a Saturday! Listed stock options expire on the Saturday following the third Friday of the expiration month at 11:59 p.m. EST. Options stop trading on the third Friday of every month. Check to see when your options expire.

If you don't close out your option position when you invest in index options, your option will expire worthless.

No, you don't have to worry about missing your favorite cartoons, because the final trading day of the week for options closes at 4:30 p.m. EST on the business day before the expiration day. By this cut-off time, you need to notify your broker whether or not you're going to exercise your option. This is why options are said to also have *time value*. This reflects any additional amount that purchasers of options are willing to pay in hopes that the changes in the underlying stock price or index price will increase the option's market value before the option expires.

The more time you have before an option expires, the more of a premium you pay. The less time you have until expiration the less the premium will cost you. Think of it this way. The more time, the more of a chance the stock price will move accordingly. The less time, the less of a chance it will get to where you want the price to go!

Options that have an expiry date longer than a year are called **leaps**.

Covered Calls versus Naked Calls (Yes, Naked!)

We've talked about what happens when you buy calls or puts. When you buy calls or puts, you either want the stock price to go up (call up), or go down (put down). Now think for a moment who might be selling you this call or put? And what strategy is the seller using?

Covered call writing is one of the few option strategies that is allowed in your RRSP.

Well, we won't get into all the various and complex strategies you can use with options, but I want you to know that they exist at least. One of the most common and conservative among option investing strategies is called *covered call writing*. Remember when you buy a call you hope that the stock price will rise and that the cost to purchase that option is the premium. Well, let's say you already own the stock.

For example, say you own 100 shares of BCE and it's trading at $49. You could sell the September 50 call at, say, $1.30. This would mean that someone bought this call from you and he or she has the right to buy the stock at $50 from you between now and the third Friday in September. So, if the buyer of your call "exercises" his or her option, you would have to sell to him or her your 100 shares of BCE at $50. Now, why would somebody want to sell the calls in the open market?

If I owned 100 shares of BCE at an average price of, say, $45 and it's now at $49, my objective might be to sell the stock at $50. If I sell the September 50 call and the call is exercised, I have to sell my stock for $50. So, I have met my objective.

Now for the good part. Not only have I reached my goal of selling my shares at $50, but I have also made an additional $130 ($1.30 x 100), which was the premium for selling the option in the first place.

Wait, it gets even better. The possibility exists that the call is not exercised and expires worthless. This mean that you get to keep the $130 premium you generated from selling the call in the first place and you also get to keep your 100 shares of BCE. Many times if this happens the investor will then sell the October 50 call to bring in another $130, let's say, and keep doing this. You will generate income each month and bring down the average price you originally paid for the stock. This strategy is called covered call writing because if you sell the option and the call gets exercised, you have to sell the stock at $50. You are covered because you already own the stock that you now have to sell.

Now, if you don't own the stock, you are not covered, meaning you're *naked*. So if the option was exercised, you'd be forced to buy the stock on the open market and then sell it at $50. If you are buying the stock in the open market, you may have to pay a lot more for the stock, say $55, and sell it for $50—a loss of $5 a share. This is called a naked, or *short* call. You can see that selling a naked call (when you don't own the underlying stock) is a much riskier strategy.

The downside to the covered call strategy is that if you write (sell) the covered call, you will not be able to participate in the upside appreciation of the stock if it occurs before your option expires. Using our example, let's say BCE goes to $60. As a covered call writer, you profit from selling your stock at $50 (remember, you sold the September $50 call) and you profited $130 from selling the option. But, you do not share in the profit above and beyond that to the $60.

Don't Forget Rights and Warrants

Rights and warrants share certain similarities with call options, which we just learned about. Each gives the holder or buyer the right to purchase additional stock at a specific price until the expiry date. Unlike options, rights and warrants are usually issued by the underlying corporation itself as a method of raising capital (options are usually created by investors).

The major difference between rights, warrants, and call options is the time to expiry. This difference in expiry is a major consideration when investment decisions are being made. Rights have the shortest life span—typically four to six weeks—while warrants tend to have a life span of three to five years. Call options, on the other hand, tend to expire within a year.

A *right* is the term applied to the privilege given to the shareholder to acquire additional shares directly from the issuing company. The quantity of shares the shareholder is allowed to acquire from the company depends on the terms set out by the company. If the shareholder decides to exercise his or her rights, there is no commission charged.

Rights are issued to shareholders in the same way as dividends; this means you have to purchase the underlying stock before the expiry date to be eligible to receive the rights.

A *warrant* is granted by the underlying company and gives the holder an option to purchase shares in the company from the issuer at a set price for a set period of time. The main speculative attraction of warrants is their leverage potential. The market price of a warrant is usually much less than the price of the underlying security and generally moves together with it. The capital appreciation of a warrant on a percentage basis can therefore greatly exceed that of the underlying security (keep in mind that this applies when the underlying security is appreciating or depreciating).

Rights and warrants, like options, will have a value assigned to them that depends on whether or not the underlying security is trading above the strike price (intrinsic value) and how much time is left before expiry (time value).

Judging the Overall Risk

With any investment strategy, but especially with options, please realize that there are many risks. Options aren't for everyone. Used wisely, options investing can be very profitable within your overall portfolio. Please consult a full-service broker to advise you.

Table 30.1 recaps the risk potential of various option transactions. Make sure you're aware of the risk you're incurring before making any investment.

Table 30.1 The Risk Scale

When you...	Maximum Profit	Maximum Loss
Buy a call	Unlimited	Premium paid
Buy a put	Strike price less premium paid	Premium paid
Write a call	Premium received	Unlimited
Write a put	Premium received	Strike price less premium received

The Least You Need To Know

➤ If you buy a call option, you want the stock to go up. You're buying the option to buy the stock (call it in) at a specific price.

➤ If you buy a put option, you want the stock to go down. You're buying the option to sell the stock (put it out) at a specific price.

➤ If you write a call, or short the call, you don't want the stock to go up.

➤ If you write a put, or short the put, you don't want the stock to go down.

"Buy a stock the way you would buy a house. Understand and like it such that you would be content to own it in the absence of any market."

—Warren Buffet

Part 7
Make That Money Grow

One of my favourite books, Think and Grow Rich (I wish it were that easy) by Napoleon Hill, has the best line I've ever read: "Opinions are the cheapest commodities on earth." You can always get an opinion on a stock, bond, or mutual fund investment from anybody. There are millions of opinions on investing: research report opinions issued by brokerage firms, rating agencies, survey companies, newsletters published by financial gurus and market wizards, and a host of TV programs telling viewers what they should and shouldn't sink their money into.

Making your own decisions about market information will enable you to have control over your financial destiny. If you are too easily influenced by the opinions of others, then all of the knowledge and investment smarts you have learned will go down the tubes.

You have the investment smarts to make your own decisions. This part tells you how to use that knowledge to make your money grow!

Your Investment Portfolio from $100 to $10,000

Now that you have all this financial information stored away in your brain (which is probably ready to burst), it's time to see how to assemble an investment portfolio. This chapter will help you finalize your investment decisions—no matter how much money you have to invest!

Where To Start

I've given you an education about what types of investments you can buy and the philosophy that you don't need a lot of money to start. The world of making a lot of money is available to everyone, rich and poor.

Making money on the Canadian stock market requires you to think about what kinds of investments are suitable for you. All of you who read this book have different levels of income and net worth, so the same investment portfolio that works well for me might not work out as well for you. I might be more of a risk-taker, and your investment approach may fall under the more conservative side.

I know you all want more from your investment programs. Some of you just want an investment program. The investment portfolios you are about to see are just guidelines. There aren't any secrets or any financial formulas to calculate. Any decision about how an investment portfolio is constructed is your decision and ultimately your responsibility. These are just suggestions. Your personal goals are different from anybody else's, but we're all looking for the same thing. It's not necessary to get rich, but we should all make our money work as hard for us as we do for it.

Bet You Didn't Know

If you have less than $100 to start out with, don't worry. There is still an investment for you—the monthly purchase plan. You can have as little as $25 each month allocated to the mutual fund of your choice. You can set this up through your broker. Remember, the earlier you start the more time your money can benefit from the power of compounding!

The $100 Portfolio

If you are just starting out, congratulations and welcome to making money on the markets. You have motivated yourself enough (and I hope I helped a little) to start an investment program. Don't worry that you're starting out with only $100 a month or even every other month. Instead, focus on how you're going to make that $100—and any additional contributions—grow. The idea is to start with $100 and continue adding as much as possible on a consistent basis. The more money you add, the more the magic of compounding can go to work for you!

The following investments are just suggestions. If you want to get your feet wet, these are a great way because most of them require no minimum investment amount, depending on which company you choose to invest in.

➤ **Money market mutual funds.**
The safest way to build your capital is to invest your $100 in a money market fund, if the fund company or bank allows you a low minimum deposit. In exchange for little to no risk of principal, you'll earn a low, competitive rate of interest.

➤ **Automatic investment plans.**
In exchange for a little more risk, take your entire $100 and invest it in a monthly purchase plan. This type of investment allows you to automatically and electronically have a set amount of money transferred from your bank account to the mutual fund of your choice. Start your automatic investment plan with your $100 deposit and pick an amount (such as $25) that you can work with to add subsequent investments. Then watch your money grow!

➤ **Dividend reinvestment programs.** In what is commonly known as a DRIP, you can invest your $100 and buy shares of stock. In order .o diversify your portfolio, a good way to start is to choose three different companies that offer DRIPs with low minimum deposits and very few transaction fees. Divide up your $100 three ways (you choose the amount) to get your DRIP program started. If possible, add at least the minimum amount allowed each month to the program.

➤ **Savings bonds.** Canada Savings Bonds have been available for sale since 1946. They can be purchased for as little as $100 and can be cashed in at any bank in Canada at any time. They're available for sale in the fall until November 1st of each year.

> If you want your $100 to benefit from the magic of compounding, your best bet would be to invest in a monthly purchase plan or a dividend reinvestment program. Savings accounts are safe; however, they pay low rates of interest.

The $1,000 Portfolio

When you can make your $100 turn into $1,000 or even if you are fortunate enough to start off with $1,000, here are a few avenues you can pursue. Remember, since some investments require initial minimum deposits of $1,000, you'll have to fully invest your $1,000. Otherwise, make sure you diversify your portfolio and allocate a certain percentage to each investment. The allocation percentage depends upon your investment objective (growth or income) and your level of risk.

➤ **Money market mutual funds.** Typically, the minimum initial deposit requirement to open money market mutual funds is $1,000. If you're a conservative investor and need liquidity (the ability to get at your cash quickly) from your investment portfolio, consider depositing your money in a money market mutual fund.

➤ **Stock and/or bond mutual funds.** Unless you go through a monthly purchase plan, many stock and bond funds require an initial deposit of $1,000 to invest. If your objective is growth, consider a stock growth fund for your $1,000. If your objective is income, consider a not-too-risky bond fund (no junk bond funds or commodity funds) for your $1,000. In either situation, make additional contributions on a monthly basis to take advantage of dollar cost averaging.

➤ **Automatic investment plans.** Since you can start with as little as $25 a month, allocate a portion—such as $50 or $100 a month—of your $1,000 to this plan. In fact, you could allocate $50 a month to a stock fund monthly purchase plan and $50 a month to a bond fund monthly purchase plan. This way you are diversifying your portfolio. Your other choices include a domestic stock fund and an international stock fund, an aggressive growth stock fund and a balanced fund. Whatever the mix, make sure it's the right one for you!

➤ **Dividend reinvestment plans.** Your $1,000 can be spread across several different DRIP stock programs. Each stock you select depends upon your investment objective (growth or income) and your risk tolerance. As an example, you could invest $100 in four different stocks, two growth stocks and two income-producing stocks, or you can invest $200 in two different stocks. The allocation strategy is up to you, but make sure you research the stocks you choose, monitor company news and performance, and that your decision is in line with your objectives.

➤ **Savings bonds.** If you're planning on using the $1,000 toward university tuition, a nice conservative investment would be a Canada Savings Bond.

The $5,000 Portfolio

Now that you have accumulated $5,000, you can either keep doing what you've been doing, or take on a little more risk by allocating some of your money into the investments listed below. The idea is to diversify your portfolio, so all of your money doesn't get put into just one investment.

➤ **Money market mutual funds—for cash needs.** Cash needs are those little "emergencies" that pop up, such as when you are laid off (not when you need to go to Las Vegas to "get away from it all" for a weekend). Most investors keep a portion of their portfolios in cash, anywhere between zero and thirty percent.

➤ **Families of mutual funds.** Now you can choose several different types of mutual funds. Because you meet the minimum initial deposit requirements, consider investing $5,000 in five different funds. You can choose from aggressive stock funds, growth stock funds, balanced funds, and international funds. Five funds aren't too many as long as you are diversified in your holdings.

➤ **Automatic investment plans.** If you have been following this plan, continue to take advantage of dollar cost averaging. You don't need to sink all $5,000 in this plan; however, make it a point to increase your monthly contribution.

➤ **Foreign stock mutual funds.** The risks are greater, but the reward is, too. In 1993, the average international stock mutual fund returned slightly above 40%. I don't advise sinking all your money into this sector because of the risks involved. The more aggressive you are in your investment objectives, the more money you can allocate to these types of funds.

➤ **Stocks.** You can start but be careful. You have more money now to actually buy one hundred shares of stock, but the risks involved are greater. You don't necessarily have to sink all $5,000 into stocks, but for those of you searching for growth, a long-term growth stock with stable performance history might be a good choice. If dividends are the name of your game, consider researching companies that provide good, steady income. In either event, you can allocate your $5,000 among a few different stocks—just make sure you do your homework! (Refer to Chapter 6 for a refresher course.)

The $10,000 or More Portfolio!

Ten grand. Congratulations. Keep chugging along, you're doing great. Remember, a quitter never wins and a winner never quits! Don't get caught up because there are more zeros after the one in your investment portfolio now. Investment success requires long-term planning.

Add to your positions. If you currently own one hundred shares of Bells and Whistles stock and want to invest more money into the same company, you would buy more shares. Therefore, you would be adding more shares to the number you already own.

➤ **Money market funds—for those emergency needs.** Make sure you have a portion of your portfolio allocated to money market funds to help cushion any financial blows. Keep a percentage of your $10,000 in cash that you feel comfortable with—but not so much that you don't take advantage of higher returns elsewhere.

➤ **Mutual funds—stock and bond funds and foreign funds.** All types of mutual funds are available to you now. If you currently are investing in mutual funds, consider allocating a significant portion to each fund. If you are new to this ball game, make sure you are well-diversified and that you meet your investment objectives.

➤ **Automatic investment plans.** If you consistently do this, it's habit-forming. Keep up with your monthly purchase plan. At this point, you may wish to increase your monthly contributions.

➤ **Stocks.** Make sure you have done your homework. If you're happy with the performance of your stocks and you are investing for the long-term, you may want to add to your positions.

➤ **Fixed-income securities.** Depending on the direction of interest rates, consider looking into these now. Remember the minimum investment requirement for each fixed-income security, the risks involved, and the tax ramifications. For example, $10,000 buys a Treasury bill, but since $10,000 is all of your portfolio, investing only in a T-bill wouldn't follow the guideline of diversification. Keep in mind the higher degree of risk, the higher the return. If you are concerned with safety of principal, you can always look into a high quality government bond instead.

What about options and futures trading as you make more money? It's up to you, as long as you know what risks are involved. As my mother always taught me, "When in doubt, don't."

The Least You Need To Know

➤ It doesn't take a lot of money to make money.

➤ If you want to reach financial security, then you have to make your investment portfolio grow. Do it slowly and mainly over a long-term period.

➤ You know the ten percent rule that I constantly drilled into everyone's head in the beginning of the book? Use it as a means to add to your investment portfolio.

Money often costs too much.

—Ralph Waldo Emerson

One More, Dude

Chapter 32

Tips on Taxes from A to Z

In this chapter

➤ Just a few basics about tax planning—year round

➤ A breakdown of how you're taxed on all investments, profit or loss!

➤ How some investments are timed

The last item on your to-do list right now is worrying about this year's or next year's tax deadline, right? (Unless it is that time of year right now, and you're knee-deep in receipts with your accountant sleeping on a cot in your living room.)

Knowing sound tax strategies is an integral part of your investment planning, and this chapter can be a big help. After all, the more money you make in investing, the more you'll have to pay to the government. By putting smart tax strategies into effect now, you can avoid hassles come tax time—and keep your hard-earned cash in your pocket.

Adding Up the Pluses and Minuses

Ideally, tax planning should be an ongoing process throughout the year, as part of an overall financial plan. You should review your particular situation regularly to ensure you've structured your finances so as to minimize your taxes. But, if you're one of those procrastinators who wait until April 29th to pull out your tax file (that is, if you have one), keep reading! This chapter will give you some tax planning suggestions that will help organize your tax file.

While the February 1997 Federal Budget proposed no tax increases, that doesn't mean next year's taxes won't increase. So don't memorize last year's tax rules. Things are always a changin'. The tax bracket you fall under and how you structure your investing requires you to be careful! If you find yourself paying more in taxes every year, don't wait until the last minute to look for some cash. You might end up having to sell some stock shares for only a slight profit, or even a loss. If you start squirreling away some extra money right now to pay for your tax bill in April, the easier it will be.

Also, if you are self-employed, go in for a financial check-up immediately! If you're making estimated payments, increase them. If you're employed full-time, either have your boss increase your withholding or put some dollars away every month in a money market fund earmarked for your tax payments. Every little bit helps.

Tax planning doesn't just concern the wealthy. You might find yourself in a new tax bracket if you planned your investments properly and made a few profits along the way.

Do It in June, Not April

Just as Bernard Baruch, legendary stock trader and millionaire, said to buy straw hats in winter and snowsuits in July, so should you begin your tax planning the June before your taxes are due! Sure, April is ten months away, but you know what our mothers always tell us. The early bird gets the worm. Assessing your tax situation when everything is a bit more relaxing allows you to take the time to make a more thorough review of your investments and how they could affect your taxes.

Go Tax-Free

An absolute must (as you learned in Chapter 4), is to set up an RRSP and make your maximum allowable contribution every year. Remember that your RRSP is a fully tax-sheltered vehicle—you can deduct your contributions from your taxable income come April.

As your tax rate increases, the value of tax-free investing increases, too. Compare yields that you would earn from investing inside an RRSP versus outside. Even the money that you earn on your RRSP investments compounds tax-free!

Listen folks, no matter what tax bracket you fall under or how small your investments, if you are planning to make your investment objectives work for you, you need to know about tax planning strategies. Familiarize yourself with any change in the tax rules and be sure to consult with a tax adviser. Tax planning is one area where it is definitely worth paying for good advice.

No Pain, No Capital Gain

When you buy low and sell high, you get a profit. That profit—known as a capital gain—has to be reported to Revenue Canada. And when you buy high and sell low, you get a loss—a capital loss. That amount of loss must be reported to Revenue Canada as well. Why would you want a loss? You'll see why in a minute.

To make tax preparation easier on you, make sure you record all of the prices at which you bought and sold your investment securities. Usually, a brokerage firm will have this information, but make sure you do too, in your financial records. Keep copies of all of your confirmation statements for all of your transactions.

In the month of January, you should receive a trading summary from your brokerage firm. This form will tell you what you currently own and what you bought and sold during the year for either a profit or a loss. In any case, you should keep track of all your trading transactions, including any capital gains and losses.

If your goal is to reduce your taxable income and/or offset any capital gains, consider selling the investment to get the capital loss. The amount will be applied to the following year's tax return.

Profits = Capital Gains

Profits are known as capital gains. Three-quarters of your capital gain is taxed at your full marginal tax rate.

What if you have a loss? I mean, what if you picked the biggest loser of all

> ### Bet You Didn't Know
>
> Capital losses can be carried backward three years to be applied against capital gains, or can be carried forward indefinitely to be used against any future capital gains.

time? (Maybe you should re-read this book!) It's called a capital loss. No investor likes losses, but there is a bright side. You can apply capital losses against your capital gains, thereby reducing the amount of tax you pay.

If, for example, you have $10,000 worth of gains in one tax year and also $10,000 worth of losses, you can net the losses against the gains. Therefore, you wouldn't have any taxable income from your investments.

Should this make you feel better about any losses you incur? Maybe. The bottom line rests with the amount of the cheque you send off to the government, or the amount you get back if you're getting a refund!

Dividends and Interest

Revenue Canada will send you a T-5 slip that details your interest and dividend income. Interest income (e.g. from all bonds and GICs) are taxed at your full marginal tax rate. Dividends that you receive are taxed more favourably than regular income such as interest income. You are entitled to a dividend gross-up and credit from dividends you receive from taxable Canadian corporations. It works like this. The amount of the dividend is grossed up by 25%. For example, if you receive $1,000 in dividends, it would be reported as $1,250 in taxable income. The $1,250 in taxable income is subject to federal tax. But, you then can claim a federal tax credit of 13.33%. Provincial tax is then deducted. (The gross-up and federal tax credit are shown on your T-5 slip.) Here is the example laid out step by step:

Canadian Dividend Gross-Up and Credit Calculations

Dividend Income:	$1,000
Gross-up (25% of $100)	250
Taxable Income	$1,250
Federal Tax	325
(e.g. 26% of $1,250)	
Federal Tax Credit	167
(13.33% of $1,250)	
Federal Tax Payable (325 – 167)	158
Provincial Tax	84
(e.g. 53% of $158 (fed. tax payable)	
Total taxes payable ($158 + $84)	$242
Net Dividend ($1,000 – $242)	$758

Now, to recap the your different types of investment income and taxation. The three types of investment income you may receive are: capital gains income, dividend income, and interest income. Interest income is taxed at your full marginal tax rate. Both capital gains and dividend income receive preferential tax treatment. Capital gains are taxed at your full marginal tax rate, but only taxed on three-quarters of the capital gain. With dividend income, you are entitled to a 25% gross-up and a federal tax credit of 13.33%.

Bet You Didn't Know

One of the best ways to accumulate income and defer paying taxes on it is to set up a Registered Retirement Savings Plan (RRSP). Not only are you able to deposit tax-deductible contributions up to a certain limit, you can also accrue interest and capital gains tax-free until they are withdrawn.

It's All in the Timing

There are two things in life that could really turn sour if you get the timing wrong. Jokes and taxes.

Timing when you buy and sell investment products does have an effect on your financial situation, either by putting you into a different tax bracket or by getting you a bigger tax refund in the mail. Either way, here are a few tips you should know. Don't limit yourself to reading these words. Always consult a tax adviser if you have any tax-related questions.

Timing your decision to sell an investment is just as important as choosing the right time to buy an investment. If, for example, it is mid-December and you have a stock that you want to sell at a loss because it isn't performing well, you could do two things:

1. Sell the additional stock for a loss and apply it to any capital gains you have. If you have no capital gains to apply the loss to, you can carry forward your loss indefinitely.

2. Watch the timing of a capital gain. It may be advantageous if you are late in a calendar year (say, December) to wait until January to sell a security and lock in a capital gain for the following year; this way you delay paying taxes for one more year.

Keep in mind that if you are selling stock to lock-in a capital loss, there may be some restrictions for purchasing the stock back in the near future. Consult your tax advisor for more details.

The Least You Need To Know

➤ Start evaluating your tax situation right now. Find out what tax bracket you are in. Even if it's the middle of July and April 30 is not for another nine months, there's no better time than the present.

➤ If you are organized in your taxes, you have better control over your investment strategies. You'll know when to take a capital gain and when to take a loss.

➤ Always, and I repeat, always consult a tax adviser if you have any complicated tax issues.

Appendix

Investment Dealers Association of
Canada (IDA)
121 King Street West, Suite 1600
Toronto, Ontario M5H 3T9
Tel: (416) 364-6133

Canadian Investor Protection Fund
(CIPF)
P.O. Box 192
200 Bay Street
Toronto, Ontario M5J 2J4
Tel: (416) 866-8366

Canada Deposit Insurance
Corporation (CDIC)
Toll-free: 1-800-461-CDIC

Provincial Securities Commissions
Alberta Securities Commission
4th Floor, Alberta Stock Exchange
Tower
300-5th Avenue S.W.
Edmonton, Alberta T2P 3C4
Tel: (403) 297-4277

British Columbia Securities
Commission
1200-865 Hornby Ave.
Vancouver, B.C. V6Z 2H4
Tel: (604) 660-4800

Manitoba Securities Commission
1130-405 Broadway Avenue
Winnipeg, Manitoba R3C 3L6
Tel: (204) 945-2548

New Brunswick Securities
Commission
133 Prince William Street, Suite 102
P.O. Box 5001
Saint John, New Brunswick E2L 4Y9
Tel: (506) 658-3060

Newfoundland Securities
Commission
Department of Justice
2nd Floor, West Block
75 O'Leary Avenue, P.O. Box 8700
St. John's, Newfoundland A1B 4J6
Tel: (409) 729-4189

NorthWest Territories Securities
Commission
Department of Justice
Government of N.W. Territories
P.O. Box 1320
Yellowknife, N.W.T. X1A 2L9
Tel: (403) 873-7490

Nova Scotia Securities Commission
Joseph How Building, 2nd Floor
1690 Hollis Street, P.O. Box 458
Halifax, Nova Scotia B3J 3J9
Tel: (902) 424-7768

Ontario Securities Commission
20 Queen St. West, Suite 1800 Box 55
Toronto, Ontario M5H 3S8
Tel: (416) 593-8200

Prince Edward Island Securities
Commission
Dept. Of Community Affairs &
Attorney General
Consumer, Corporate & Insurance
Division
95 Rochford Street, 4th Floor,
P.O. Box 2000
Charlottetown, PEI C1A 7N8
Tel: (902) 368-4550

Quebec Securities Commission
Stock Exchange Tower,
800 Victoria Square
P.O. Box 246, 17th Floor
Montreal, Quebec H4Z 1G3
Tel: (514) 873-5326

Saskatchewan Securities
Commission
T.D. Bank Building, Suite 850
800-1920 Broad Street

Regina, Saskatchewan S4P 3V7
Tel: (306) 787-5645

Yukon Territory Securities
Commission
Government of Yukon Territory
P.O. Box 2703
Whitehorse, Yukon Territory
Y1A 2C6
Tel: (403) 667-5811

Stock Exchanges in Canada

The Alberta Stock Exchange
300-5th Avenue S.W., 21st Floor
Calgary, Alberta T2P 3C4
Tel: (403) 974-7400

The Montreal Stock Exchange*
800 Victoria Square, P.O. Box 61,
4th Floor
Montreal, Quebec H4Z 1A9
Tel: (514) 871-2424

The Toronto Stock Exchange*
Exchange Tower
2 First Canadian Place
P.O. Box 450, 4th Floor
Toronto, Ontario M5X 1J2
Tel: (416) 947-4700

The Vancouver Stock Exchange
Stock Exchange Tower
609 Granville Street, P.O. Box 10333
Vancouver, B.C. V7Y 1H1
Tel: (604) 689-3334

The Winnipeg Stock Exchange
1 Lombard Place, Room 2901
Winnipeg, Manitoba R3B 0Y2
Tel: (204) 987-7070

The Winnipeg Commodity
Exchange*
500-360 Main
Winnipeg, Manitoba R3C 3Z4
Tel: (204) 925-5000

*Futures contracts are traded on
these exchanges

Selected Mutual Fund Companies: Top Ten by assets under management

(from largest to smallest)
Please note that all of the following
mutual fund companies have offices
across Canada. You can reach your
nearest office by calling the toll-free
numbers as listed.

Investors Group Inc.
1 Canada Centre
447 Portage Avenue
Winnipeg, Manitoba R3C 3B6
Toll-free: 1-888-746-6344

Trimark Investment Management Inc.
One First Canadian Place
Suite 5600, P.O. Box 487
Toronto, Ontario M5X 1E5
Toll free: 1-800-465-3399

Royal Mutual Funds Inc.
Toll-free: 1-800-463-3863

Mackenzie Financial Corporation
Toll free: 1-800-387-0780

Templeton Management Limited
Toll-free: 1-800-387-0830

TD Asset Management Inc.
P.O. Box 100
Toronto Dominion Centre
Toronto, Ontario M5K 1G8
Toll-free: 1-800-268-8166

AGF Group of Funds
P.O. Box 50
Toronto Dominion Bank Centre
Toronto, Ontario M5K 1E9
Toll-free: 1-800-268-8583

Fidelity Investments
Toll-free: 1-888-203-4778

CIBC Securities Inc.
Toll-free: 1-800-465-3863

CT (Canada Trust) Investment
Management
Toll-free: 1-800-386-3757

Financial Planning Sources

*Deloitte & Touche Canadian Guide to
Personal Financial Management* by
John Budd, Claude Rinfret, Nicholas
Seed, and Danielle Lacasse Brien
This workbook contains more than
30 straightforward tear-out forms
that form the foundation of a per-
sonalized financial plan. Published
by Prentice Hall Canada. Available at
most major bookstores across
Canada for approximately $19.95.

60 Minute Financial Planner
by Dana Shilling. Published by
Prentice Hall. Retails for approximately $26.95

"Every man is the architect of his own fortune."

—Appius Claudius

Money Talks—Learn the Language

Accrued interest This is the interest collected on a bond since the last interest payment was made. The buyer of the bond pays not only the market price but also the accrued interest. This should be shown on a trade confirmation.

Analyst This is a person who has been trained to investigate all of the facts concerning a stock, bond, mutual fund, future or option. An analyst often gives opinions and advice to help a potential investor decide what to do.

Annual Report This is a financial statement issued by a company that shows all of its pluses and minuses, including whether the company made a profit or not.

Annual or Annualized Return Expresses the rate of return for a time-frame that is greater than one year. The rate of return is calculated in terms of a twelve-month period.

Annual Yield The amount of money, percentage of return in dividends, or interest an investor receives from an investment. This figure is then calculated on an annual basis.

Annuity A contract usually sold by life insurance companies that guarantees an income to the beneficiary or annuitant at some time in the future.

Appreciation That fake smile you put on your face when your in-laws bring over the Christmas fruitcake, or, in the investment world, what is known as price improvement.

Asked or Offering Price The lowest price which any seller will accept for a security that you want to buy. You, as the buyer, would buy the investment at the asked or offering price.

Asset allocation How you carve up your investment pie. Represented usually in percentages, such as the percentage you have in stocks, bonds, mutual funds, etc.

Assets What you own.

At a discount Below par value, typically $1,000, in the world of bond investing. If a bond is selling at 95 ($950) and par is 100 ($1,000), then the bond is selling at a discount.

At a premium Above par value, typically $1,000, in the world of bond investing. If a bond is selling at 105 ($1,050) and par is 100 ($1,000), then the bond is selling at a premium.

At auction Where to buy antique furniture—oops, sorry. How Treasury securities are bought.

At par Equal to face value, which is usually $1,000.

At the close The final few milliseconds when the trading day stops.

At the market Market order.

At the opening Opposite of at the close. You would get the best price possible if you were to buy or sell a security when the market opened.

Averages Also known as indices. The TSE 300 is the one most often used in Canada. They represent a way of measuring the trend of security prices.

Averaging down Buying more of a security at a lower price than the original investment. Aim: to reduce the average cost per unit.

Balance sheet Found in the annual report, it lists the pluses and minuses of a company. You should make one for yourself, too!

Balanced funds A mutual fund that diversifies its securities by purchasing many kinds of stocks and bonds.

Bank Rate The minimum rate at which the Bank of Canada makes short-term advances to the chartered banks.

Basis point A measurement of change, whether up or down, in the current yield equal to one one-hundredth of 1% on bonds or bills.

Bear Market A market where prices drop rather sharply. Pessimism, growing unemployment, and sometimes a recession are common. Opposite of bull market.

Bid and Asked A quote.

Bid price This is the highest quoted price that any potential buyer will pay you for a security that you are trying to sell.

Block An exceptionally large chunk of stock purchased, typically ten thousand shares or more.

Blue chip The stock of a leading company which is known for superior management.

Board Lot A regular trading unit which has uniformly been decided upon by stock exchanges.

Bond An IOU issued by corporations, the federal and provincial government, foreign governments, and city municipalities. These entities borrow money from investors and promise to pay them back in full plus interest at a later date.

Broker A person who handles your order to buy and sell securities.

Bull Market An advancing market, where everything is on the upswing. Opposite of a bear market.

Business cycle A regularly recurring period that all businesses go through. Shows where the country is in terms of recession, depression, recovery, and expansion.

Buy order An order to buy a security that you specify.

Call An option that gives the option holder the right—but not the obligation—to buy the underlying stock.

Callable A feature on a bond that says the issuer can redeem the bond before maturity.

Canadian Investor Protection Fund (CIPF) A fund set up by the stock exchanges and the Investment Dealers Association to protect investors from losses resulting from the bankruptcy of a member firm.

Capital gain or loss Profit or loss from the sale of an investment.

Cash dividend A dividend paid on an investment in cash or by check.

Central Bank A body established by a national government to regulate currency and monetary policy on a national-international level. In Canada, it is the Bank of Canada; in the United states, the Federal Reserve Board; in the U.K., the Bank of England.

Closed-end fund Opposite of an open-end mutual fund. The fund's shares are traded on a securities exchange where the number of shares outstanding is limited.

Closing price The price at which the final transaction of a security took place on a particular business day.

Commodity exchange An organization of traders who buy and sell contracts for future delivery of commodities, such as grain, sugar, coffee, gold, and soybeans.

Common stock An investment that represents ownership interest in a corporation.

Compounding It is a mathematical process of finding the final value of an investment when the compound interest is applied. It's a matter of taking the interest earned on the interest earned on the principal investment. Get out your calculators!

Consumer Price Index It is an economic report that is looked upon as a good indicator of inflation.

Corporate bond A bond issued by a corporation. The corporation borrows the money from the lenders (investors) and promises to pay them back their "loan" at a specified date plus interest.

Convertible A bond, debenture or preferred share which may be exchanged by the owner, usually for the common stock of the same company, in accordance with the terms of the conversion privilege.

Covered Writer The writer of an option who also holds a position that is equivalent to, but on the opposite side of, the market from the short option position.

Credit rating Typically used in describing the credit risk involved in a bond investment. Indicated by a letter, usually given by one of the large credit rating companies, such as Moody's and Standard & Poor's.

Current yield Annual bond interest divided by the market price per bond.

Cyclical stocks Stocks that move in the same direction as the business cycle. When business conditions are improving, cyclical stocks tend to follow and vice-versa.

Day order An order to buy (or sell) an investment, which, if not executed, expires at the end of the trading day.

Deficit The money the government—or even a company—pays out in excess of what it takes in over a given period.

Depression A prolonged period of sharply reduced business activity. Typically characterized by high unemployment, low production, and a major drop in consumer buying.

Discount In the world of bond investing, it is the amount by which a bond sells below its face value. If the face value of the bond is $1,000 and it is selling for $950, it is selling at a discount. Opposite of premium.

Diversification The spreading of investment funds among classes of securities and localities in order to distribute the risk. Don't put all of your eggs in one basket.

Dividend The proportion of a company's net earnings paid to its stockholders.

Dividend Tax Credit System A procedure to encourage Canadians to invest in preferred and common shares of taxable, dividend-paying Canadian corporations.

Dividend yield Expressed as a percent. Divide the dividend payment by the market price of the stock.

Dollar cost averaging This is when a fixed dollar amount is invested on a periodic basis into one or more investments, thereby enabling the investor to average the purchase of shares (if it's a stock or mutual fund) over the long haul.

Dow Jones Industrial Average A popular gauge of the US stock market based on the average closing prices of thirty US blue-chip stocks.

Due date Maturity date.

Earnings per share This is a company's net income minus preferred dividends divided by the outstanding shares of stock. Also known as EPS.

Equities Refers to ownership of property, such as having equity in your home or owning stocks.

Exercise Price The price at which a warrant can be exchanged for a share of the underlying security. For an option, it is the price at which the underlying security can be purchased, in the case of a call, or sold, in the case of a put, by the option holder. Synonymous with strike price.

Ex-dividend A divorced dividend. No, really, it is the date where the buyer of a stock must own the stock in order to receive the dividend.

Execute an order To fulfill an order to buy or sell a security.

Expiration date The last day on which a stock option may be exercised.

Face value The value of the bond that appears on the face of the bond. Remember, face value is not an indication of market value.

Federal Reserve System The central banking system of the United States made up of twelve Federal Reserve banks and supervised by the Federal Reserve Board.

Financial statement Another term for balance sheet.

Fixed-income Securities Securities that generate a predictable stream of interest or dividend income, such as bonds, debentures and preferred shares.

Fluctuations Variations in the market price of a security. Means it goes up and down.

Forward contract Contracts where two parties agree to the purchase and sale of a commodity at some future time and at a specific price.

Fundamental Analysis Analysis based on factors such as earnings growth and value.

Futures A contract in which the seller agrees to deliver a specified commodity or financial instrument at a specified price sometime in the future.

Gross Domestic Product The market value of the country's total output of goods and services.

Growth stock The stock issued by a corporation whose earnings have increased consistently over a number of years.

Guaranteed Investment Certificate (GIC) A deposit instrument most commonly available from trust companies and banks, requiring a minimum investment at a predetermined rate of interest for a stated term. Generally non-redeemable prior to maturity but there can be exceptions.

Hedging The temporary purchase or sale of a contract (either futures or options) calling for future delivery of a specific quantity of an investment at an agreed price to offset a present position.

Index In economics, it is a statistical benchmark or yardstick, if you will, expressed in terms of percentage of a base year or years.

Index fund A fund comprising securities that will produce (hopefully) a return that replicates a designated securities index.

Inflation A phase of the business cycle characterized by changing economic conditions, including sky-high prices and a loss of purchasing power. If you've been to the grocery store recently, you'll know what I'm talking about.

Initial Public Offering (IPO) A new issue of securities offered to the public for investment for the very first time. IPOs must adhere to strict government regulations as to how the investments are sold to the public.

Interest The amount a borrower pays a lender for the use of his or her money.

Interest rate risk When interest rates rise (or fall), the market value of a bond declines (or rises). Interest rate risk is associated with these fluctuations.

In-the-money In options investing, it is the striking price that is below the market price of the stock.

Intrinsic Value That portion of a warrant or call option's price that represents the amount by which the market price of a security exceeds the price at which the warrant or call option may be exercised (exercised price).

Investment objectives Before you invest, you need them. They should be long-term, risk/return objectives developed principally from careful consideration of what you want to do with your money and where you want to go.

Investment portfolio A securities portfolio.

Lender I need money. You let me borrow it. You are the lender.

Leverage A condition where you get the maximum bang for your buck.

Liabilities The amount of money that you, a company, or the government owes to others.

Limit order An order to buy (sell) a stated amount of a security at a specific or better price.

Liquidity When you have sufficient cash available at the time you need it. The ability to get at your money quickly. If you need money but you can't sell your investment because there isn't a buyer, the investment is said to be illiquid.

Load The commissions and sales charges associated with a mutual fund. Opposite of no-load.

Management Expense Ratio The total expense of operating a mutual fund expressed as a percentage of the fund's net asset value. It includes the management fee as well as other expenses like brokerage fees, audit, legal fees, etc., which are charged directly to the fund. Published rates of return are calculated after the management expense ratio has been deducted.

Margin The amount paid by a client when he uses credit to buy a security, the balance being loaned by his or her broker against acceptable collateral.

Market order An order to buy (sell) a security at the best price possible.

Market price The last reported price at which an investment sold.

Maturity The date on which a loan comes due and is to be paid off.

Money Market That part of the capital market in which short-term financial obligations are bought and sold. These include treasury bills and other federal government securities maturing in three years or less and Commercial Paper, Bankers' Acceptances, Guaranteed Investment Certificates and other instruments with a year or less left to maturity. Longer term securities, when their term shortens to the limits mentioned, are also traded in the money market.

Mortgage Backed Securities (MBS) Similar to bonds, the current $5,000 units with five-year terms are backed by a share in a pool of home mortgages insured under the National Housing Act. Units pay interest and part principal each month. They trade in the bond market at prices reflecting current interest rates.

Mutual fund company A company that uses its customers' deposits to invest in securities of other companies through their mutual funds and pools the money together into a fund that is based on specific criteria, such as investment objectives and risk tolerance.

Naked Writer A seller of an option contract who does not own an offsetting position in the underlying security or a suitable alternative.

NASDAQ Stands for National Association of Securities Dealers Automated Quotations. A techno-geek automated information network which provides brokers with quotes on securities (typically stocks).

Net worth The total amount of equity/assets that you have after you calculate what you own against what you owe.

New York Stock Exchange Known as the NYSE or the "Big Board," this is an exchange where hundreds of securities trade every day.

No-load fund A mutual fund that does not carry any commissions or sales charges.

Noncallable securities Securities which cannot be redeemed before the date of maturity.

Odd lot An amount of stock bought (or sold) that is less than one hundred shares.

Offer The price at which a person is willing to sell.

Open order An order to buy (or sell) at a stipulated price which remains effective until it is executed.

Opening price A security's price at the first trade of the day.

Over-the-Counter (OTC) A market for securities made up of securities dealers who may or may not be members of a recognized stock exchange. Over-the-counter is mainly a market conducted over the telephone. Also called the unlisted, inter-dealer or street market.

P/E Ratio Price earnings ratio. This measures whether a stock is over-valued or not. You take the stock's market price and divide it by its current or estimated future earnings.

Par value This is the amount to be received in cash at maturity of a bond.

Point A point means $1. If XYZ Company stock rises three points, it means it rose $3.

Position Think of it as a market commitment of what you hold. If you own one hundred shares of stock, the one hundred shares are your position.

Preferred stock Securities which represent an ownership interest (like stock) but have preference over the other shares in terms of dividends.

Premium The amount by which a security sells over its face value.

Price The market value of anything being offered for sale.

Prime Rate The interest rate chartered banks charge to their most credit-worthy borrowers.

Principal The dollar amount of your initial investment on which you earn interest.

Profit The money that you have remaining after all costs of operating a business are paid, or when you buy low and sell high.

Prospectus A legal document that explains the complete history and current status of an investment security.

Purchasing power The goods and services that you can buy given any amount of money. If there is inflation, you will have a loss in purchasing power of some goods.

Put option An option that gives the investor the right-but not the obligation to sell the underlying security.

Quote "I think, therefore I am." Oh, in investing? It is the highest bid to buy and the lowest offer to sell a security.

Rally A quick rise following a decline in the general price level of the market.

Registered Retirement Savings Plan (RRSP) A vehicle available to individuals to defer tax on specified amounts of money to be used for retirement. The holder invests money in one or more of a variety of investment vehicles which are held in trust under the plan. Income tax on contributions and earnings within the plan are deferred until the money is withdrawn at retirement. RRSPs can be transferred into Registered Retirement Income Funds.

Registered Retirement Income Fund (RRIF) A tax-deferred vehicle available to Registered Retirement Savings Plan holders. The plan holder invests the funds in the RRIF and must withdraw a certain amount each year. Income tax would be due on the funds withdrawn.

Return The amount of money that you receive annually from an investment typically expressed as a percentage.

Risk Any chance of loss.

Round lot When you buy one hundred shares of stock, that is known as a round lot. It's a unit of trading. See also odd lot.

Rule of 72 A mathematical formula used to determine how long it takes to double your money. Divide the rate of return by 72. Your answer will give you the number of years it takes.

Safekeeping fee A fee that a bank or brokerage firm will charge its customers who keep their stock and bond certificates in the vault.

Savings accounts An account in a bank that earns a pretty low rate of interest.

SEC The securities and Exchange Commission, a federal body established by the United States Congress, to protect investors in the U.S. In Canada there is no national regulatory authority; instead, securities legislation is provincially administered.

Security Note, stock, bond, or any type of investment product.

Settlement date The date on which the final consummation of a transaction takes place and when the money is due!

Short sale This is a trade made by investors who believe the market is going to take a tumble. They borrow the stock from the brokerage firm that is selling at its current price. These investors hope that the stock will drop in price so they can buy back the shares.

Speculation A risk taken in order to achieve a greater return.

Spousal RRSP A special type of RRSP in which one spouse contributes to a plan registered in the beneficiary spouse's name. The contributor receives the tax deduction. See Registered Retirement Savings Plan.

Spread The difference between the bid price and the asked (offering) price.

Stock A certificate of ownership. See Common stock or Preferred stock.

SRO Short for self-regulatory organization, such as the Investment Dealers Association of Canada and the principal stock exchanges.

Stock split A division made of the stock (decided upon by the company's board of directors) to either create more shares or reduce the number of shares (which is known as a reverse stock split.)

Stockholder If you buy stock, you are a stockholder.

Stop order An order to buy (or sell) at a price above (or below) the current market price.

Street name Securities belonging to a client of a brokerage firm registered in the name of the brokerage firm.

T-Bills A colloquialism for government treasury bills.

Technical analysis An approach by market wizards (with graph paper) who chart price movements and volatility to determine the best time to buy and/or sell a security.

Time Value The amount, if any, by which the current market price of a right, warrant, or option exceeds its intrinsic value.

Total return The aggregate increase in the value of the portfolio resulting from calculating all of the pluses and minuses.

Trader A person who actively buys and sells investment securities.

Treasury Bills Short-term government debt issued in denominations ranging from $1,000 to $1,000,000. Treasury bills do not pay interest, but are sold at a discount and mature at Par (100% of face value). The difference between the purchase price and par at maturity represents the lender's (purchaser's) income in lieu of interest.

Underlying security The shares of stock (or other security) subject to the exercise of an option.

Volume The total number of shares traded during a given period.

Warrant A certificate giving the holder the right to purchase securities at a stipulated price within a specified time limit. Warrants are usually issued with a new issue of securities as an inducement or sweetener to investors to buy the new issue.

Wealth What you are working to accumulate.

Wilshire 5000 index An all-equity, very broad-based index comprising five thousand stocks.

Yield The return of an investment expressed as a percentage.

Yield curve A visual illustration and representation of the term structure of interest rates.

Yield to maturity The return provided by a bond to its maturity date.

Zero-coupon bond A bond that has no interest payments, which you buy at a discount. You should receive the face value of the bond upon maturity.

Index

About the Author

Stephen Nelson is a graduate of the Economics program at the University of Western Ontario, and presently works as a Senior Investment Advisor at TD Evergreen, TD Bank's full-service brokerage firm. His clients include individuals, institutions, and non-profit organizations. Stephen has been servicing his clients for over nine years and has built a wealth of knowledge in fixed income and equity markets.

Stephen can be reached at 416-982-8670, or by e-mail at **nelsos3@tdbank.ca**.

Acknowledgments

I would especially like to thank my assistant, Janet Yu, for the tremendous time and effort she put into this project.

I would also like to thank the following people: Bill McKeown, Mike Dilworth, Dave Cairns, Ed Kusins, Denis Veres, Mike O'Rourke, Pete Ribeiro, Alfred Jay, Chris Bacon, Adam Smith, Joe Dayian, Dave Nelson, Frank Kastelic, Dave Huebel, Jeff Young, Sandy Knapp, Mike Guerriere.